the unbeatable Squirrel Girl

Like I'm the Only Squirrel in the World

the unbeatab

COLLECTION EDITOR: **JENNIFER GRÜNWALD**
ASSISTANT EDITOR: **CAITLIN O'CONNELL**
ASSOCIATE MANAGING EDITOR: **KATERI WOODY**
EDITOR, SPECIAL PROJECTS: **MARK D. BEAZLEY**
VP PRODUCTION & SPECIAL PROJECTS: **JEFF YOUNGQUIST**
SVP PRINT, SALES & MARKETING: **DAVID GABRIEL**
BOOK DESIGNER: **JAY BOWEN**

EDITOR IN CHIEF: **AXEL ALONSO**
CHIEF CREATIVE OFFICER: **JOE QUESADA**
PUBLISHER: **DAN BUCKLEY**
EXECUTIVE PRODUCER: **ALAN FINE**

THE UNBEATABLE SQUIRREL GIRL VOL. 5: LIKE I'M THE ONLY SQUIRREL IN THE WORLD. Contains material originally published in magazine form as THE UNBEATABLE SQUIRREL GIRL #12-16. First printing 2017. ISBN# 978-1-302-90328-2. Published by MARVEL WORLDWIDE, INC., a subsidiary of MARVEL ENTERTAINMENT, LLC. OFFICE OF PUBLICATION: 135 West 50th Street, New York, NY 10020. Copyright © 2017 MARVEL No similarity between any of the names, characters, persons, and/or institutions in this magazine with those of any living or dead person or institution is intended, and any such similarity which may exist is purely coincidental. **Printed in Canada. ALAN FINE**, President, Marvel Entertainment; DAN BUCKLEY, President, TV, Publishing & Brand Management; JOE QUESADA, Chief Creative Officer; TOM BREVOORT, SVP of Publishing; DAVID BOGART, SVP of Business Affairs & Operations, Publishing & Partnership; C.B. CEBULSKI, VP of Brand Management & Development, Asia; DAVID GABRIEL, SVP of Sales & Marketing, Publishing; JEFF YOUNGQUIST, VP of Production & Special Projects; DAN CARR, Executive Director of Publishing Technology; ALEX MORALES, Director of Publishing Operations; SUSAN CRESPI, Production Manager; STAN LEE, Chairman Emeritus. For information regarding advertising in Marvel Comics or on Marvel.com, please contact Vit DeBellis, Integrated Sales Manager, at vdebellis@marvel.com. For Marvel subscription inquiries, please call 888-511-5480. **Manufactured between 1/27/2017 and 2/28/2017 by SOLISCO PRINTERS, SCOTT, QC, CANADA.**

10 9 8 7 6 5 4 3 2 1

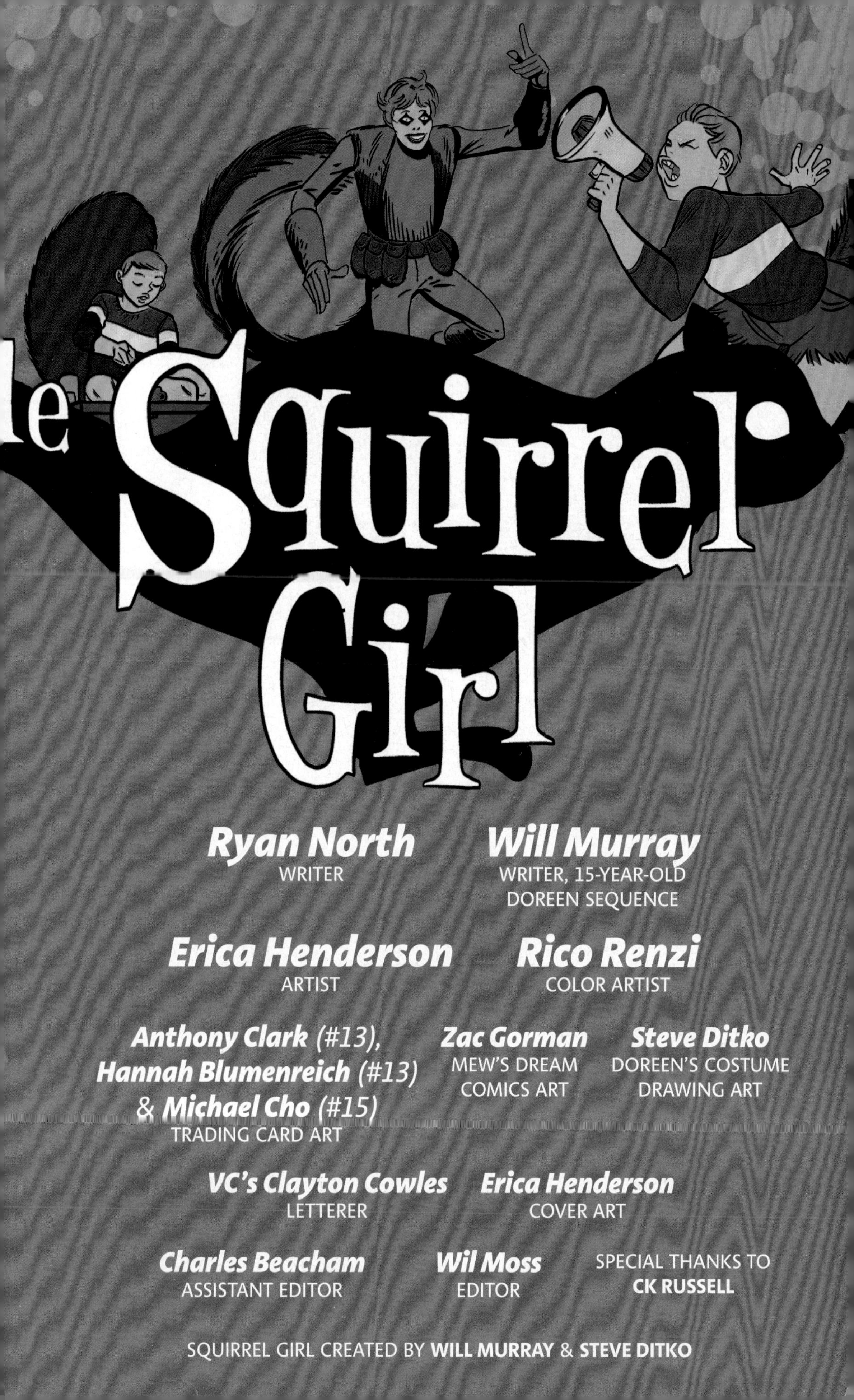
le Squirrel Girl

Ryan North
WRITER

Will Murray
WRITER, 15-YEAR-OLD DOREEN SEQUENCE

Erica Henderson
ARTIST

Rico Renzi
COLOR ARTIST

Anthony Clark (#13), **Hannah Blumenreich** (#13) & **Michael Cho** (#15)
TRADING CARD ART

Zac Gorman
MEW'S DREAM COMICS ART

Steve Ditko
DOREEN'S COSTUME DRAWING ART

VC's Clayton Cowles
LETTERER

Erica Henderson
COVER ART

Charles Beacham
ASSISTANT EDITOR

Wil Moss
EDITOR

SPECIAL THANKS TO **CK RUSSELL**

SQUIRREL GIRL CREATED BY **WILL MURRAY** & **STEVE DITKO**

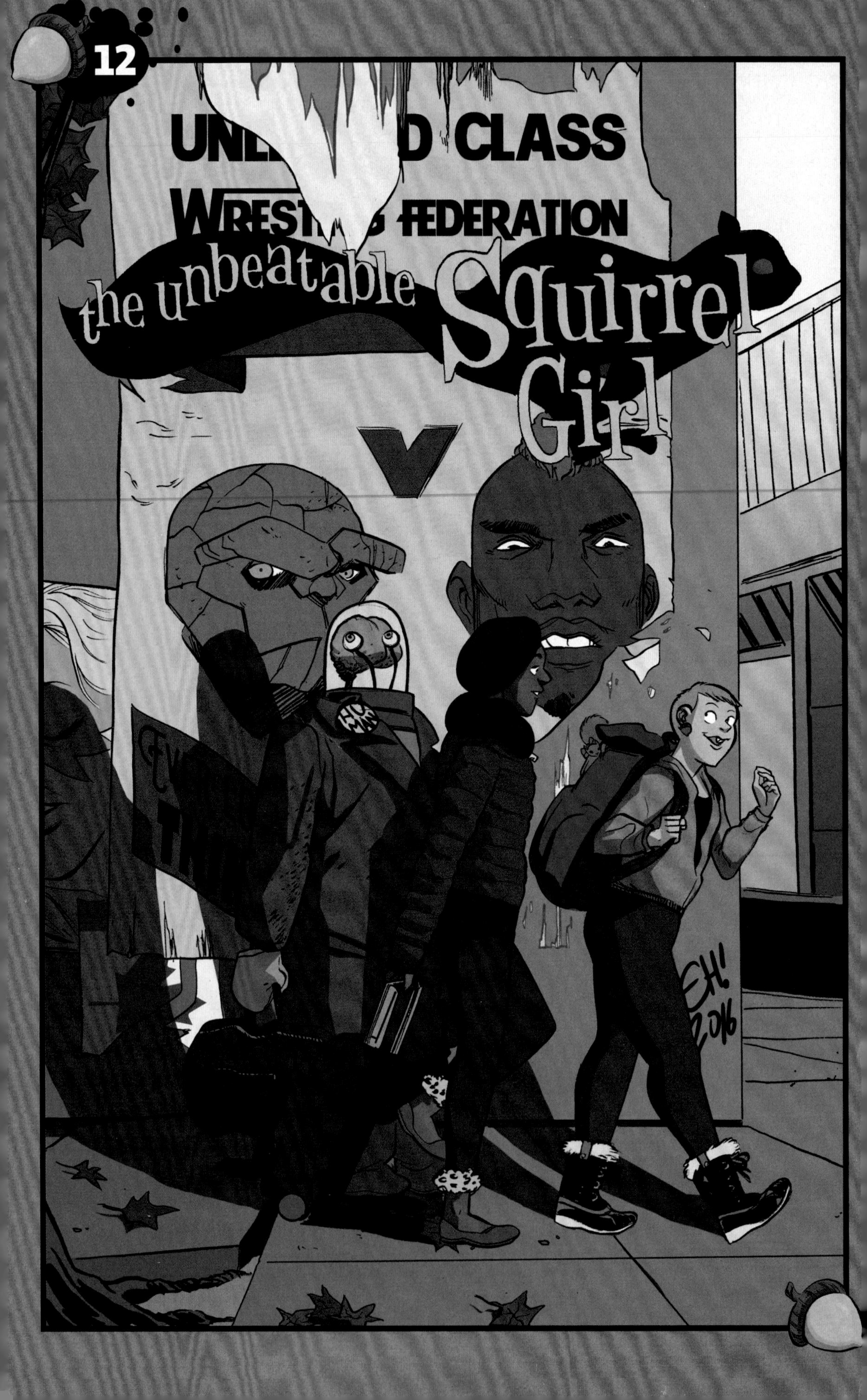
12
UNLE D CLASS
WREST G FEDERATION
the unbeatable Squirrel Girl
EH! 2016

Doreen Green isn't just a second-year computer science student: she secretly also has all the powers of both squirrel and girl! She uses her amazing abilities to fight crime **and** be as awesome as possible. You know her as...**The Unbeatable Squirrel Girl!** Find out what she's been up to, with...

Squirrel Girl *in a nutshell*

search!

#braindrain

#canada

#nopowernoproblems

#maureengreen

Squirrel Girl @unbeatablesg
Whew, I just had THE BEST NIGHT'S SLEEP OF ALL TIME. For some reason I feel like I could take on the world?

Squirrel Girl @unbeatablesg
Like, I woke up energized and jazzed, as if I really had just defeated a super villain and saved the world...IN MY SLEEP!! Felt great tbh

Squirrel Girl @unbeatablesg
But hah hah that's impossible so oh well

> **Spider-Man** @aspidercan
> @unbeatablesg actually there's a doctor strange bad guy named "nightmare" that you could've technically fought in your dreams!!!
>
> **Spider-Man** @aspidercan
> @unbeatablesg doc strange isn't on here though otherwise we could ask him
>
> **Squirrel Girl** @unbeatablesg
> @aspidercan A guy with a doctorate in strangeness doesn't hang out online here? WEIRD
>
> **Squirrel Girl** @unbeatablesg
> @aspidercan YOU'D THINK HE'D FIT RIGHT IN

Tony Stark @starkmantony ✓
@unbeatablesg Hey, how's that robot brain in a jar guy you patched up working out?

> **Squirrel Girl** @unbeatablesg
> @starkmantony Brain Drain? Great! Well on his way to becoming a real hero, actually! Still mega nihilistic but in a cool way
>
> **Squirrel Girl** @unbeatablesg
> @starkmantony We're going out on patrol together in a bit actually
>
> **Tony Stark** @starkmantony ✓
> @unbeatablesg Shouldn't you not mention when you're going out on patrol, so the criminal element won't know?
>
> **Squirrel Girl** @unbeatablesg
> @starkmantony good point my dude, one sec

Squirrel Girl @unbeatablesg
HELLO CRIMINALS, THIS IS JUST TO ANNOUNCE THAT I AM ON PATROL ALWAYS AND WILL DEFINITELY CATCH YOU DOING A CRIME, SO DON'T DO THEM

> **Spider-Man** @aspidercan
> @unbeatablesg holy crap can i use that

Squirrel Girl @unbeatablesg
@starkmantony Tony are you there I just had the best idea!! Tony tony tony

> **Tony Stark** @starkmantony ✓
> @unbeatablesg Hey.

Squirrel Girl @unbeatablesg
@starkmantony TONY. BRAINSTORM. What if you changed your name from "Tony Stark" to--HEAR ME OUT--..."Ira."

Tony Stark @starkmantony ✓
@unbeatablesg "Ira Stark"?

Squirrel Girl @unbeatablesg
@starkmantony IRA ONMANN.

Tony Stark @starkmantony ✓
@unbeatablesg oh my god

Squirrel Girl @unbeatablesg
@starkmantony Tony I'm going on vacation so I just wanted to give you something to remember me by

Squirrel Girl @unbeatablesg
@starkmantony just a little memento

Squirrel Girl @unbeatablesg
@starkmantony for my good friend

Squirrel Girl @unbeatablesg
@starkmantony ira onmann

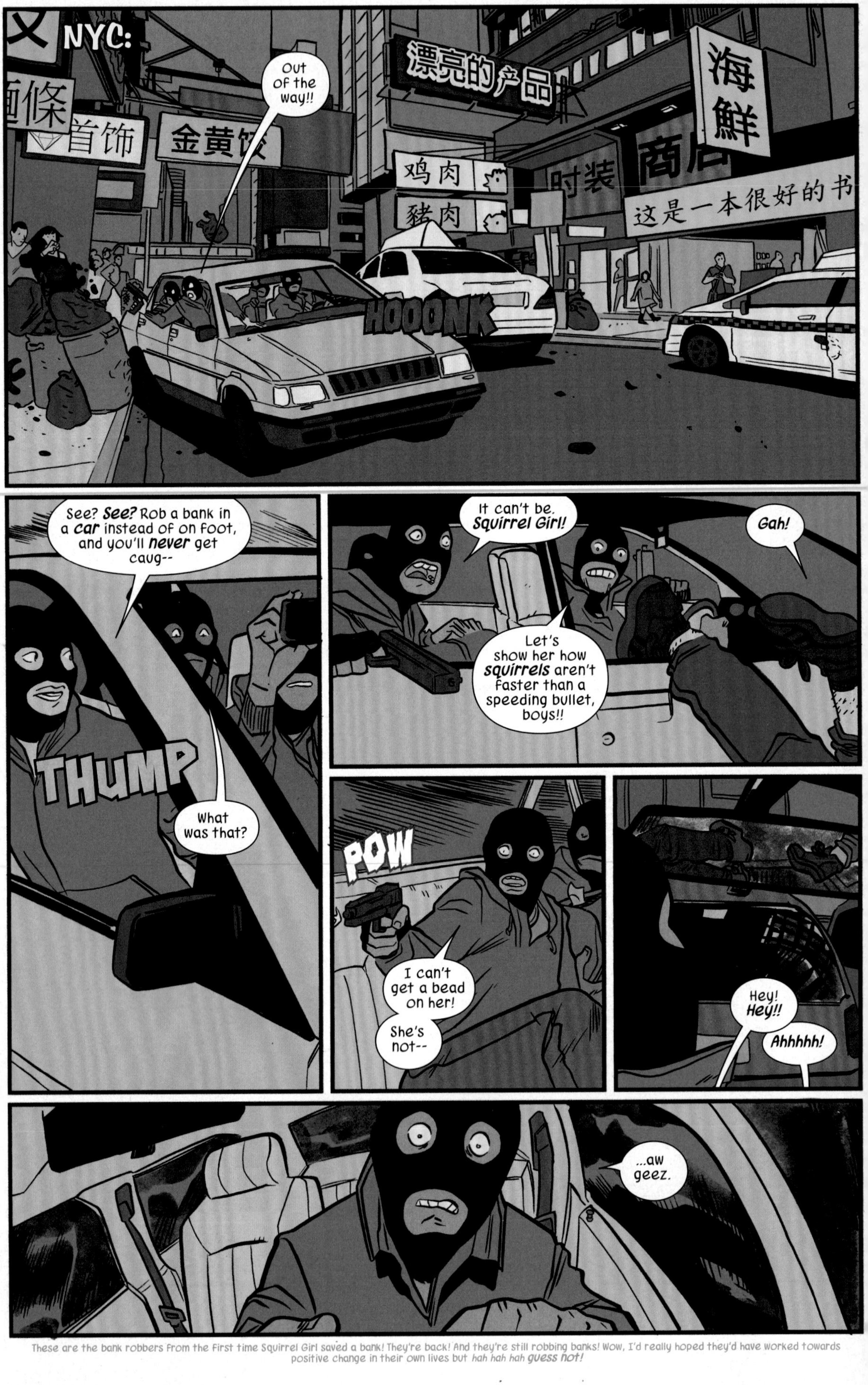

NYC:
Out of the way!!
漂亮的产品
海鲜
首饰
金黄饺
鸡肉
豬肉
时装
这是一本很好的书
HOOONK
See? See? Rob a bank in a car instead of on foot, and you'll never get caug--
THUMP
What was that?
It can't be. Squirrel Girl!
Gah!
Let's show her how squirrels aren't faster than a speeding bullet, boys!!
POW
I can't get a bead on her!
She's not--
Hey! Hey!!
Ahhhhh!
...aw geez.

These are the bank robbers from the first time Squirrel Girl saved a bank! They're back! And they're still robbing banks! Wow, I'd really hoped they'd have worked towards positive change in their own lives but *hah hah hah* ***guess not!***

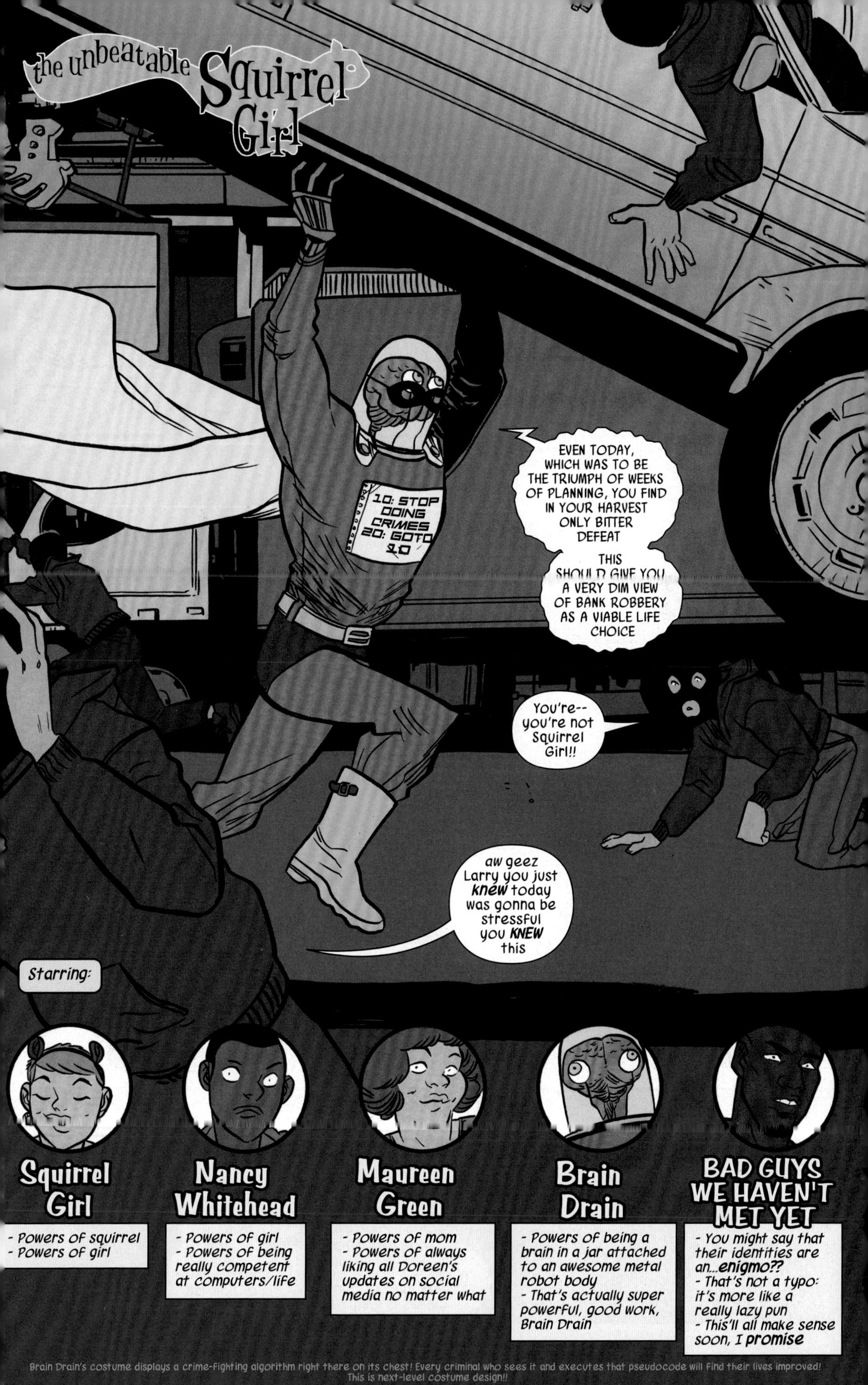
the unbeatable Squirrel Girl
10: STOP DOING CRIMES 20: GOTO 10
EVEN TODAY, WHICH WAS TO BE THE TRIUMPH OF WEEKS OF PLANNING, YOU FIND IN YOUR HARVEST ONLY BITTER DEFEAT
THIS SHOULD GIVE YOU A VERY DIM VIEW OF BANK ROBBERY AS A VIABLE LIFE CHOICE
You're-- you're not Squirrel Girl!!
aw geez Larry you just *knew* today was gonna be stressful you *KNEW* this
Starring:
Squirrel Girl
- Powers of squirrel
- Powers of girl
Nancy Whitehead
- Powers of girl
- Powers of being really competent at computers/life
Maureen Green
- Powers of mom
- Powers of always liking all Doreen's updates on social media no matter what
Brain Drain
- Powers of being a brain in a jar attached to an awesome metal robot body
- That's actually super powerful, good work, Brain Drain
BAD GUYS WE HAVEN'T MET YET
- You might say that their identities are an...*enigmo??*
- That's not a typo: it's more like a really lazy pun
- This'll all make sense soon, I *promise*

Brain Drain's costume displays a crime-fighting algorithm right there on its chest! Every criminal who sees it and executes that pseudocode will find their lives improved! This is next-level costume design!!

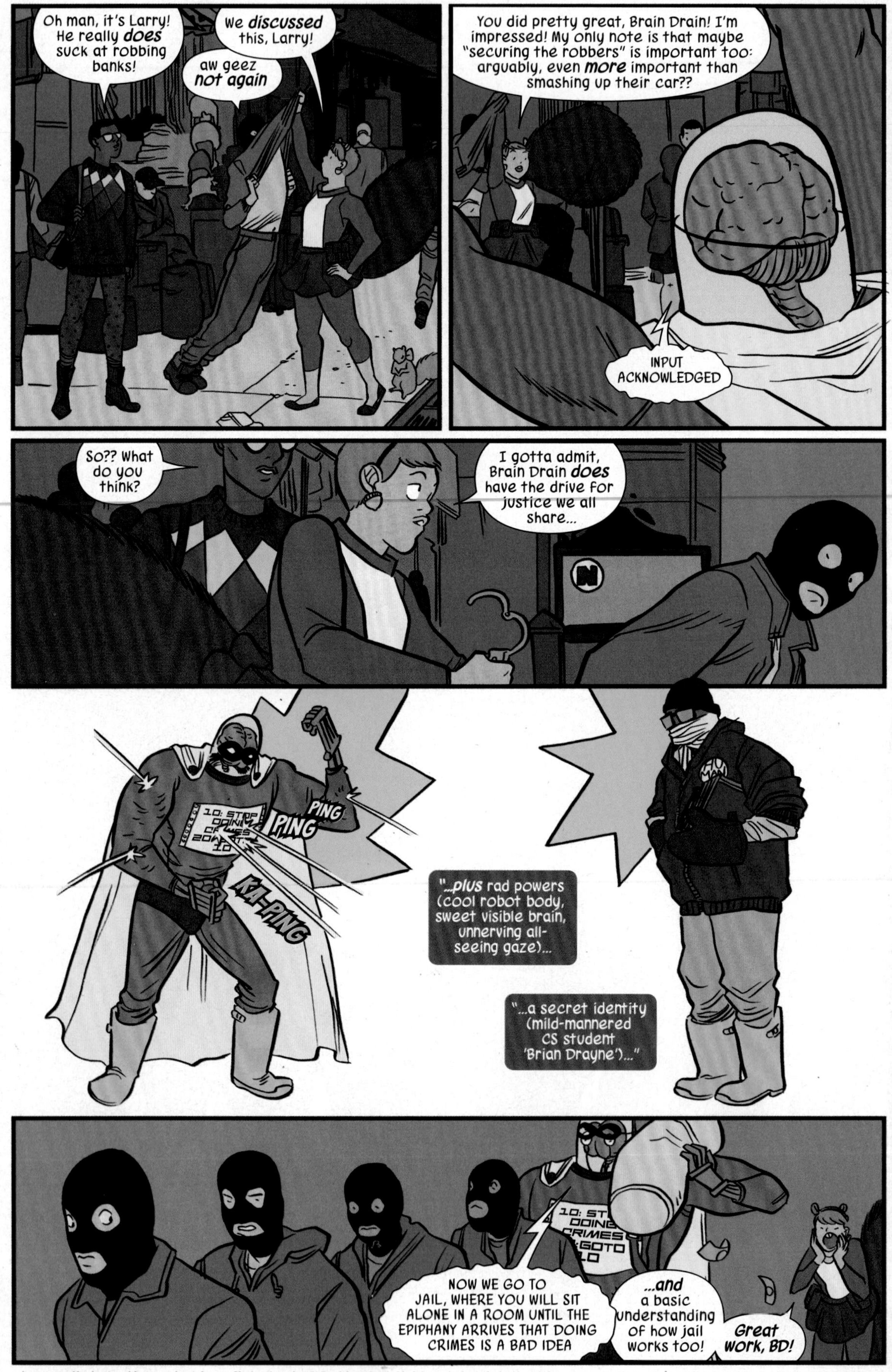
Oh man, it's Larry! He really *does* suck at robbing banks!
We *discussed* this, Larry!
aw geez *not again*
You did pretty great, Brain Drain! I'm impressed! My only note is that maybe "securing the robbers" is important too: arguably, even *more* important than smashing up their car??
INPUT ACKNOWLEDGED
So?? What do you think?
I gotta admit, Brain Drain *does* have the drive for justice we all share...
PING
PING
KA-PING
"...*plus* rad powers (cool robot body, sweet visible brain, unnerving all-seeing gaze)...
"...a secret identity (mild-mannered CS student 'Brian Drayne')..."
NOW WE GO TO JAIL, WHERE YOU WILL SIT ALONE IN A ROOM UNTIL THE EPIPHANY ARRIVES THAT DOING CRIMES IS A BAD IDEA
...*and* a basic understanding of how jail works too!
Great work, BD!

Larry was the bank robber way back in our first volume's #3! Fun Larry Fact: his interests include both getting money for free *and* recidivism. Not a good look on you, Larry!

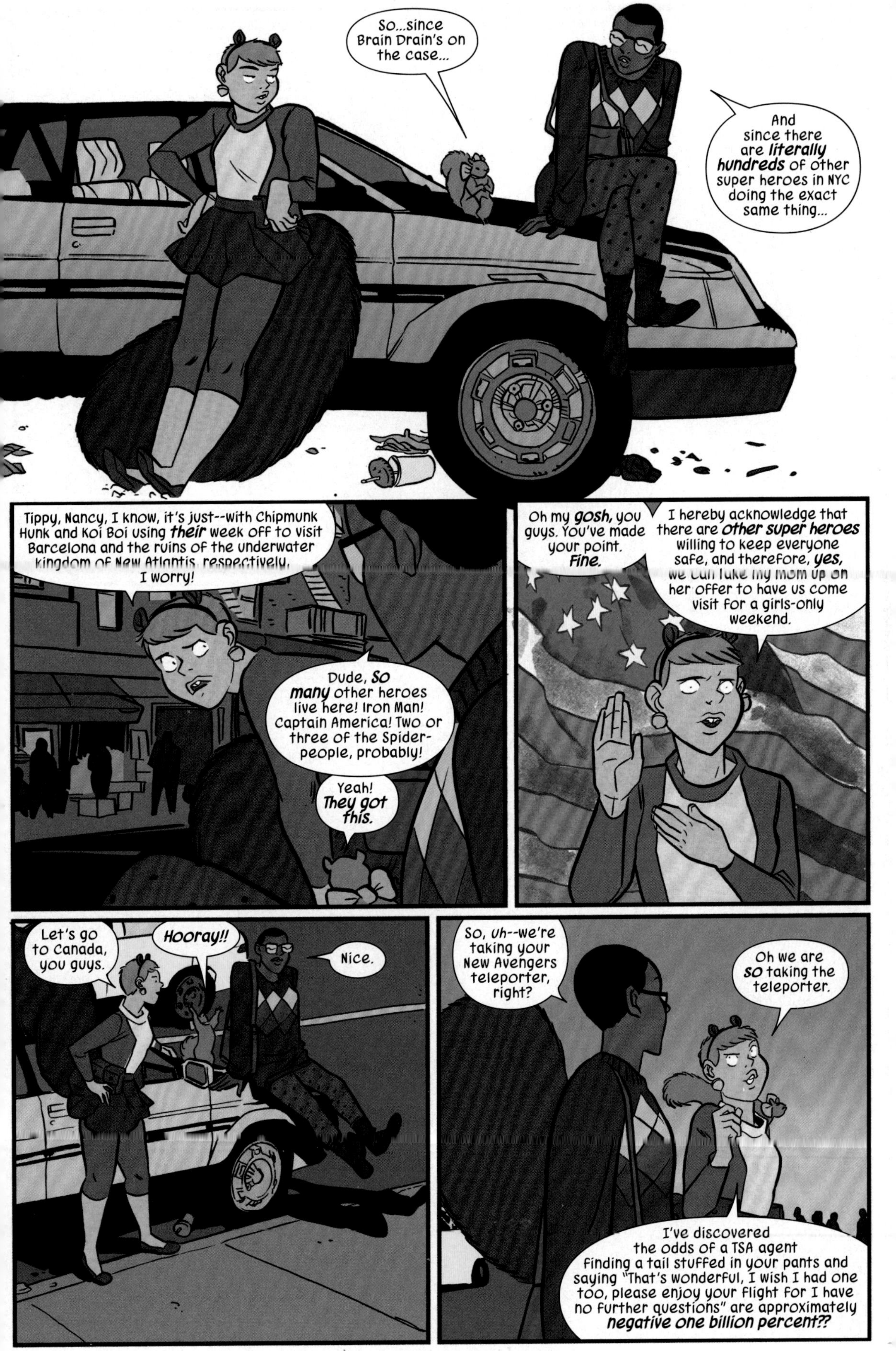
So...since Brain Drain's on the case...
And since there are literally hundreds of other super heroes in NYC doing the exact same thing...
Tippy, Nancy, I know, it's just--with Chipmunk Hunk and Koi Boi using their week off to visit Barcelona and the ruins of the underwater kingdom of New Atlantis, respectively, I worry!
Dude, SO many other heroes live here! Iron Man! Captain America! Two or three of the Spider-people, probably!
Yeah! They got this.
Oh my gosh, you guys. You've made your point. Fine.
I hereby acknowledge that there are other super heroes willing to keep everyone safe, and therefore, yes, we can take my mom up on her offer to have us come visit for a girls-only weekend.
Let's go to Canada, you guys.
Hooray!!
Nice.
So, uh--we're taking your New Avengers teleporter, right?
Oh we are SO taking the teleporter.
I've discovered the odds of a TSA agent finding a tail stuffed in your pants and saying "That's wonderful, I wish I had one too, please enjoy your flight for I have no further questions" are approximately negative one billion percent??

TSA agents freak out even if you wear *shoes* when you're not supposed to! They are clearly not yet woke enough for tails.

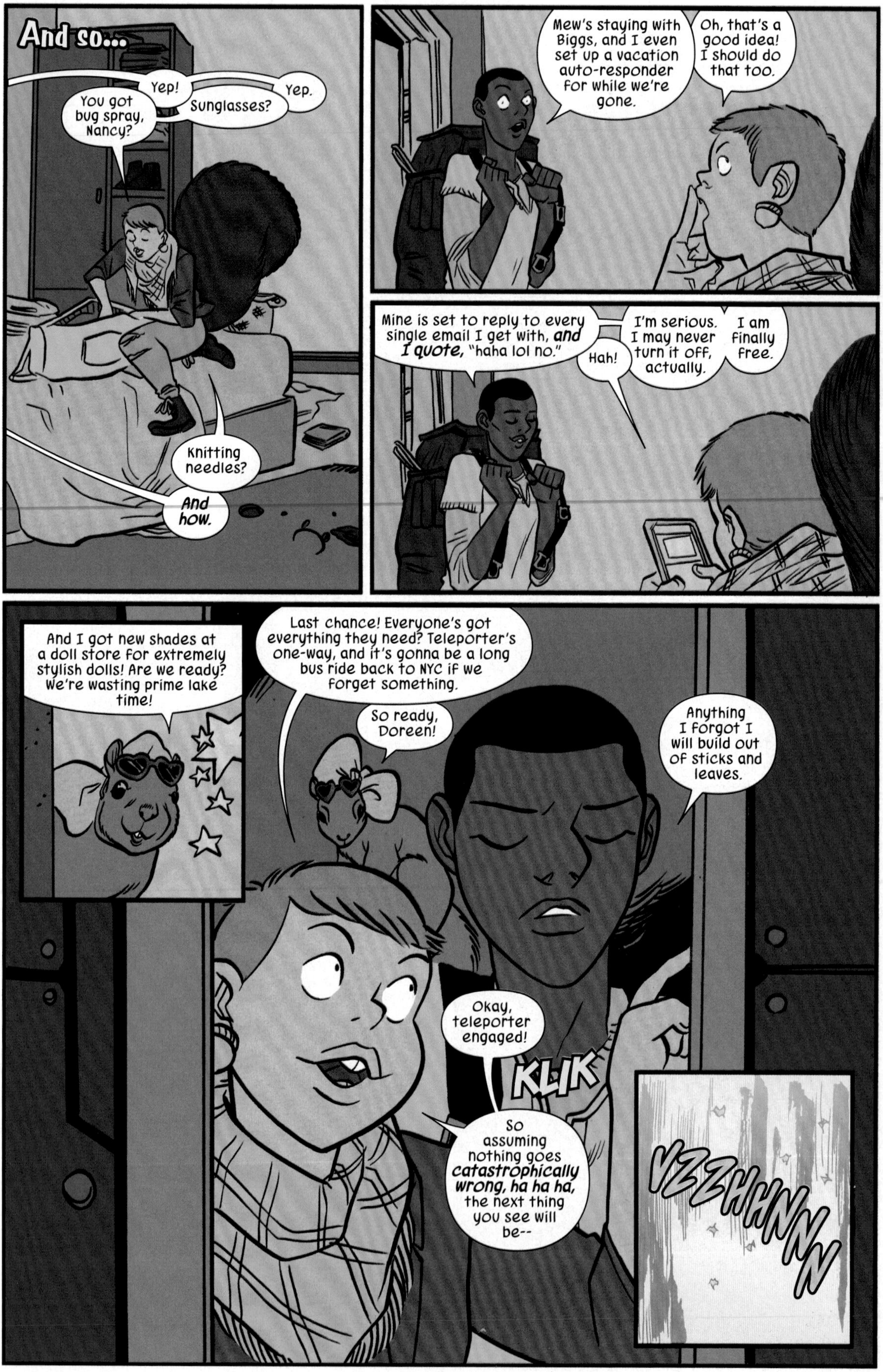
And so...
You got bug spray, Nancy?
Yep!
Sunglasses?
Yep.
Knitting needles?
And how.
Mew's staying with Biggs, and I even set up a vacation auto-responder for while we're gone.
Oh, that's a good idea! I should do that too.
Mine is set to reply to every single email I get with, and I quote, "haha lol no."
Hah!
I'm serious. I may never turn it off, actually.
I am finally free.
And I got new shades at a doll store for extremely stylish dolls! Are we ready? We're wasting prime lake time!
Last chance! Everyone's got everything they need? Teleporter's one-way, and it's gonna be a long bus ride back to NYC if we forget something.
So ready, Doreen!
Anything I forgot I will build out of sticks and leaves.
Okay, teleporter engaged!
KLIK
So assuming nothing goes catastrophically wrong, ha ha ha, the next thing you see will be--
VZZHHNNN

Other email autoresponses that have no possible downsides include "haha seriously?? tell me more!!", "interesting, let's follow up on this tomorrow!", and "who are you and how did you get this email?". Like I said, no possible downsides!!

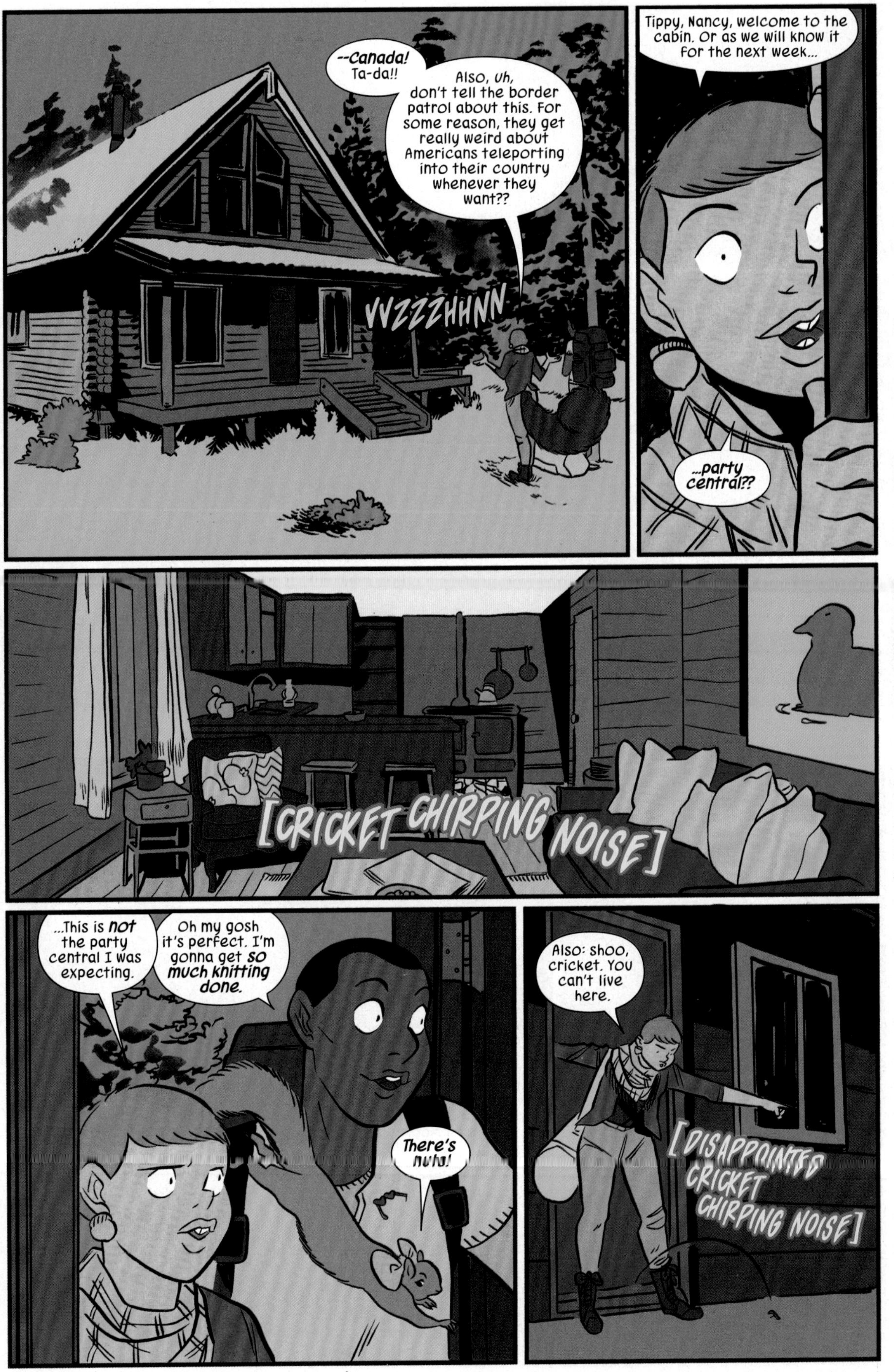
--Canada! Ta-da!!
Also, uh, don't tell the border patrol about this. For some reason, they get really weird about Americans teleporting into their country whenever they want??
VVZZZHHNN
Tippy, Nancy, welcome to the cabin. Or as we will know it for the next week...
...party central??
[CRICKET CHIRPING NOISE]
...This is *not* the party central I was expecting.
Oh my gosh it's perfect. I'm gonna get *so much knitting done.*
There's nuts!
Also: shoo, cricket. You can't live here.
[DISAPPOINTED CRICKET CHIRPING NOISE]

Also I'm sorry I mentioned catastrophic failures as we were literally stepping into a teleporter: that was bad timing and I apologize. It was really just a completely catastrophic failure of timing on my part. ...Sorry again.

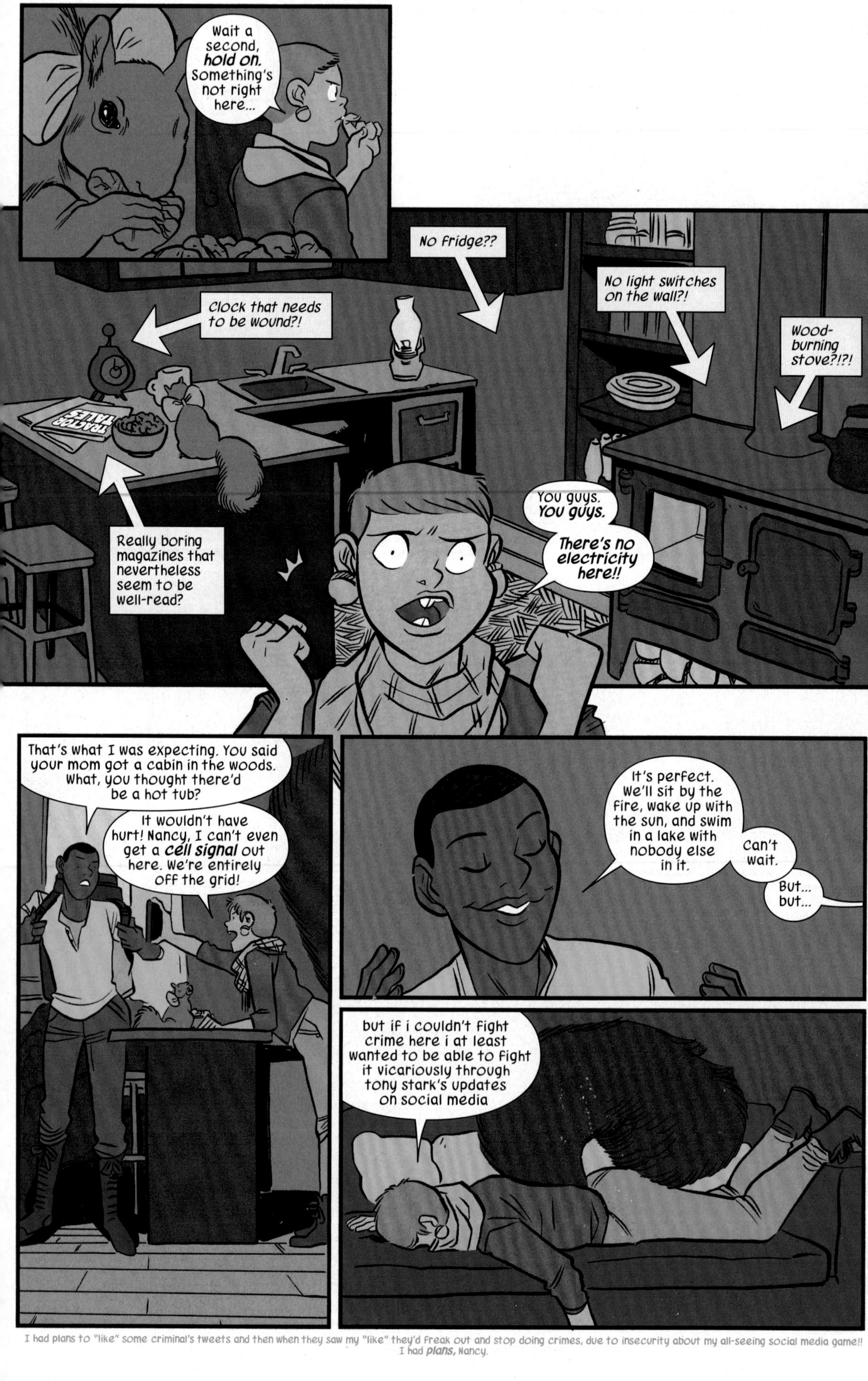
Wait a second, **hold on.** Something's not right here...
No fridge??
Clock that needs to be wound?!
No light switches on the wall?!
Wood-burning stove?!?!
TRACTOR TALES
Really boring magazines that nevertheless seem to be well-read?
You guys. **You guys.**
There's no electricity here!!
That's what I was expecting. You said your mom got a cabin in the woods. What, you thought there'd be a hot tub?
It wouldn't have hurt! Nancy, I can't even get a **cell signal** out here. We're entirely off the grid!
It's perfect. We'll sit by the fire, wake up with the sun, and swim in a lake with nobody else in it.
Can't wait.
But... but...
but if i couldn't fight crime here i at least wanted to be able to fight it vicariously through tony stark's updates on social media

I had plans to "like" some criminal's tweets and then when they saw my "like" they'd freak out and stop doing crimes, due to insecurity about my all-seeing social media game!! I had ***plans,*** Nancy.

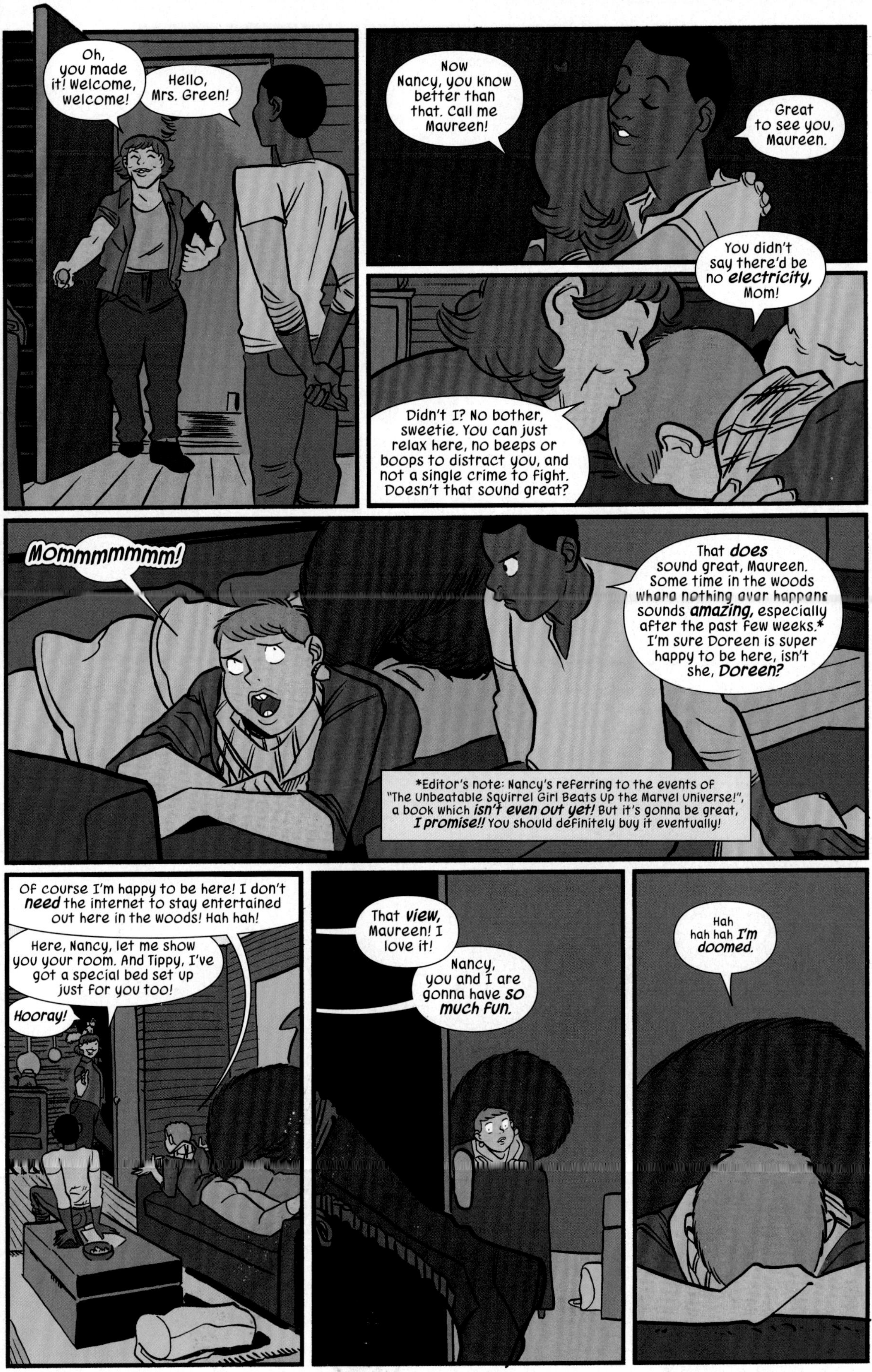
Oh, you made it! Welcome, welcome!
Hello, Mrs. Green!
Now Nancy, you know better than that. Call me Maureen!
Great to see you, Maureen.
You didn't say there'd be no *electricity,* Mom!
Didn't I? No bother, sweetie. You can just relax here, no beeps or boops to distract you, and not a single crime to fight. Doesn't that sound great?
MOMMMMMMM!
That *does* sound great, Maureen. Some time in the woods where nothing ever happens sounds *amazing,* especially after the past few weeks.* I'm sure Doreen is super happy to be here, isn't she, *Doreen?*
*Editor's note: Nancy's referring to the events of "The Unbeatable Squirrel Girl Beats Up the Marvel Universe!", a book which *isn't even out yet!* But it's gonna be great, *I promise!!* You should definitely buy it eventually!
Of course I'm happy to be here! I don't *need* the internet to stay entertained out here in the woods! Hah hah!
Here, Nancy, let me show you your room. And Tippy, I've got a special bed set up just for you too!
Hooray!
That *view,* Maureen! I love it!
Nancy, you and I are gonna have *so much fun.*
Hah hah hah *I'm doomed.*

You can also take out our new book from the library! You might think that people in the business of selling books would be against places where you can read books for free, but here is a secret: libraries are awesome, librarians are even *more* awesome, and both are among the greatest things civilization has given us. ***No apologies; it's true.***

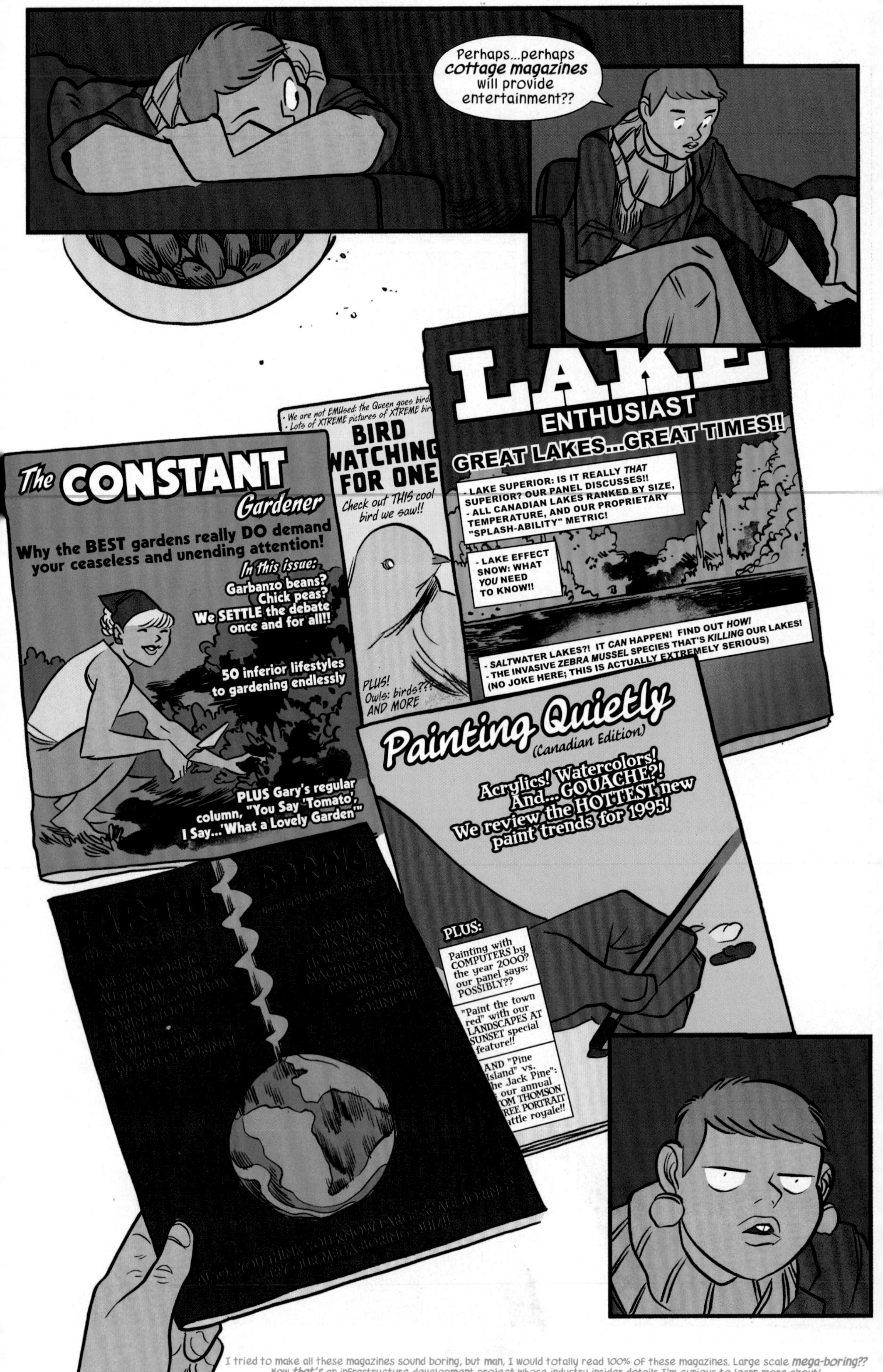
Perhaps...perhaps *cottage magazines* will provide entertainment??
The CONSTANT Gardener
Why the BEST gardens really DO demand your ceaseless and unending attention!
In this issue:
Garbanzo beans? Chick peas? We SETTLE the debate once and for all!!
50 inferior lifestyles to gardening endlessly
PLUS Gary's regular column, "You Say 'Tomato', I Say...'What a Lovely Garden'"
• We are not EMUsed: the Queen goes bird
• Lots of XTREME pictures of XTREME bir
BIRD WATCHING FOR ONE
Check out THIS cool bird we saw!!
PLUS! Owls: birds??? AND MORE
LAKE ENTHUSIAST
GREAT LAKES...GREAT TIMES!!
- LAKE SUPERIOR: IS IT REALLY *THAT* SUPERIOR? OUR PANEL DISCUSSES!!
- ALL CANADIAN LAKES RANKED BY SIZE, TEMPERATURE, AND OUR PROPRIETARY "SPLASH-ABILITY" METRIC!
- LAKE EFFECT SNOW: WHAT *YOU* NEED TO KNOW!!
- *SALTWATER* LAKES?! IT *CAN* HAPPEN! FIND OUT *HOW!*
- THE INVASIVE *ZEBRA MUSSEL* SPECIES THAT'S *KILLING* OUR LAKES!
(NO JOKE HERE; THIS IS ACTUALLY EXTREMELY SERIOUS)
Painting Quietly
(Canadian Edition)
Acrylics! Watercolors! And... GOUACHE?! We review the HOTTEST new paint trends for 1995!
PLUS:
Painting with COMPUTERS by the year 2000? our panel says: POSSIBLY??
"Paint the town red" with our LANDSCAPES AT SUNSET special feature!!
AND "Pine Island" vs. "The Jack Pine": our annual TOM THOMSON TREE PORTRAIT battle royale!!

I tried to make all these magazines sound boring, but man, I would totally read 100% of these magazines. Large scale *mega-boring??* Now *that's* an infrastructure development project whose industry insider details I'm curious to learn more about!

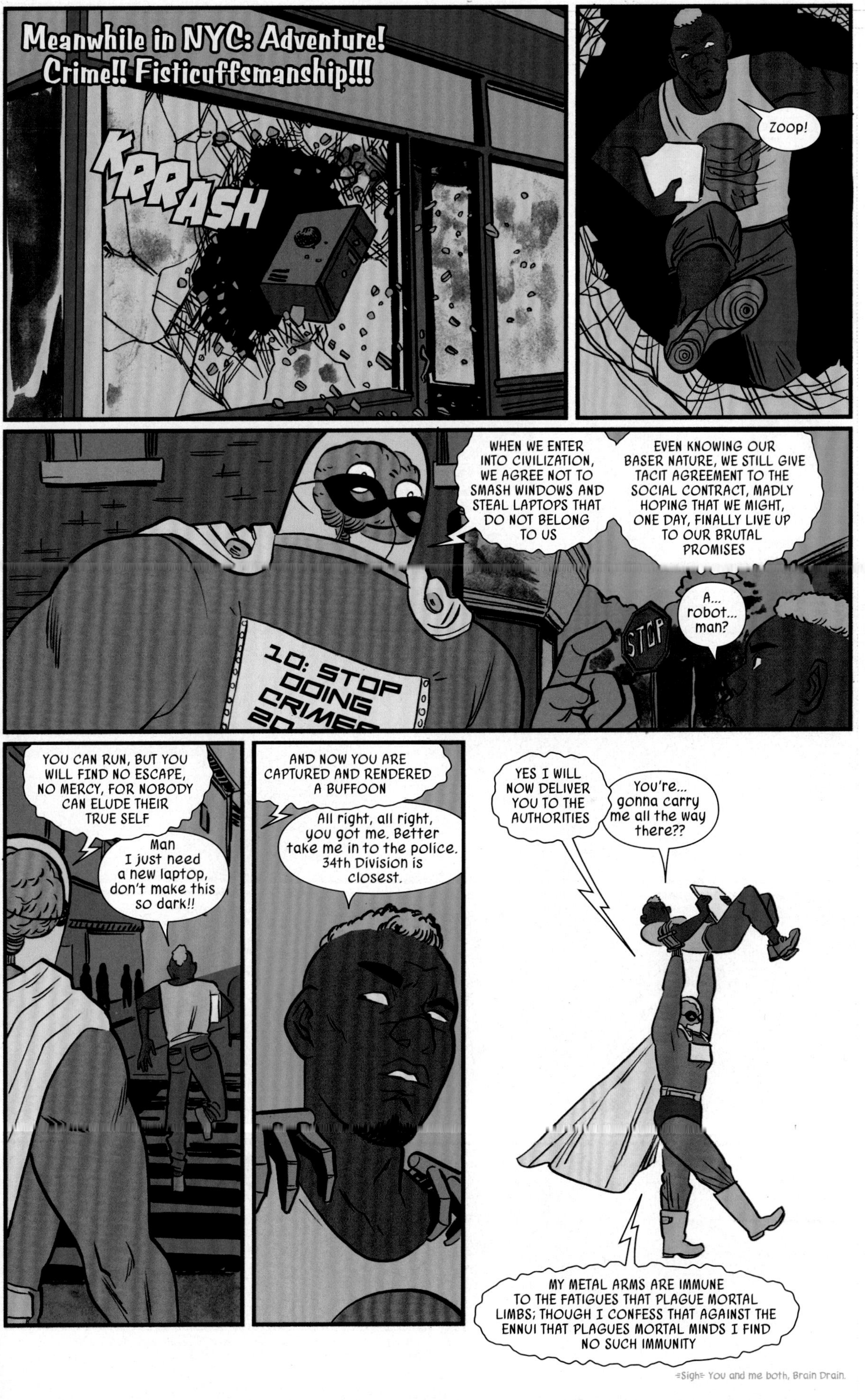

Meanwhile in NYC: Adventure! Crime!! Fisticuffsmanship!!!
KRRASH
Zoop!
WHEN WE ENTER INTO CIVILIZATION, WE AGREE NOT TO SMASH WINDOWS AND STEAL LAPTOPS THAT DO NOT BELONG TO US
EVEN KNOWING OUR BASER NATURE, WE STILL GIVE TACIT AGREEMENT TO THE SOCIAL CONTRACT, MADLY HOPING THAT WE MIGHT, ONE DAY, FINALLY LIVE UP TO OUR BRUTAL PROMISES
A... robot... man?
STOP
10: STOP DOING CRIMES
YOU CAN RUN, BUT YOU WILL FIND NO ESCAPE, NO MERCY, FOR NOBODY CAN ELUDE THEIR TRUE SELF
Man I just need a new laptop, don't make this so dark!!
AND NOW YOU ARE CAPTURED AND RENDERED A BUFFOON
All right, all right, you got me. Better take me in to the police. 34th Division is closest.
YES I WILL NOW DELIVER YOU TO THE AUTHORITIES
You're... gonna carry me all the way there??
MY METAL ARMS ARE IMMUNE TO THE FATIGUES THAT PLAGUE MORTAL LIMBS; THOUGH I CONFESS THAT AGAINST THE ENNUI THAT PLAGUES MORTAL MINDS I FIND NO SUCH IMMUNITY
=Sigh= You and me both, Brain Drain.

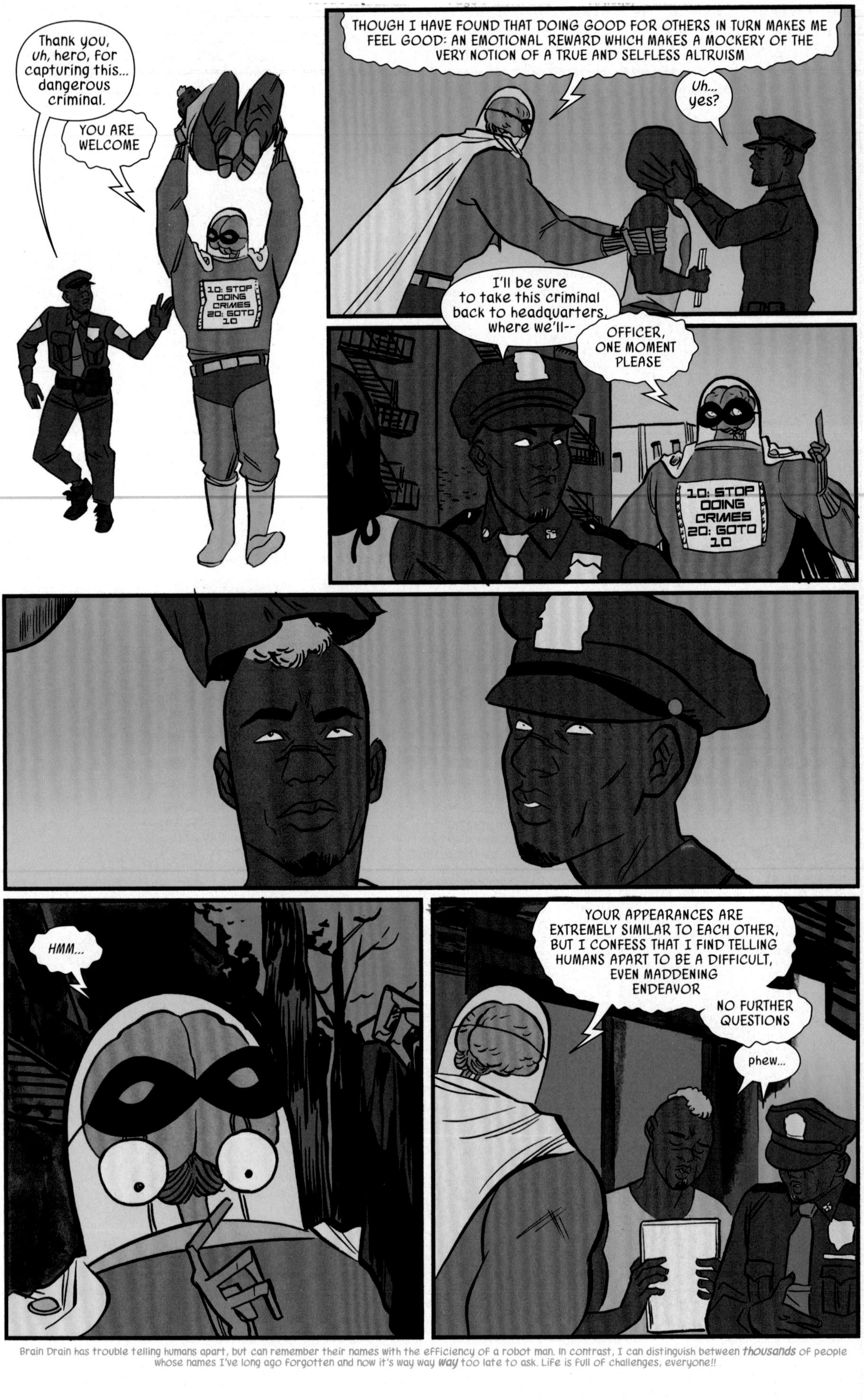

Thank you, uh, hero, for capturing this... dangerous criminal.
YOU ARE WELCOME
10: STOP DOING CRIMES 20: GOTO 10
THOUGH I HAVE FOUND THAT DOING GOOD FOR OTHERS IN TURN MAKES ME FEEL GOOD: AN EMOTIONAL REWARD WHICH MAKES A MOCKERY OF THE VERY NOTION OF A TRUE AND SELFLESS ALTRUISM
Uh... yes?
I'll be sure to take this criminal back to headquarters, where we'll--
OFFICER, ONE MOMENT PLEASE
10: STOP DOING CRIMES 20: GOTO 10
HMM...
YOUR APPEARANCES ARE EXTREMELY SIMILAR TO EACH OTHER, BUT I CONFESS THAT I FIND TELLING HUMANS APART TO BE A DIFFICULT, EVEN MADDENING ENDEAVOR
NO FURTHER QUESTIONS
phew...

Brain Drain has trouble telling humans apart, but can remember their names with the efficiency of a robot man. In contrast, I can distinguish between ***thousands*** of people whose names I've long ago forgotten and now it's way way ***way*** too late to ask. Life is full of challenges, everyone!!

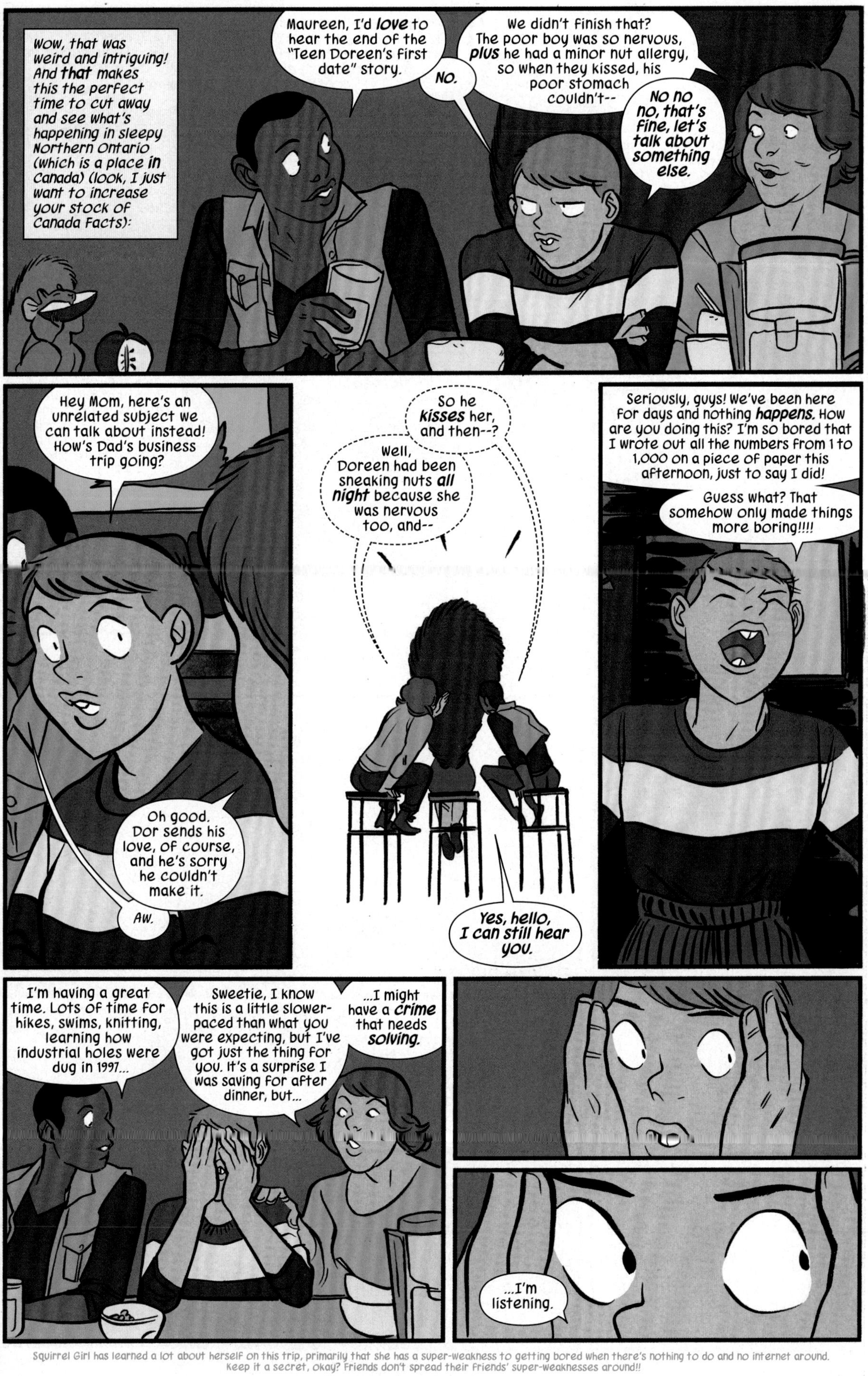

Wow, that was weird and intriguing! And that makes this the perfect time to cut away and see what's happening in sleepy Northern Ontario (which is a place in Canada) (look, I just want to increase your stock of Canada Facts):
Maureen, I'd love to hear the end of the "Teen Doreen's first date" story.
NO.
We didn't finish that? The poor boy was so nervous, plus he had a minor nut allergy, so when they kissed, his poor stomach couldn't--
No no no, that's fine, let's talk about something else.
Hey Mom, here's an unrelated subject we can talk about instead! How's Dad's business trip going?
Oh good. Dor sends his love, of course, and he's sorry he couldn't make it.
AW.
So he kisses her, and then--?
Well, Doreen had been sneaking nuts all night because she was nervous too, and--
Yes, hello, I can still hear you.
Seriously, guys! We've been here for days and nothing happens. How are you doing this? I'm so bored that I wrote out all the numbers from 1 to 1,000 on a piece of paper this afternoon, just to say I did!
Guess what? That somehow only made things more boring!!!!
I'm having a great time. Lots of time for hikes, swims, knitting, learning how industrial holes were dug in 1997...
Sweetie, I know this is a little slower-paced than what you were expecting, but I've got just the thing for you. It's a surprise I was saving for after dinner, but...
...I might have a crime that needs solving.
...I'm listening.

Squirrel Girl has learned a lot about herself on this trip, primarily that she has a super-weakness to getting bored when there's nothing to do and no internet around. Keep it a secret, okay? Friends don't spread their friends' super-weaknesses around!!

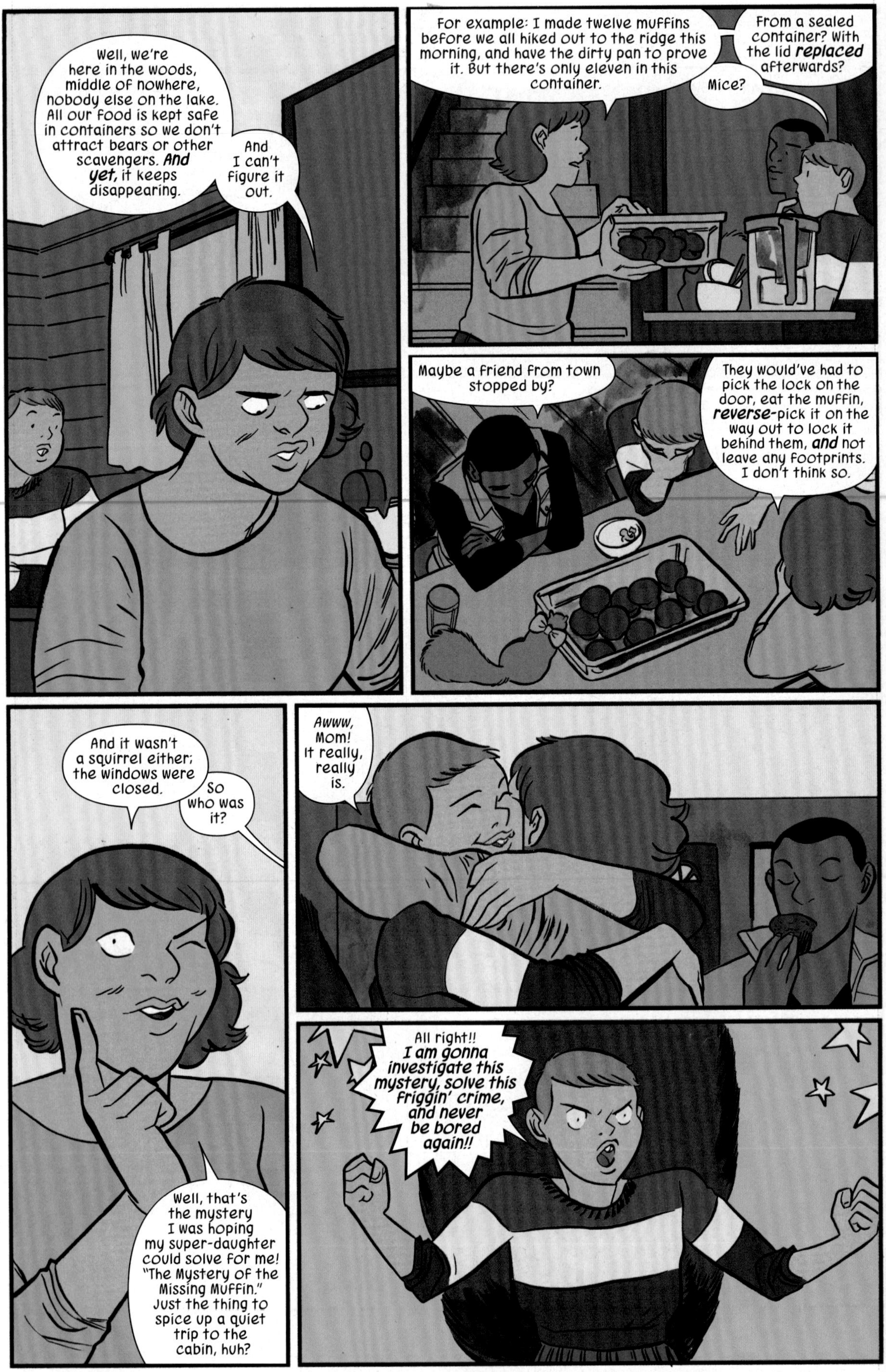
Well, we're here in the woods, middle of nowhere, nobody else on the lake. All our food is kept safe in containers so we don't attract bears or other scavengers. **And yet,** it keeps disappearing.
And I can't figure it out.
For example: I made twelve muffins before we all hiked out to the ridge this morning, and have the dirty pan to prove it. But there's only eleven in this container.
Mice?
From a sealed container? With the lid *replaced* afterwards?
Maybe a friend from town stopped by?
They would've had to pick the lock on the door, eat the muffin, **reverse**-pick it on the way out to lock it behind them, **and** not leave any footprints. I don't think so.
And it wasn't a squirrel either; the windows were closed.
So who was it?
Well, that's the mystery I was hoping my super-daughter could solve for me! "The Mystery of the Missing Muffin." Just the thing to spice up a quiet trip to the cabin, huh?
Awww, Mom! It really, really is.
All right!! ***I am gonna investigate this mystery, solve this friggin' crime, and never be bored again!!***

Alternative titles for this case: "The Case of the Cupcake Caper," "Just Desserts," and "The Mysterious Muffin of Skellington Bay" (did you know: if a bay doesn't have a name, you can ***probably*** just name that bay??)

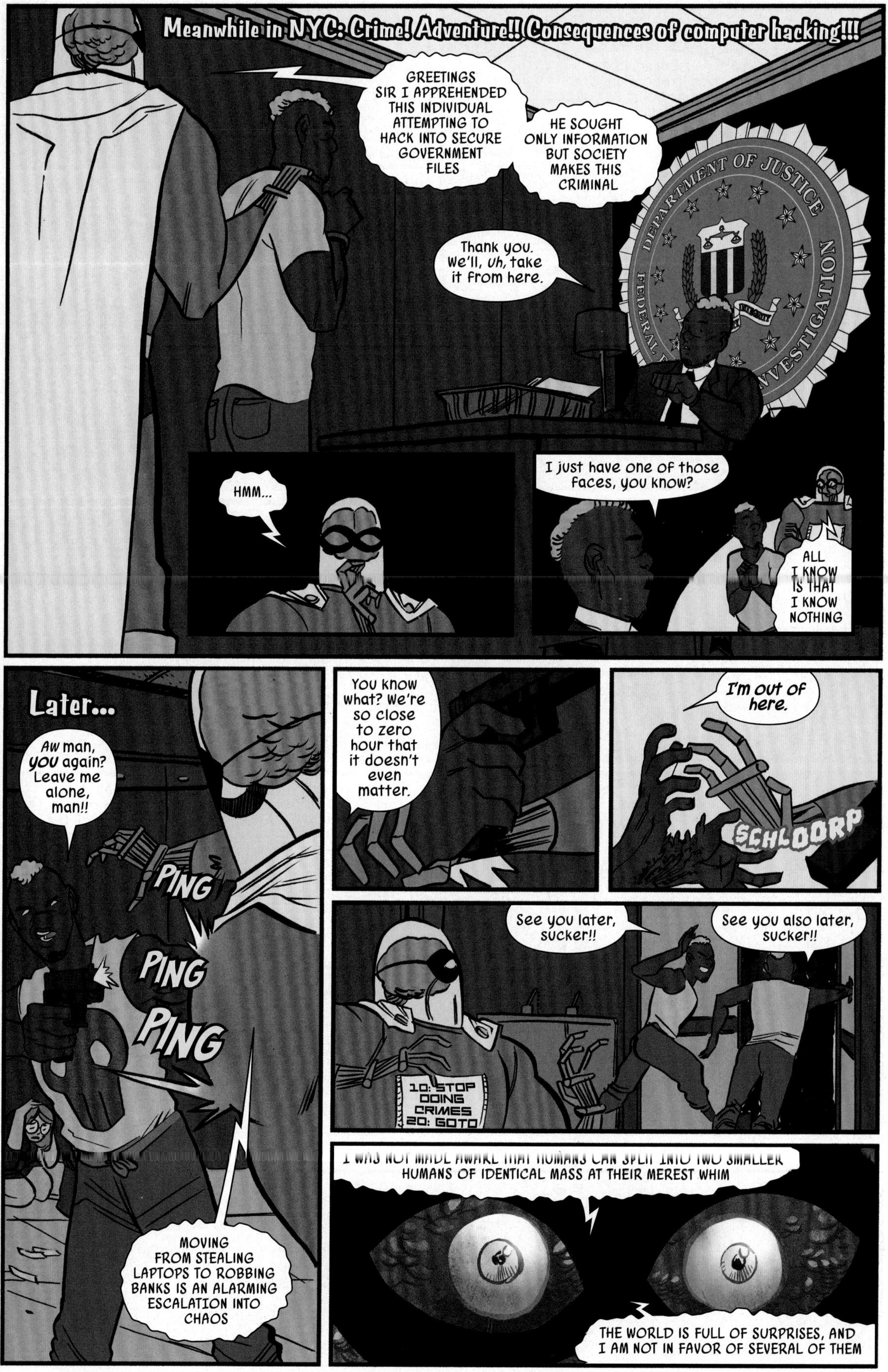
Meanwhile in NYC: Crime! Adventure!! Consequences of computer hacking!!!
GREETINGS SIR I APPREHENDED THIS INDIVIDUAL ATTEMPTING TO HACK INTO SECURE GOVERNMENT FILES
HE SOUGHT ONLY INFORMATION BUT SOCIETY MAKES THIS CRIMINAL
Thank you. We'll, uh, take it from here.
DEPARTMENT OF JUSTICE
FEDERAL BUREAU OF INVESTIGATION
HMM...
I just have one of those faces, you know?
ALL I KNOW IS THAT I KNOW NOTHING
Later...
Aw man, you again? Leave me alone, man!!
PING
PING
PING
MOVING FROM STEALING LAPTOPS TO ROBBING BANKS IS AN ALARMING ESCALATION INTO CHAOS
You know what? We're so close to zero hour that it doesn't even matter.
I'm out of here.
SCHLOORP
See you later, sucker!!
See you also later, sucker!!
10: STOP DOING CRIMES 20: GOTO
I WAS NOT MADE AWARE THAT HUMANS CAN SPLIT INTO TWO SMALLER HUMANS OF IDENTICAL MASS AT THEIR MEREST WHIM
THE WORLD IS FULL OF SURPRISES, AND I AM NOT IN FAVOR OF SEVERAL OF THEM

HOWEVER I HAVE BEEN TOLD THAT SOMETIMES THE SURPRISES ARE KITTENS AND ICE CREAM, SO I HOLD OUT HOPE, EVER DREAMING OF THE ICE CREAM KITTEN IN MY FUTURE

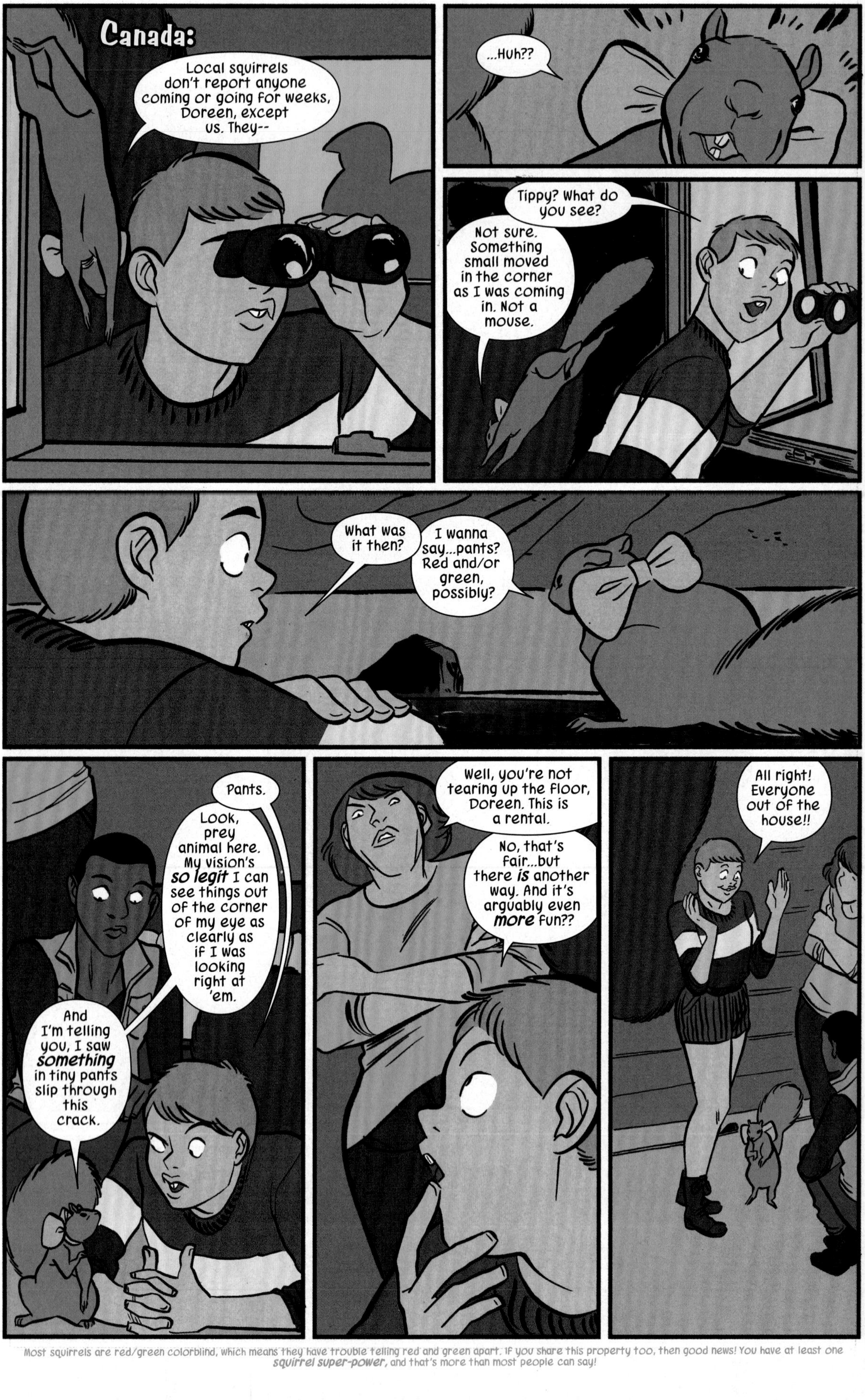
Canada:
Local squirrels don't report anyone coming or going for weeks, Doreen, except us. They--
...Huh??
Tippy? What do you see?
Not sure. Something small moved in the corner as I was coming in. Not a mouse.
What was it then?
I wanna say...pants? Red and/or green, possibly?
Pants.
Look, prey animal here. My vision's so legit I can see things out of the corner of my eye as clearly as if I was looking right at 'em.
And I'm telling you, I saw something in tiny pants slip through this crack.
Well, you're not tearing up the floor, Doreen. This is a rental.
No, that's fair...but there is another way. And it's arguably even more fun??
All right! Everyone out of the house!!

Most squirrels are red/green colorblind, which means they have trouble telling red and green apart. If you share this property too, then good news! You have at least one *squirrel super-power,* and that's more than most people can say!

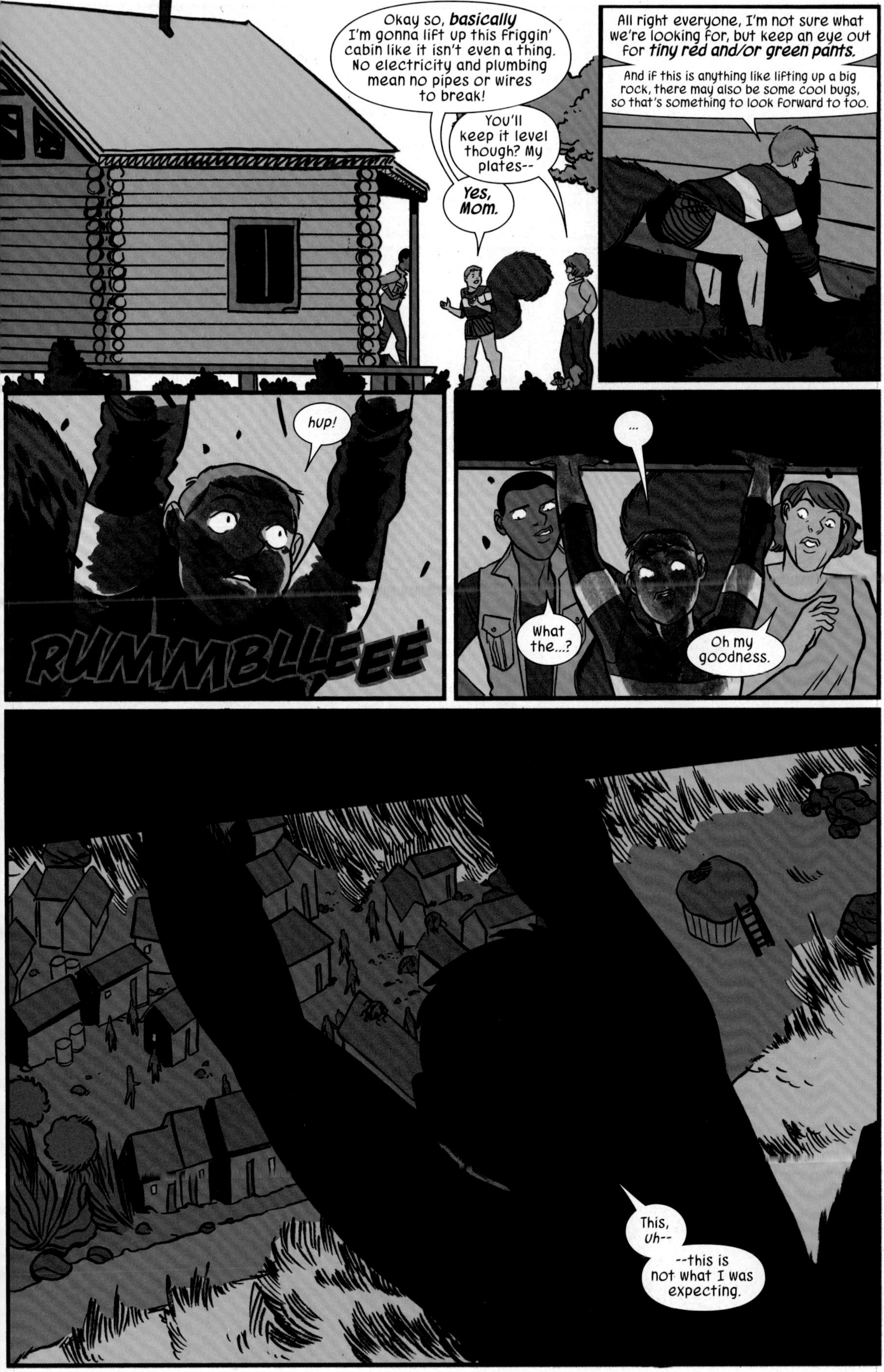

Okay so, **basically** I'm gonna lift up this friggin' cabin like it isn't even a thing. No electricity and plumbing mean no pipes or wires to break!
You'll keep it level though? My plates--
Yes, Mom.
All right everyone, I'm not sure what we're looking for, but keep an eye out for ***tiny red and/or green pants.***
And if this is anything like lifting up a big rock, there may also be some cool bugs, so that's something to look forward to too.
hup!
RUMMBLLEEE
...
What the...?
Oh my goodness.
This, uh--
--this is not what I was expecting.

Honestly: I'm not sure what I was expecting, but I feel confident in saying that "a tiny village beneath the floorboards" is the polar opposite of that.

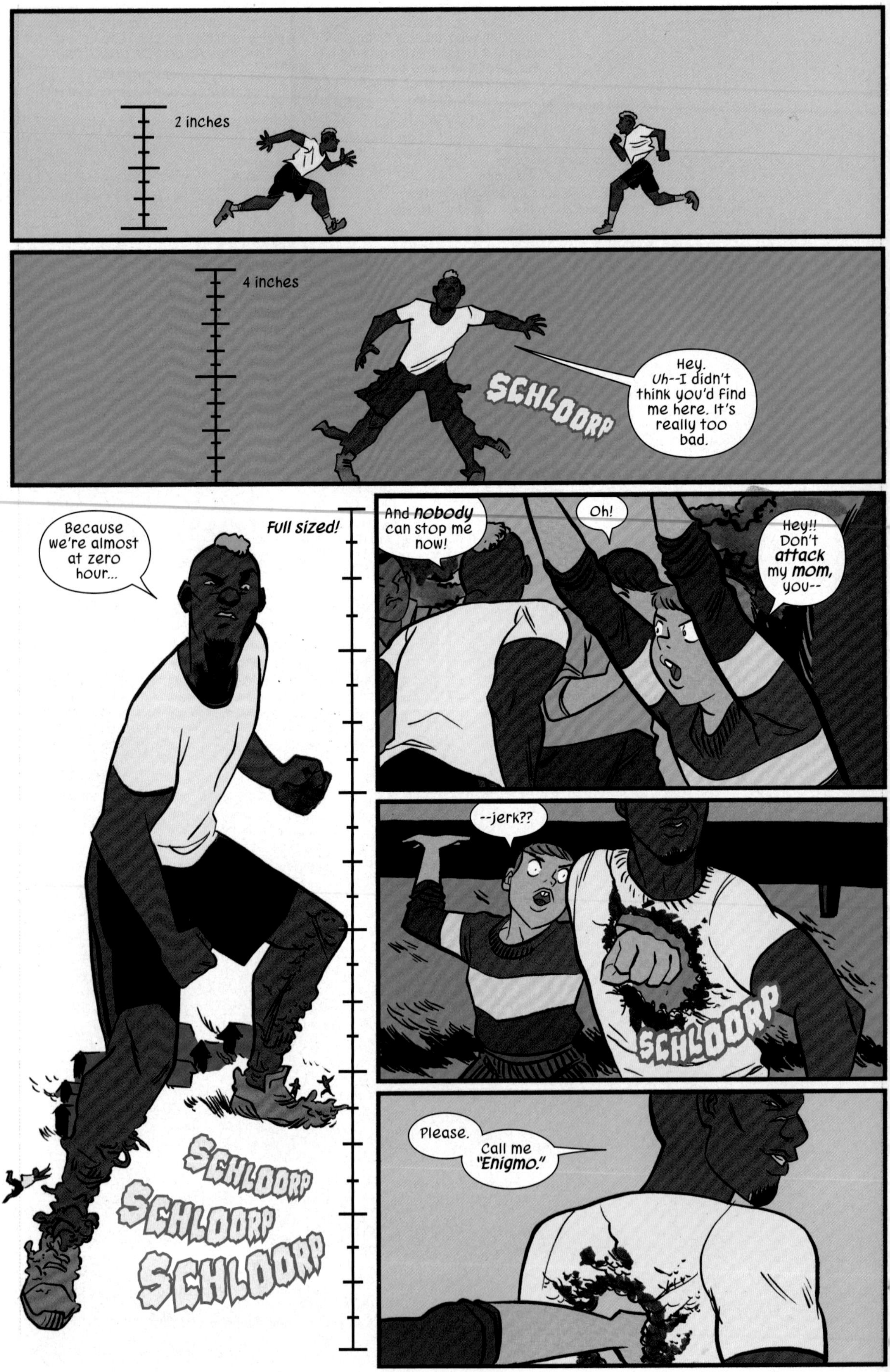
2 inches
4 inches
SCHLOORP
Hey.
Uh--I didn't think you'd find me here. It's really too bad.
Because we're almost at zero hour...
Full sized!
SCHLOORP
SCHLOORP
SCHLOORP
And *nobody* can stop me now!
Oh!
Hey!! Don't *attack* my *mom,* you--
--jerk??
SCHLOORP
Please.
Call me *"Enigmo."*

Enigmo. No, like "enigma," but with an "o." Enigmo. Look, do you have a pen? I can write it--no, it's not "Edward Nigmo"! You're thinking of another guy, and you're not even remembering him that accurately!!

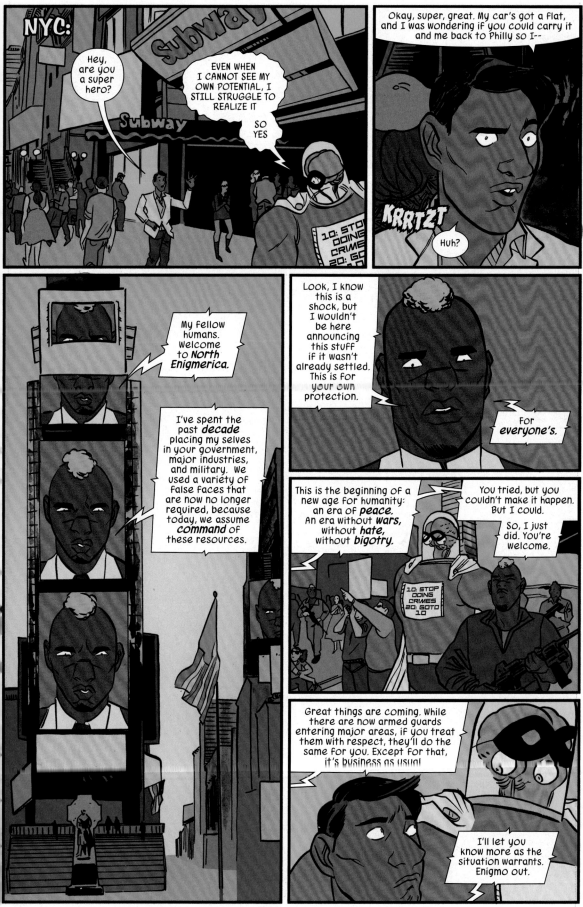

NYC:

Hey, are you a super hero?

EVEN WHEN I CANNOT SEE MY OWN POTENTIAL, I STILL STRUGGLE TO REALIZE IT

SO YES

10: STOP DOING CRIME 20: GO

Okay, super, great. My car's got a flat, and I was wondering if you could carry it and me back to Philly so I--

KRRTZT

Huh?

My fellow humans. Welcome to North Enigmerica.

I've spent the past decade placing my selves in your government, major industries, and military. We used a variety of false faces that are now no longer required, because today, we assume command of these resources.

Look, I know this is a shock, but I wouldn't be here announcing this stuff if it wasn't already settled. This is for your own protection.

For everyone's.

This is the beginning of a new age for humanity: an era of peace. An era without wars, without hate, without bigotry.

You tried, but you couldn't make it happen. But I could.

So, I just did. You're welcome.

10: STOP DOING CRIMES 20: GOTO 10

Great things are coming. While there are now armed guards entering major areas, if you treat them with respect, they'll do the same for you. Except for that, it's business as usual.

I'll let you know more as the situation warrants. Enigmo out.

Well, looks like that's it for NYC! But now let's cut back to what everyone's really concerned about: the quiet northern nation of Canada!!

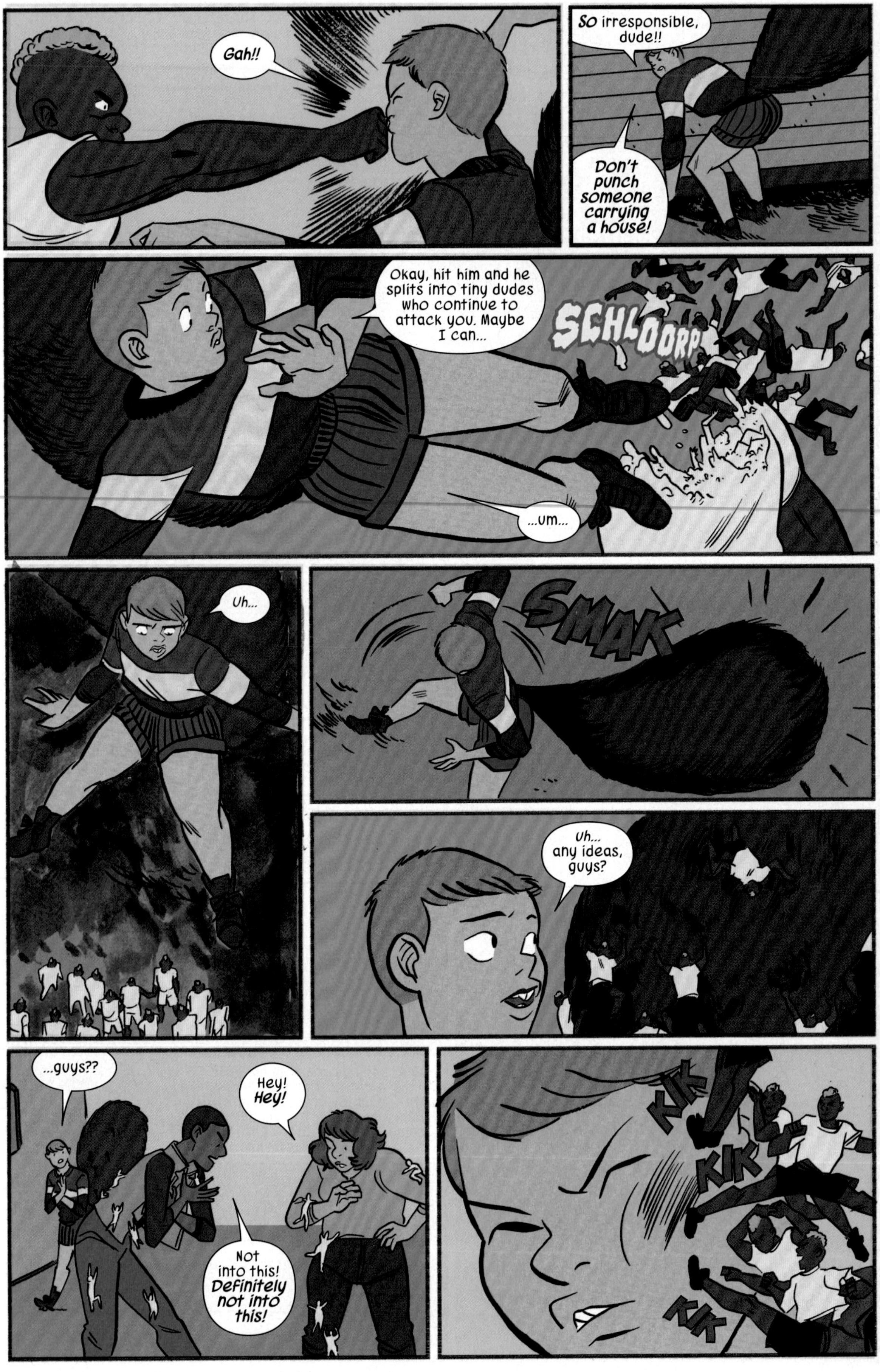
Gah!!
SO irresponsible, dude!!
Don't punch someone carrying a house!
Okay, hit him and he splits into tiny dudes who continue to attack you. Maybe I can...
SCHLOORP
...um...
Uh...
SMAK
Uh... any ideas, guys?
...guys??
Hey! Hey!
Not into this! Definitely not into this!
KIK
KIK
KIK

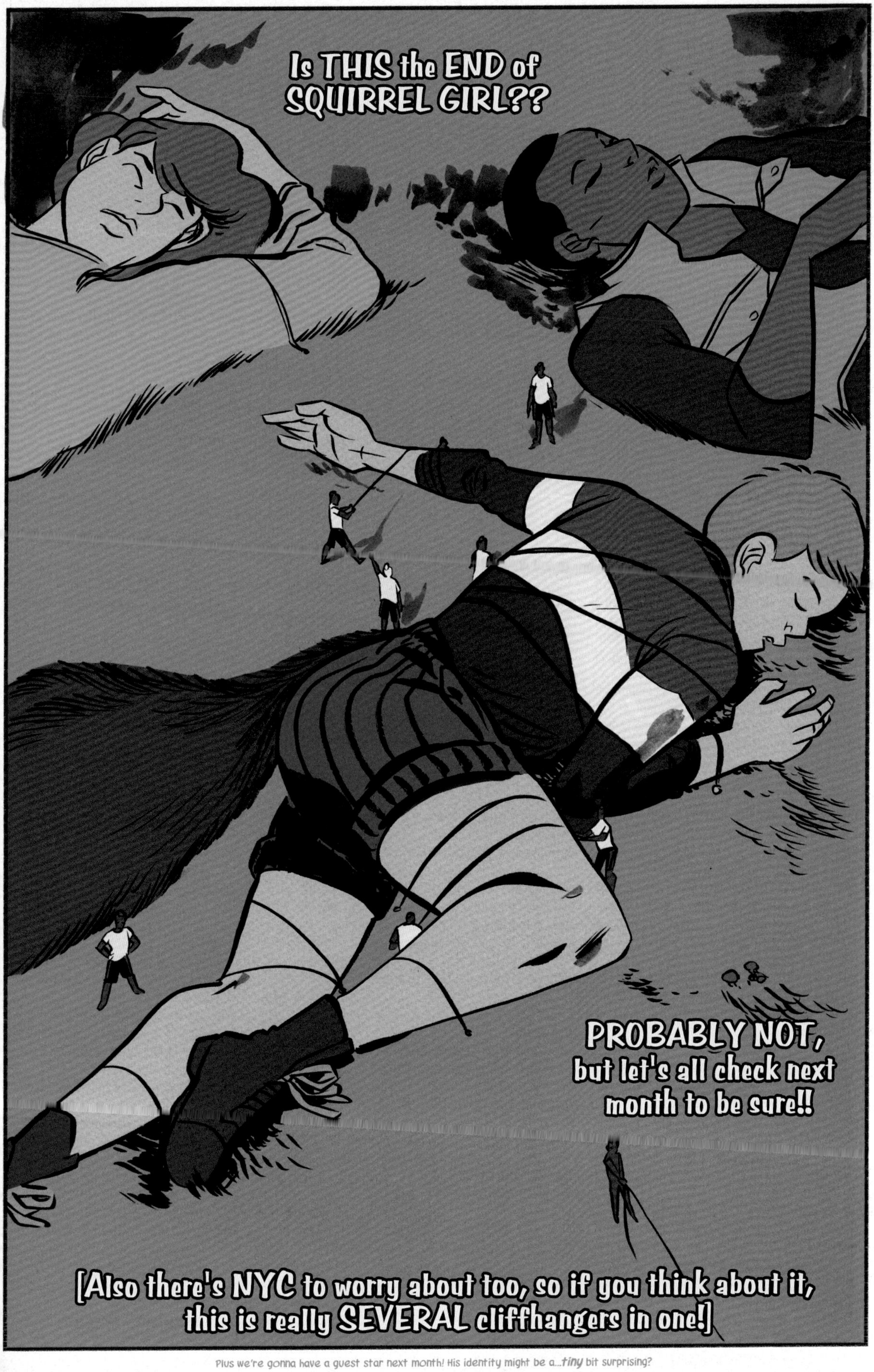

Plus we're gonna have a guest star next month! His identity might be a...*tiny* bit surprising?

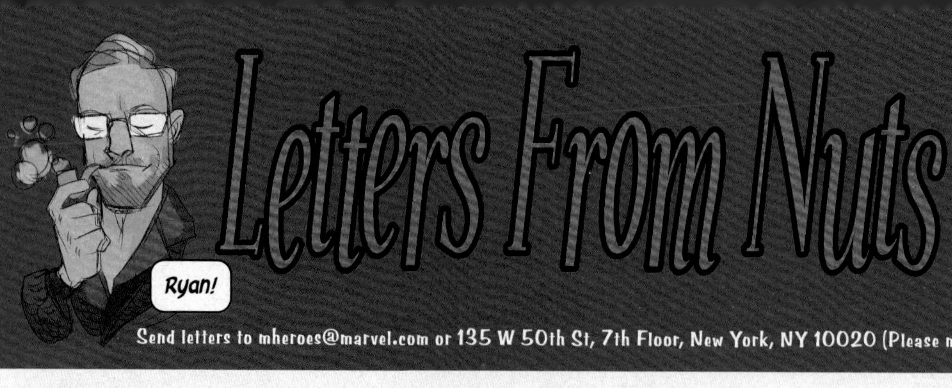
Ryan!

Letters From Nuts

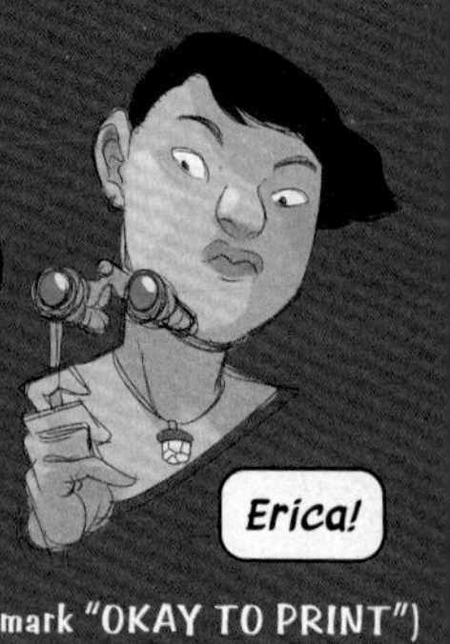
Erica!

Send letters to mheroes@marvel.com or 135 W 50th St, 7th Floor, New York, NY 10020 (Please mark "OKAY TO PRINT")

Hey, Squirrelly Friends!

I just got done reading SG #11, and I feel like every new issue reminds me how much I love this friggin' series! This issue had everything that makes SQUIRREL GIRL so unique and enjoyable, from the rad humor to the organic way that you weave fun facts and actual computer science terms into the story in a plot-relevant way.

Which actually brings me to a point! (Yay for segues!) I should preface this by saying that I totally understand that you were going for a computer science angle on this, but would you believe me if I told you that there is an even more efficient way to count on one hand? It's true, dudes! In American Sign Language, you can actually count up to 999 before having to bring in a second hand! Pretty neat, right?

Anyway, I loved, loved, loved the issue, and I cannot wait to see Erica and Ryan at NYCC this year. Keep being your awesome selves!

Peace out, Squirrel Scouts,
Shani

RYAN: I know a bit of ASL and I considered mentioning that style of finger-counting, but it didn't fit the computer science theme of the issue! Alas. You already know this, Shani, but guess what, everyone else? ASL is an amazing language. When my wife and I are at a party and we want to see if the other one wants to go home, we sometimes catch the other's eye and discreetly sign "GO [to] HOUSE?" It's really easy: you can sign "GO" by pointing your index fingers on each hand at each other and rotating them around each other in a rolling motion, and "HOUSE" is just making your hands form the roof of a house and then bringing them down for the walls. Do it really quick and nobody will even know you're the kind of person who leaves a party to go home because you get sleepy sometimes! Technically we should be saying "GO HOME?" but the sign for HOME is less discreet.

ERICA: Hey guys, I know a lot about computer science and sign language as well! Just don't ask me any questions about them. What fun we're having talking about things we all know about. Anyway, did you know that New York Comic Con will be the FIRST TIME Ryan and I are doing a convention together??

Dear Erica and Ryan,

I have been reading and re-reading SQUIRREL GIRL many times over the last month or two, and am on a bit of a squirre(vangelica)l mission to share its wonders with my comics-loving friends.

I stayed at a lovely place called Looking Stead in the Lake District (UK) last weekend where RED SQUIRRELS ARE AN ACTUAL FEATURE. Attached is a pic of my view at breakfast.

I have no idea if she's capable of kicking butts (crime being somewhat rare in them parts), but the other half of the theme song still seems to hold true.

P.S. The "squirrel" homonym puns don't work that well in the UK due to the difference in pronunciation. We're generally "squi-RUhl" more than "squrl." But that is like the only complaint I have about your comic so just keep being hilarious and I am sorry for bringing it up.

Unless Doreen comes to the UK, in which case IT IS ON (between squirrels, maybe).

Very much love,
Kevin

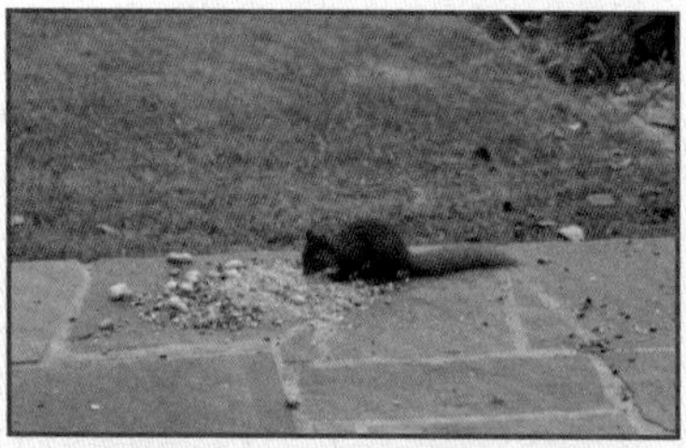

RYAN: I think Erica and I both SOMETIMES do a deliberate "Squir-RELL Guir-RELL" in the way we've heard people from the UK and Germany try to pronounce it so it rhymes. Two syllables for both "squirrel" and "girl"! It's actually very charming. Also, Kevin: Is crime rare in the parts where you saw the squirrels by chance, or could it be...the squirrels are the ones KEEPING the crime rate low?? Just something to think about in case you're planning to start stealing everyone's stuff in what I can tell you now is the delightful-looking Looking Stead in the Lake District.

ERICA: I love seeing other types of squirrels in the wild. I've always lived on the upper east coast so it's mostly eastern greys for me. Toronto is full of black squirrels. It's so cool. We'll be out in Leeds for the Thought Bubble comic convention later this year. I look forward to seeing what sorts of squirrels that trip will bring.

Dear Nutty Buddies,

After nearly two years, I was beginning to wonder when Erica was going to need a break, and I dreaded the idea of someone else coming along to try and fill her shoes. So let me just say how pleasantly surprised I was with guest artist Jacob Chabot's work in issue #11! And even without his sister from another mister, Ryan knocked another great issue out of the park too, so kudos to both of you. From Doc Ock to Kraven the College Administrator, this issue really felt like an homage to Squirrel Girl co-creator Steve Ditko in so many ways. I mean, if Doreen signaling "9 o'clock" in binary hand signs while defeating one of Doctor Strange's oldest villains, who in turn is wrapped in the symbiotic flesh of one of Spider-Man's most powerful adversaries isn't a totally kick-butt tribute to one of Marvel's great artist-creators, then I don't know what is! And thankfully, Erica wasn't completely absent from this issue either, and I'm not just talking about the final panel she drew. Her comment in the letters page about the best ever Nomad phase has secured her the highest place in my esteem for all time. Now, if you could just figure out a way to bring him back from the dead, Nomad would be in his "Lazarus Lorenzo Lamas" phase which, of course, would be even better!

Darryl Etheridge
St. Catharines, ON

P.S. I have to ask, do Doreen and/or Tippy-Toe ever watch AMC's *The Walking Dead* and, if so, how do they feel about Daryl Dixon's favorite snack?

RYAN: Here is a thing: I wrote this issue because I like to have one-shot issues between arcs where we can try something a little different, and it was already completely scripted when we realized Erica would need time off to focus on the UNBEATABLE SQUIRREL GIRL BEATS UP THE MARVEL UNIVERSE! book we're working on (which we already mentioned in the comic itself so it's not like I need to mention it again here BUT STILL). And by complete luck, the next issue to be drawn already had a stand-alone story where a different art style would fit perfectly WITHIN the narrative of the comic itself! Even that last panel of Doreen sleeping was already scripted; all we changed was to have that one drawn by Erica. So it worked out really well AND Jacob knocked it out of the friggin' park.

As for *The Walking Dead*, I've only played the Clementine games, so I'll have to defer to Erica's encyclopedia knowledge of television on this one.

ERICA: Haha. It wasn't even a break. It was "OH NO I STILL HAVE HALF OF THIS 105 PAGE OGN TO DRAW AND THERE'S THE MONTHLY BOOK TOO? WHY DID I AGREE TO THIS?" It was sort of the opposite of a break. Anyway, luckily I was heading to Heroes Con (run by our very own Rico Renzi) right as we decided to get a fill-in, so I spent the weekend scouting. I didn't even realize Jacob was there until the

con after-party and he was in my top two to do it. Serendipity!

Interestingly enough, even though I am always bingeing TV shows and horror movies while I work (it just helps having something else going on while I draw), I never got around to *The Walking Dead*. I haven't even played the game yet! Ask me any questions about *Community* or the *Hellraiser* series, though. Fun Fact: I don't put anything on while I do layouts because there's too much critical thinking there. Movies that I always work well to: *Resident Evil, Naked Lunch*.

Ryan and Erica,

This is the first letter I have EVER written to comic creators, and it starts out a little funny, but trust me, it will make sense in a minute. I am a huge SG fan, even more so since you two started working on it. I am also a STAR WARS fan. I have read everything, and I mean everything STAR WARS. Even stuff like the book where the Emperor's illegitimate triclops son finds the glove of Darth Vader on an underwater planet and it gives him the ability to use Force Lightning. Now Marvel has STAR WARS and the comics are great, and I love them. But on the days where USG and a STAR WARS comic come out at the same time, I look at them both. And without ANY hesitation at all, I pick up your comic and devour it while Poe looks on sadly or Luke just sits there waiting for me to get on with his story. I would once again like to impress how much your comic means to me and the joy it brings. I have loved STAR WARS since I was 4, about 30 years now, but now it has to wait so I can see the awesome adventures the Unbeatable, CS-loving Squirrel Girl and her amazing friends are up to. (Also, I can count to 31 on my fingers now! You guys rock!) Keep up the great work and May the squirrels be with you!

Brad Woolwine
Austin, TX

RYAN: Aw, Brad, this is great! Thank you. But now I really want to know about this triclops son and what his deal is. Was he a duoclops like most of us, who just overachieved? A quadroclops who lost an eye? Now I'm gonna have to read the STAR WARS book, "The Tale of the Triclops and the Underwater Lightning Glove," which is what I sincerely hope that book was called.

ERICA: Fun Fact: When I was a kid I always insisted on playing as Han Solo but also I had a lightsaber (large stick). I think all of us had lightsabers actually, as long as there were enough sticks.

Hi!

I just wanted to say how much I love your comics! I can see myself in Doreen (and Squirrel Girl) and I feel like if I were a super hero, I'd be like her. I am currently working on a Squirrel Girl costume for Halloween, despite somehow being "too old for dressing up"... I mean, you can never be too old for free candy, right? Also, I NEED to see Squirrel Girl say, "Quick! To the Squirrel Scooter!" :)

Nina G.
Milwaukee, WI
(P.S. Go Great Lakes Avengers!)

RYAN: Nina, you gotta send us pictures of your costume! You ARE never too old for candy (just ask my friend Joey, who – somehow?? – manages to survive on eating mostly candy) (KIDS: do not do this, there are Consequences) (ADULTS: don't do it either, I don't know how Joey hasn't turned into a giant Swedish Berry by now).

Speaking of the Great Lakes and their avenging thereof, I met Zac Gorman (he's writing the new GREAT LAKES AVENGERS book! It's gonna come out soon!) and we discussed SECRETS about Squirrel Girl, and now I'm super excited to see what the GLA get up to.

ERICA: WHAT? THERE ARE SECRETS? WHY DON'T I KNOW THESE SECRETS? Don't say that it's because they're secret, RYAN. Anyway, it is August as I type this and I'm already stressing out because my fiancé and I haven't planned out our matching Halloween costumes yet, so don't worry. Anyway, cosplay tips: Costume 1 is a halter body suit. Costume 2 is a tennis dress with capri leggings (because I got really excited that they make sports dresses but then I was like "these are so short you're literally jumping around and now everybody has seen your butt").

Ryan,

Some suggestions for Nancy Whitehead catchphrases:

Go for the eyes, Mew!

Stuck with ANSI? Here comes Nancy!

It's time to knit sweaters and pet Mew.

It's time to count stitches and engage in at times heated, albeit always rational, discourse!

Also, does Nancy have a middle name and does it start with "P" because then her catchphrase could be "You've got an NP problem to deal with now, buddy." /slickt/

That sound effect is an HP RPN calculator opening.

Erica, you are perfect in every conceivable way appropriate to the appreciation of your work by an old married man.

Please never stop,
Gary

RYAN: These are all solid catchphrases and I see nothing wrong with any of them! I do like the idea of Nancy taunting a bad guy by saying "Things are about to get hard for you, buddy. NP HARD." Fun Fact: I attended a lecture by Professor Cook – who introduced the P vs NP problem, which remains the greatest open question in computer science at the University of Toronto! If you ask ME, P does NOT equal NP, but I, uh, don't know how to prove it. For those of us who don't have a ready knowledge of computer research to refer to, know this: Nancy's tagline is extremely excellent and if she ever fought someone who studied computational complexity theory, they would be very impressed by it.

ERICA: Gary is a smart guy. Real smart.

Dear Ryan and Erica,

I'm 9 years old and I LOVE, LOVE, LOVE the SQUIRREL GIRL comics! They're so funny! My dad and I go to our favorite comic book store and buy SQUIRREL GIRL comics along with my mom. I just recently had a SG comic book marathon with my guinea pig, Twix. She jumps around happily while I read out loud to her. Twix is going to be Tippy-Toe, my dad and mom are going to probably be squirrels, and I'll be Squirrel Girl for Halloween. Quick question: Does Twix look a bit like Tippy-Toe? Keep up the great work with these comics!!! (Attached is a picture of Twix.) #<3SG4EVER

Your Squirrel Girl Fans,
Isabel Mendoza and Twix
Las Vegas, Nevada

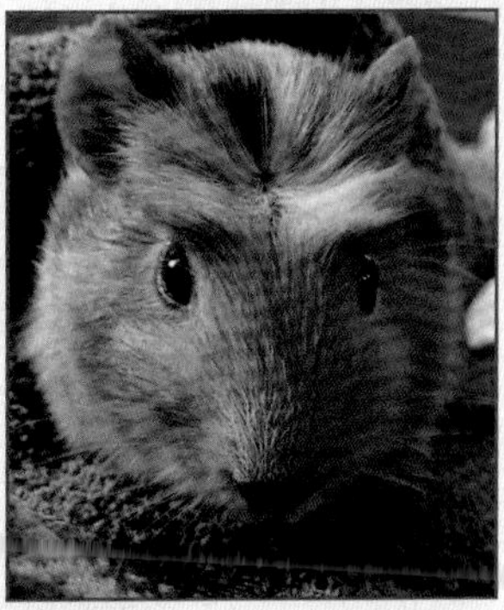

RYAN: TWIX LOOKS SUPER CUTE AND I CAN DEFINITELY SEE THE RESEMBLANCE. Also I love that you and Twix are going as Squirrel Girl and Tippy, respectively, and your parents are going as unnamed squirrels. That's what they get for not calling more exciting characters sooner!

ERICA: Dear Isabel, please send us pictures of Twix in a little bow. I suggest a tiny clip-on since I think most rodents will not deal well with a ribbon tied around them (Tippy-Toe is not most rodents). Also send us photos of ALL OF YOU IN COSTUME.

Next Issue:

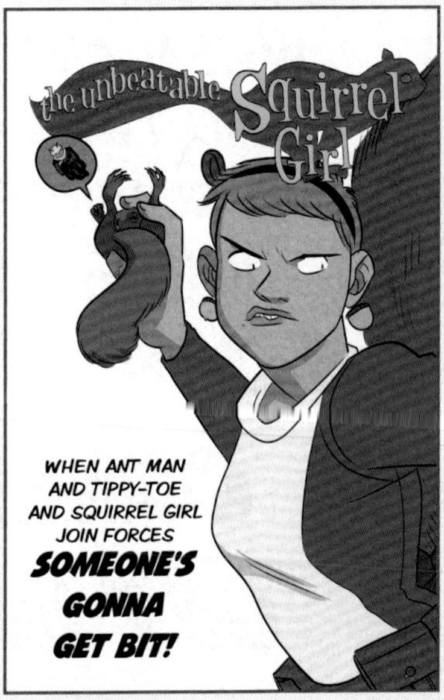

the unbeatable Squirrel Girl
WHEN ANT MAN AND TIPPY-TOE AND SQUIRREL GIRL JOIN FORCES
SOMEONE'S GONNA GET BIT!

Attention, Squirrel Scouts! Make sure to check out our production blog, **unbeatablesquirrelgirl.tumblr.com**, where we post behind-the-scenes stuff on how the book gets made, along with all sorts of cool things *you* make: fanart, cosplay, whatever!

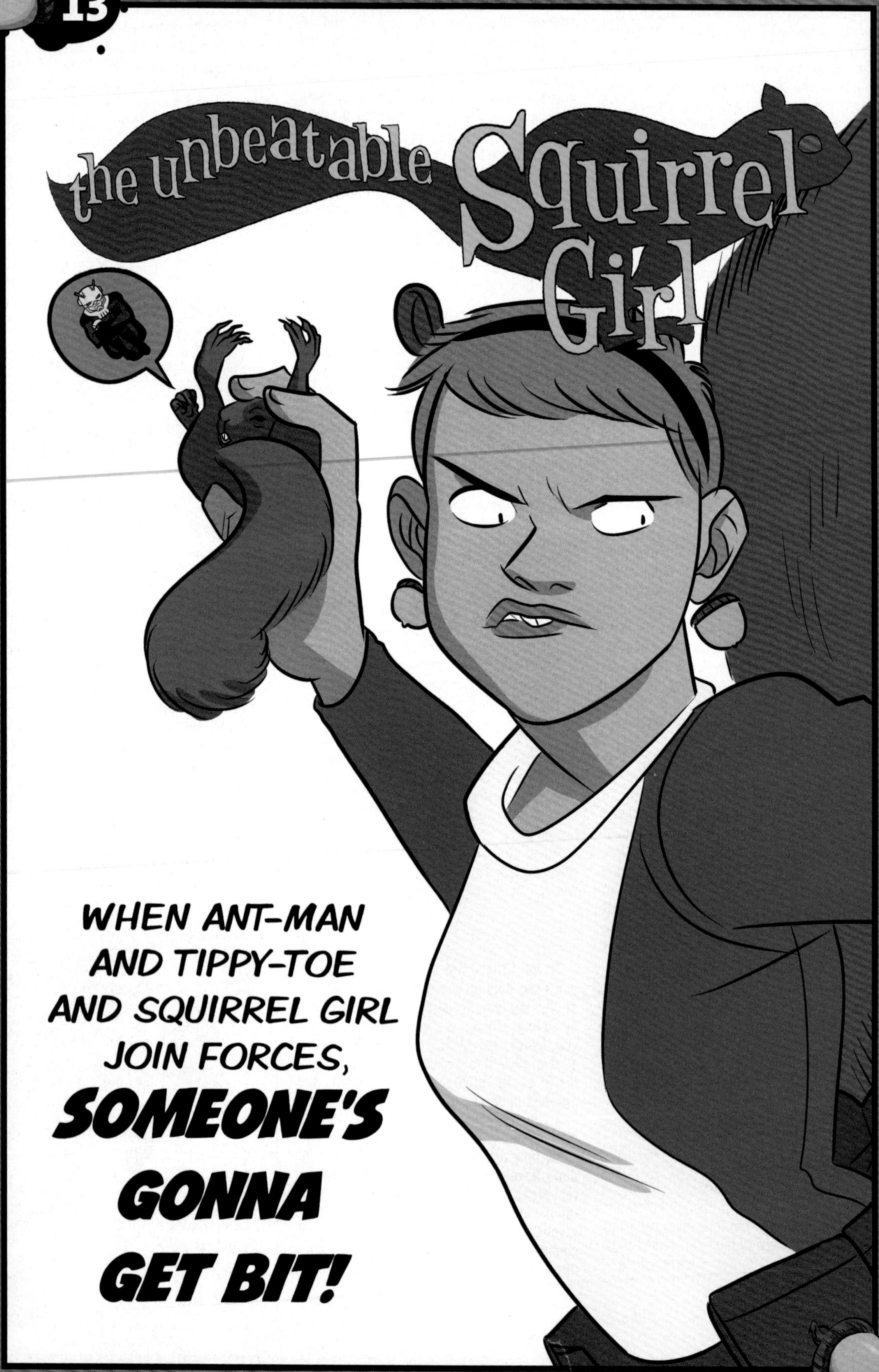
the unbeatable Squirrel Girl
WHEN ANT-MAN AND TIPPY-TOE AND SQUIRREL GIRL JOIN FORCES,
SOMEONE'S GONNA GET BIT!

Doreen Green isn't just a second-year computer science student: she secretly also has all the powers of both squirrel and girl! She uses her amazing abilities to fight crime and be as awesome as possible. You know her as... ***The Unbeatable Squirrel Girl!*** *Find out what she's been up to, with...*

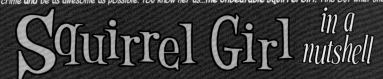

Squirrel Girl *in a nutshell*

Squirrel Girl @unbeatablesg
guys i'm SO BORED, i'm up here in CANADA but there's NOTHING TO DO except read boring magazines

Squirrel Girl @unbeatablesg
and the magazines are SO BORING that i can no longer use punctuation or capital letters

Squirrel Girl @unbeatablesg
boredom has literally sucked the ability to use punctuation out of me

Squirrel Girl @unbeatablesg
science thought it couldn't be done

Squirrel Girl @unbeatablesg
but here we are

Squirrel Girl @unbeatablesg
me with internet: HI I'M COOL AND CAN DISCUSS SEVERAL INTERESTING SUBJECTS!!!
me without internet: i wonder what bark tastes like

Squirrel Girl @unbeatablesg
me with internet: I HAVE SEVERAL HOT TAKES ABOUT TODAY'S NEWS!!
me without internet: so it's decided: i can sneeze at least 3 different ways

Squirrel Girl @unbeatablesg
me with internet: CAN'T WAIT TO CHILL WITH MY PAL TONY STARK ON SOCIAL MEDIA
me without internet: me and that rock are bffs, don't @ me

Squirrel Girl @unbeatablesg
me with internet: WOW SO THAT'S WHAT MY ROBOT PAL BRAIN DRAIN IS DOING IN NYC!
me without internet: i have unsolicited opinions on gardening

Squirrel Girl @unbeatablesg
UPDATE: guys it's a few hours later and things are more interesting now!! There's a CRIME going on!

Squirrel Girl @unbeatablesg
Someone is stealing muffins from my mom!! It's the CASE of the MISSING MUFFINS and I am ON IT

Squirrel Girl @unbeatablesg
also yes I am aware of how pathetic this sounds but listen, I NEED THIS

Squirrel Girl @unbeatablesg
UPDATE 2: okay it turns out there's a whole city of tiny men living beneath our rental cottage who can split apart and back together

Squirrel Girl @unbeatablesg
and who are attacking us on sight for some reason that I don't know!! WHOA!!

Squirrel Girl @unbeatablesg
Anyway I queued these all to post when I'm back in a place that has FRIGGIN' DATA but I should really get back to it

Squirrel Girl @unbeatablesg
Can't fake being knocked out FOREVER, you know?

Squirrel Girl @unbeatablesg
Plus, these tiny Enigmos who are trying to tie me to the ground aren't gonna let me use my phone indefinitely, I'm pretty sure

search!

#canadafacts
#dontatme
#gardening
#thatsapaddlin
#enigmos

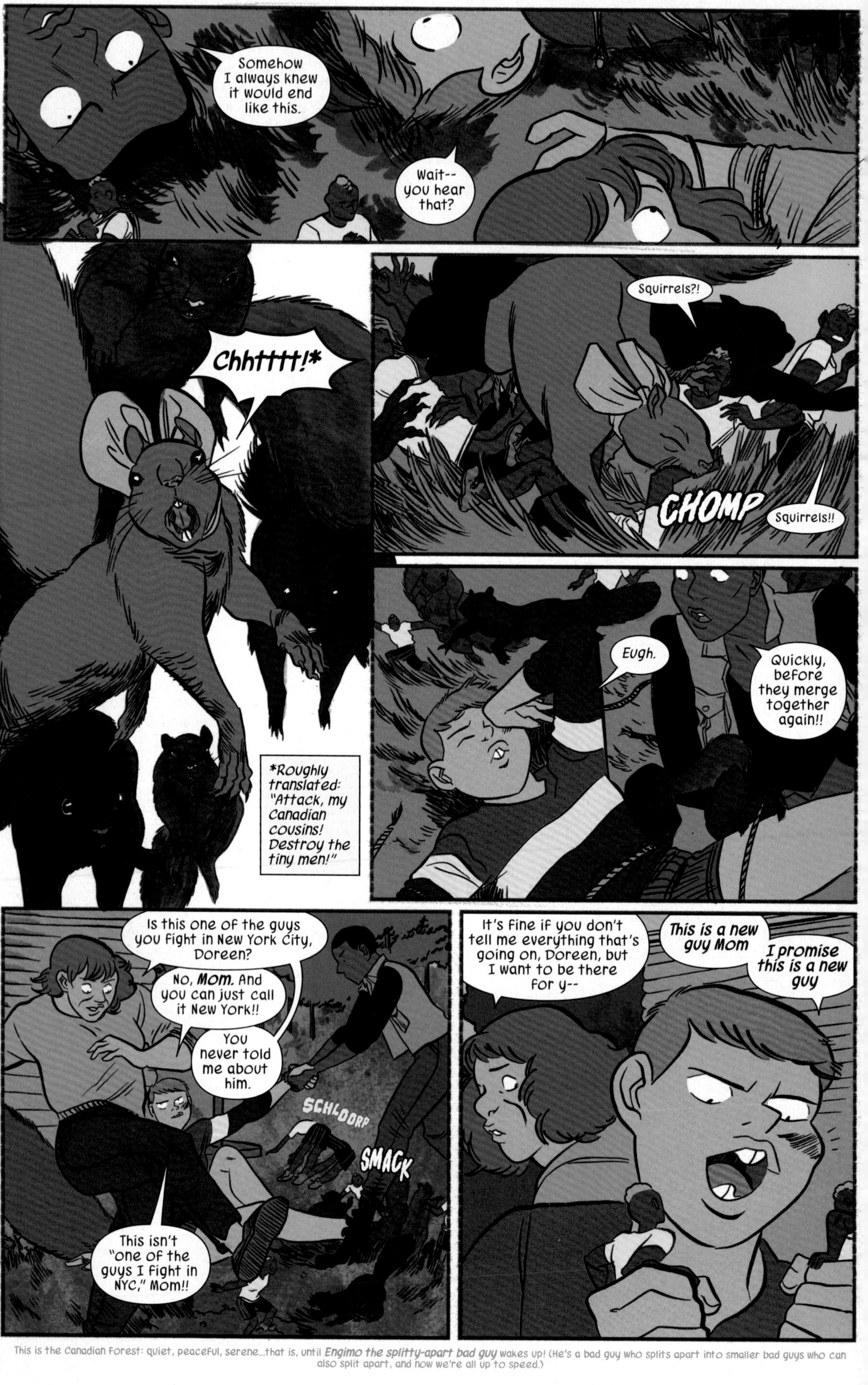
Somehow I always knew it would end like this.
Wait-- you hear that?
Chhtttt!*
*Roughly translated: "Attack, my Canadian cousins! Destroy the tiny men!"
Squirrels?!
CHOMP
Squirrels!!
Eugh.
Quickly, before they merge together again!!
Is this one of the guys you fight in New York City, Doreen?
No, Mom. And you can just call it New York!!
You never told me about him.
SCHLOORP
SMACK
This isn't "one of the guys I fight in NYC," Mom!!
It's fine if you don't tell me everything that's going on, Doreen, but I want to be there for y--
This is a new guy Mom
I promise this is a new guy

This is the Canadian Forest: quiet, peaceful, serene...that is, until ***Engimo the splitty-apart bad guy*** wakes up! (He's a bad guy who splits apart into smaller bad guys who can also split apart, and now we're all up to speed.)

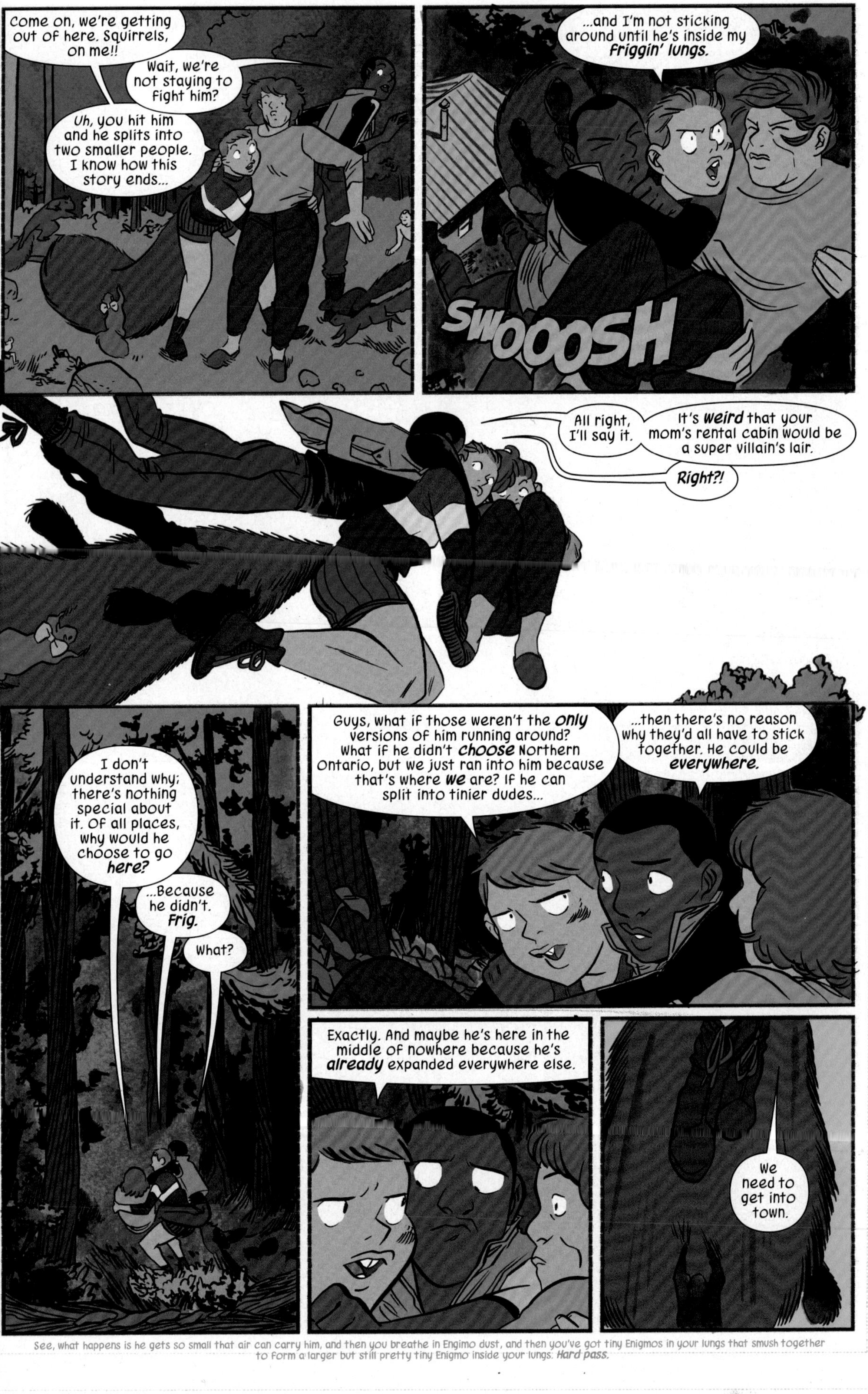

Come on, we're getting out of here. Squirrels, on me!!
Wait, we're not staying to fight him?
Uh, you hit him and he splits into two smaller people. I know how this story ends...
...and I'm not sticking around until he's inside my *friggin' lungs.*
SWOOOSH
All right, I'll say it.
It's *weird* that your mom's rental cabin would be a super villain's lair.
Right?!
I don't understand why; there's nothing special about it. Of all places, why would he choose to go *here?*
...Because he didn't. *Frig.*
What?
Guys, what if those weren't the *only* versions of him running around? What if he didn't *choose* Northern Ontario, but we just ran into him because that's where *we* are? If he can split into tinier dudes...
...then there's no reason why they'd all have to stick together. He could be *everywhere.*
Exactly. And maybe he's here in the middle of nowhere because he's *already* expanded everywhere else.
We need to get into town.

See, what happens is he gets so small that air can carry him, and then you breathe in Engimo dust, and then you've got tiny Enigmos in your lungs that smush together to form a larger but still pretty tiny Enigmo inside your lungs. ***Hard pass.***

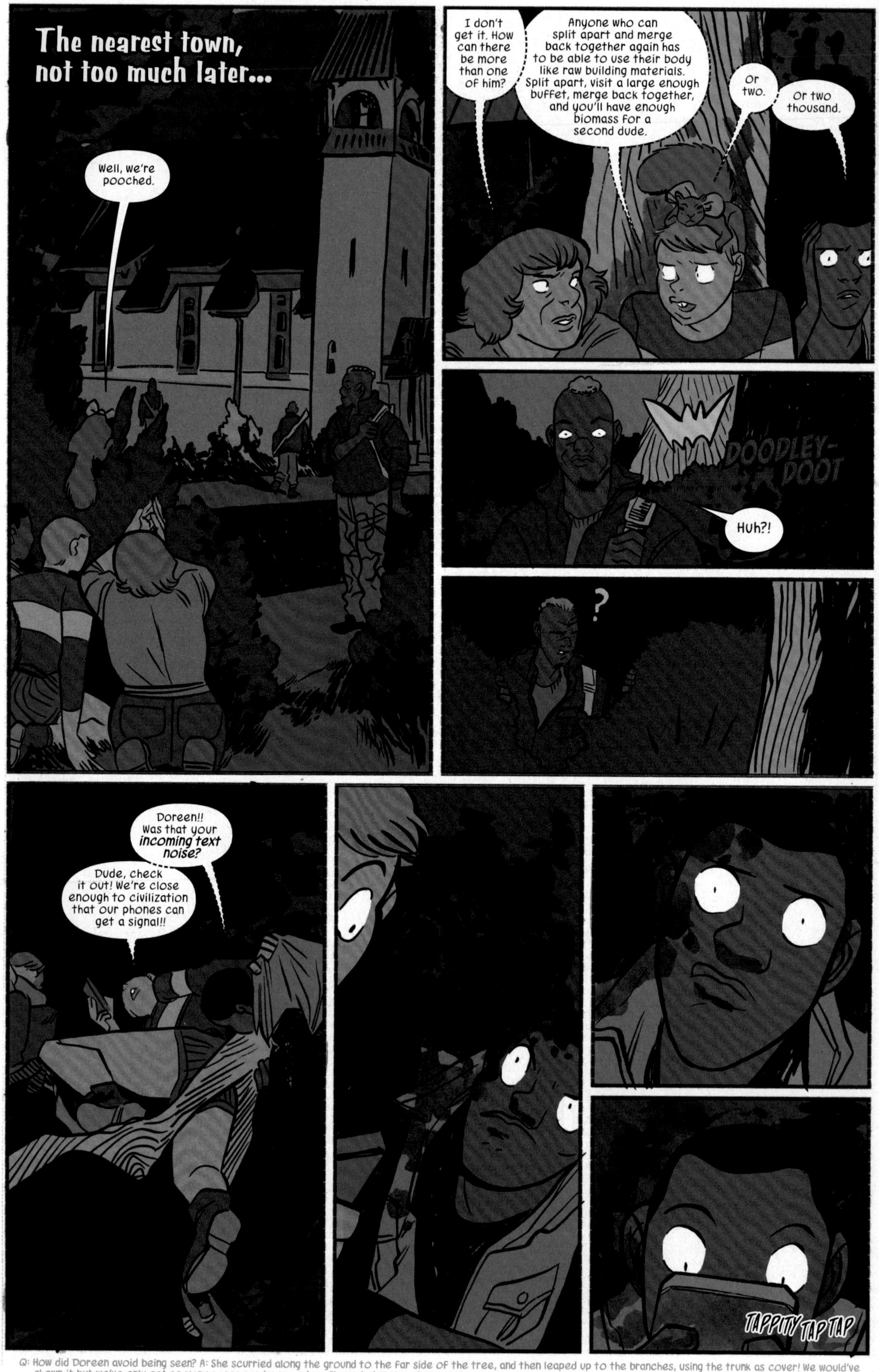

The nearest town, not too much later...
Well, we're pooched.
I don't get it. How can there be more than one of him?
Anyone who can split apart and merge back together again has to be able to use their body like raw building materials. Split apart, visit a large enough buffet, merge back together, and you'll have enough biomass for a second dude.
Or two.
Or two thousand.
DOODLEY-DOOT
Huh?!
?
Doreen!! Was that your *incoming text noise?*
Dude, check it out! We're close enough to civilization that our phones can get a signal!!
TAPPITY TAP TAP

Q: How did Doreen avoid being seen? A: She scurried along the ground to the far side of the tree, and then leaped up to the branches, using the trunk as cover! We would've shown it but we've only got so many pages per issue, and we figured y'all already knew the specifics of tree-based stealth! You're ***Squirrel Girl readers.*** You got this!

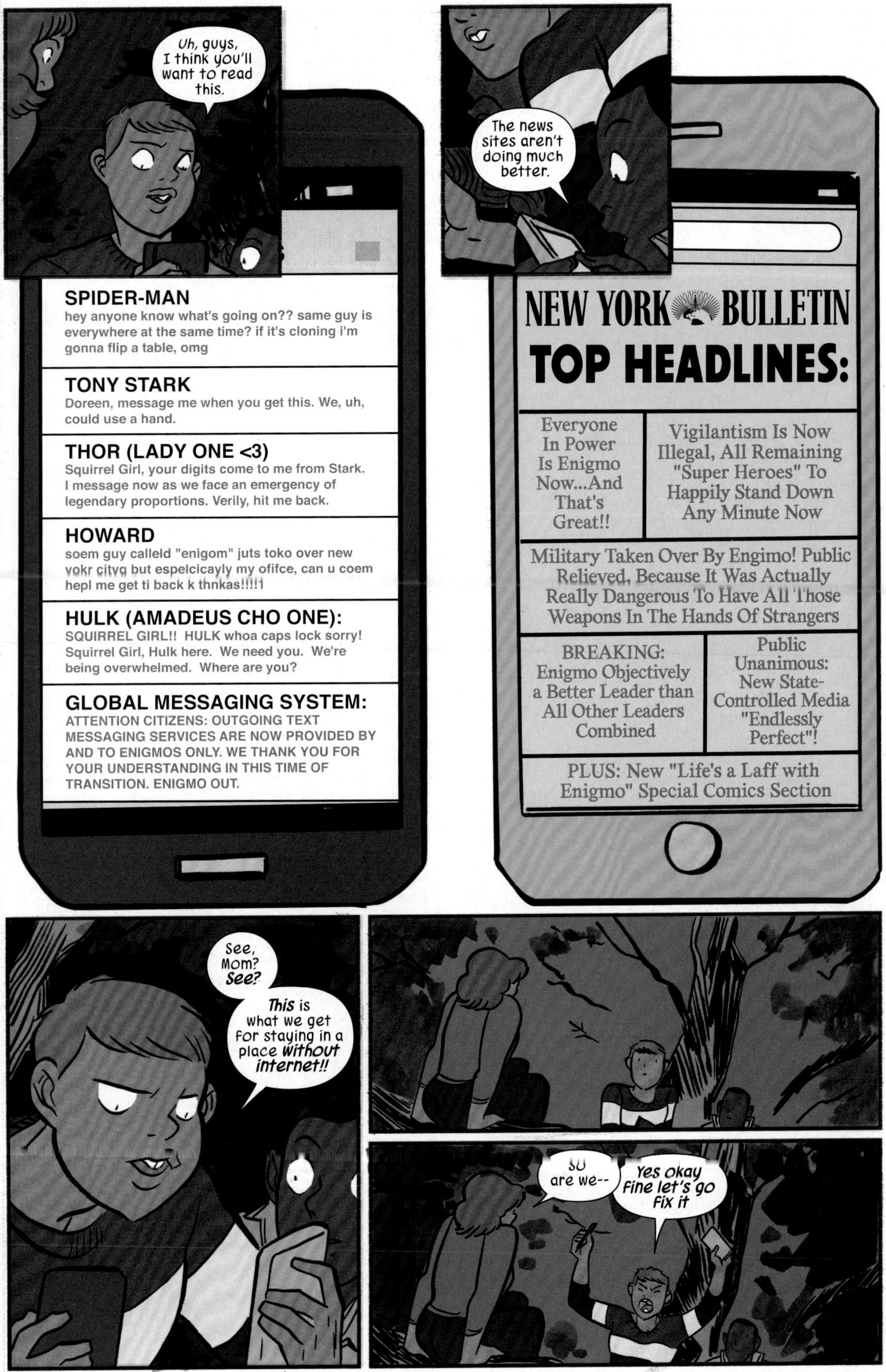

Uh, guys, I think you'll want to read this.
SPIDER-MAN
hey anyone know what's going on?? same guy is everywhere at the same time? if it's cloning i'm gonna flip a table, omg
TONY STARK
Doreen, message me when you get this. We, uh, could use a hand.
THOR (LADY ONE <3)
Squirrel Girl, your digits come to me from Stark. I message now as we face an emergency of legendary proportions. Verily, hit me back.
HOWARD
soem guy calleld "enigom" juts toko over new vokr cityq but espelcicayly my ofifce, can u coem hepl me get ti back k thnkas!!!!1
HULK (AMADEUS CHO ONE):
SQUIRREL GIRL!! HULK whoa caps lock sorry! Squirrel Girl, Hulk here. We need you. We're being overwhelmed. Where are you?
GLOBAL MESSAGING SYSTEM:
ATTENTION CITIZENS: OUTGOING TEXT MESSAGING SERVICES ARE NOW PROVIDED BY AND TO ENIGMOS ONLY. WE THANK YOU FOR YOUR UNDERSTANDING IN THIS TIME OF TRANSITION. ENIGMO OUT.
The news sites aren't doing much better.
NEW YORK BULLETIN
TOP HEADLINES:
Everyone In Power Is Enigmo Now...And That's Great!!
Vigilantism Is Now Illegal, All Remaining "Super Heroes" To Happily Stand Down Any Minute Now
Military Taken Over By Engimo! Public Relieved, Because It Was Actually Really Dangerous To Have All Those Weapons In The Hands Of Strangers
BREAKING: Enigmo Objectively a Better Leader than All Other Leaders Combined
Public Unanimous: New State-Controlled Media "Endlessly Perfect"!
PLUS: New "Life's a Laff with Enigmo" Special Comics Section
See, Mom? See?
This is what we get for staying in a place without internet!!
So are we--
Yes okay fine let's go fix it

alos he kcikde me in teh btutt adn caleld me "quackres," whikc, like, *heollo* I'ev hearfd rthem all ebfore! I've herads thme aloi befoer, sqyulkrel guril!! waugh!!! anywya hti me bakc

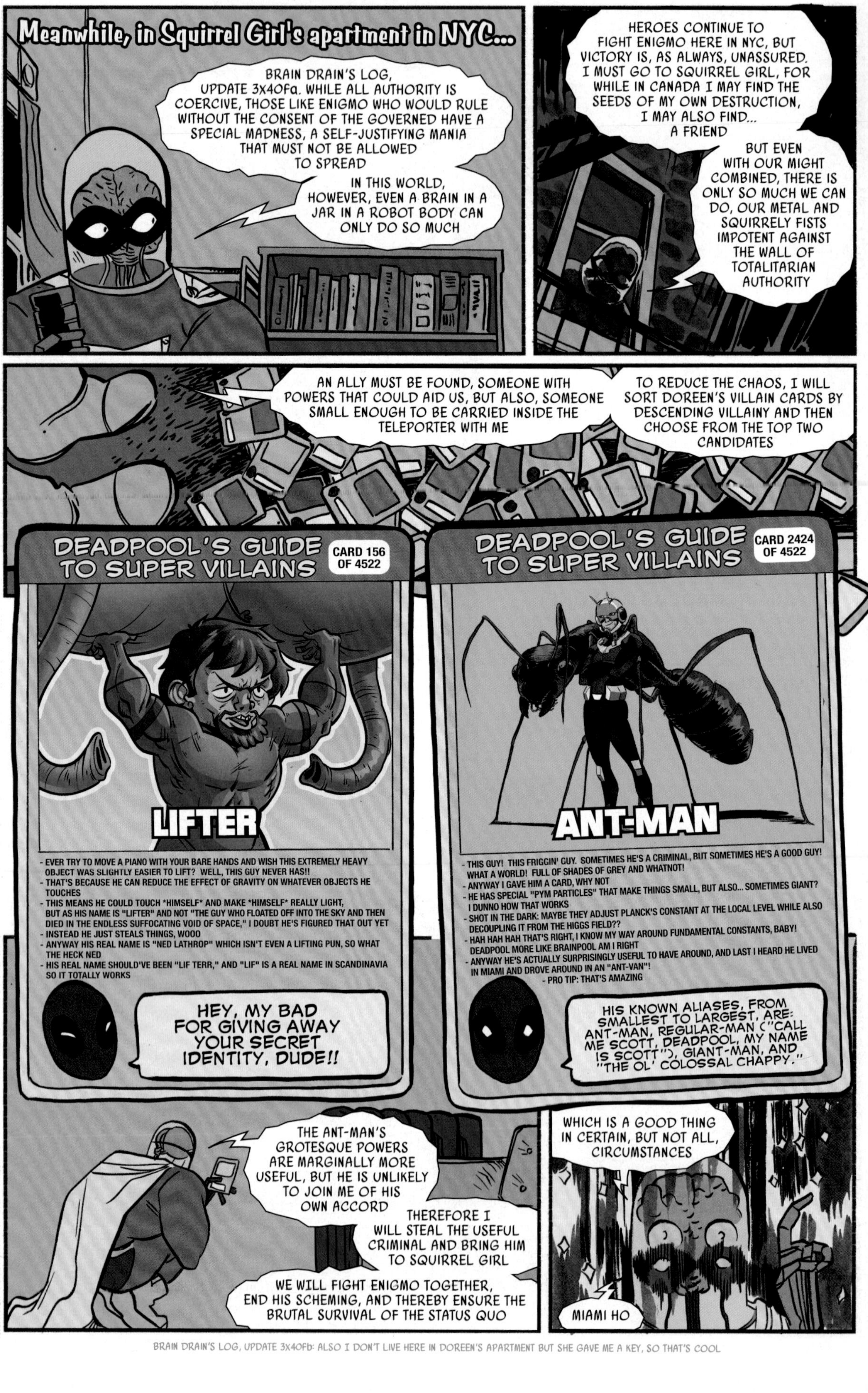
Meanwhile, in Squirrel Girl's apartment in NYC...
BRAIN DRAIN'S LOG, UPDATE 3x40Fa. WHILE ALL AUTHORITY IS COERCIVE, THOSE LIKE ENIGMO WHO WOULD RULE WITHOUT THE CONSENT OF THE GOVERNED HAVE A SPECIAL MADNESS, A SELF-JUSTIFYING MANIA THAT MUST NOT BE ALLOWED TO SPREAD
IN THIS WORLD, HOWEVER, EVEN A BRAIN IN A JAR IN A ROBOT BODY CAN ONLY DO SO MUCH
HEROES CONTINUE TO FIGHT ENIGMO HERE IN NYC, BUT VICTORY IS, AS ALWAYS, UNASSURED. I MUST GO TO SQUIRREL GIRL, FOR WHILE IN CANADA I MAY FIND THE SEEDS OF MY OWN DESTRUCTION, I MAY ALSO FIND... A FRIEND
BUT EVEN WITH OUR MIGHT COMBINED, THERE IS ONLY SO MUCH WE CAN DO, OUR METAL AND SQUIRRELY FISTS IMPOTENT AGAINST THE WALL OF TOTALITARIAN AUTHORITY
AN ALLY MUST BE FOUND, SOMEONE WITH POWERS THAT COULD AID US, BUT ALSO, SOMEONE SMALL ENOUGH TO BE CARRIED INSIDE THE TELEPORTER WITH ME
TO REDUCE THE CHAOS, I WILL SORT DOREEN'S VILLAIN CARDS BY DESCENDING VILLAINY AND THEN CHOOSE FROM THE TOP TWO CANDIDATES
DEADPOOL'S GUIDE TO SUPER VILLAINS
CARD 156 OF 4522
LIFTER
- EVER TRY TO MOVE A PIANO WITH YOUR BARE HANDS AND WISH THIS EXTREMELY HEAVY OBJECT WAS SLIGHTLY EASIER TO LIFT? WELL, THIS GUY NEVER HAS!!
- THAT'S BECAUSE HE CAN REDUCE THE EFFECT OF GRAVITY ON WHATEVER OBJECTS HE TOUCHES
- THIS MEANS HE COULD TOUCH *HIMSELF* AND MAKE *HIMSELF* REALLY LIGHT, BUT AS HIS NAME IS "LIFTER" AND NOT "THE GUY WHO FLOATED OFF INTO THE SKY AND THEN DIED IN THE ENDLESS SUFFOCATING VOID OF SPACE," I DOUBT HE'S FIGURED THAT OUT YET
- INSTEAD HE JUST STEALS THINGS, WOOO
- ANYWAY HIS REAL NAME IS "NED LATHROP" WHICH ISN'T EVEN A LIFTING PUN, SO WHAT THE HECK NED
- HIS REAL NAME SHOULD'VE BEEN "LIF TERR," AND "LIF" IS A REAL NAME IN SCANDINAVIA SO IT TOTALLY WORKS
HEY, MY BAD FOR GIVING AWAY YOUR SECRET IDENTITY, DUDE!!
DEADPOOL'S GUIDE TO SUPER VILLAINS
CARD 2424 OF 4522
ANT-MAN
- THIS GUY! THIS FRIGGIN' GUY. SOMETIMES HE'S A CRIMINAL, BUT SOMETIMES HE'S A GOOD GUY! WHAT A WORLD! FULL OF SHADES OF GREY AND WHATNOT!
- ANYWAY I GAVE HIM A CARD, WHY NOT
- HE HAS SPECIAL "PYM PARTICLES" THAT MAKE THINGS SMALL, BUT ALSO... SOMETIMES GIANT? I DUNNO HOW THAT WORKS
- SHOT IN THE DARK: MAYBE THEY ADJUST PLANCK'S CONSTANT AT THE LOCAL LEVEL WHILE ALSO DECOUPLING IT FROM THE HIGGS FIELD??
- HAH HAH HAH THAT'S RIGHT, I KNOW MY WAY AROUND FUNDAMENTAL CONSTANTS, BABY! DEADPOOL MORE LIKE BRAINPOOL AM I RIGHT
- ANYWAY HE'S ACTUALLY SURPRISINGLY USEFUL TO HAVE AROUND, AND LAST I HEARD HE LIVED IN MIAMI AND DROVE AROUND IN AN "ANT-VAN"!
- PRO TIP: THAT'S AMAZING
HIS KNOWN ALIASES, FROM SMALLEST TO LARGEST, ARE: ANT-MAN, REGULAR-MAN ("CALL ME SCOTT, DEADPOOL, MY NAME IS SCOTT"), GIANT-MAN, AND "THE OL' COLOSSAL CHAPPY."
THE ANT-MAN'S GROTESQUE POWERS ARE MARGINALLY MORE USEFUL, BUT HE IS UNLIKELY TO JOIN ME OF HIS OWN ACCORD
THEREFORE I WILL STEAL THE USEFUL CRIMINAL AND BRING HIM TO SQUIRREL GIRL
WE WILL FIGHT ENIGMO TOGETHER, END HIS SCHEMING, AND THEREBY ENSURE THE BRUTAL SURVIVAL OF THE STATUS QUO
WHICH IS A GOOD THING IN CERTAIN, BUT NOT ALL, CIRCUMSTANCES
MIAMI HO

BRAIN DRAIN'S LOG, UPDATE 3x40Fb: ALSO I DON'T LIVE HERE IN DOREEN'S APARTMENT BUT SHE GAVE ME A KEY, SO THAT'S COOL

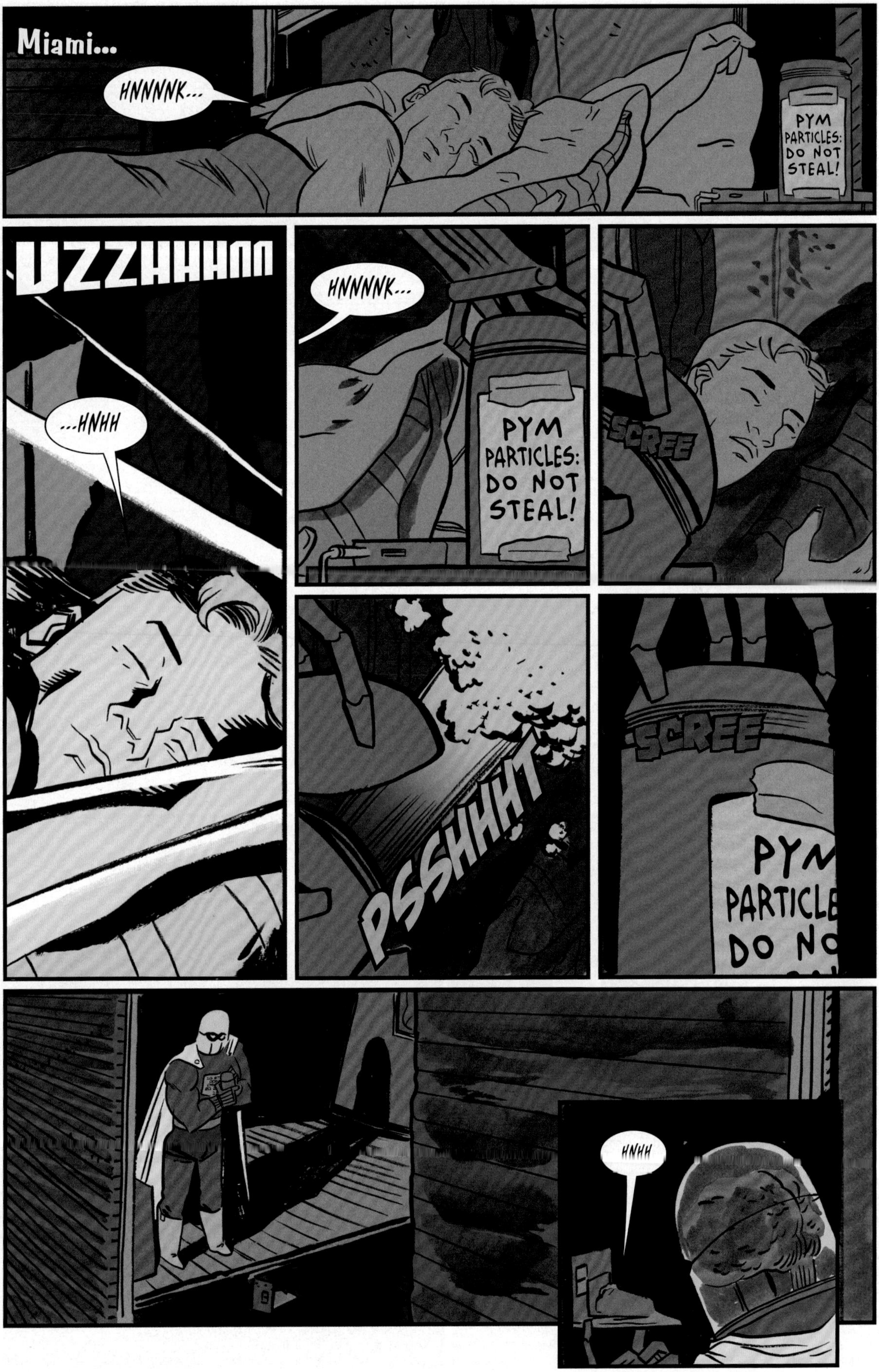
Miami...
HNNNNK...
PYM PARTICLES: DO NOT STEAL!
...HNH
HNNNNK...
PYM PARTICLES: DO NOT STEAL!
SCREE
PSSHHHT
SCREE
PYM PARTICLE DO NO
HNHH

Those *"HNNNNK"* and *"HNHH"* are snoring sound effects. I created them by listening to someone snore as they slept while taking detailed notes!!

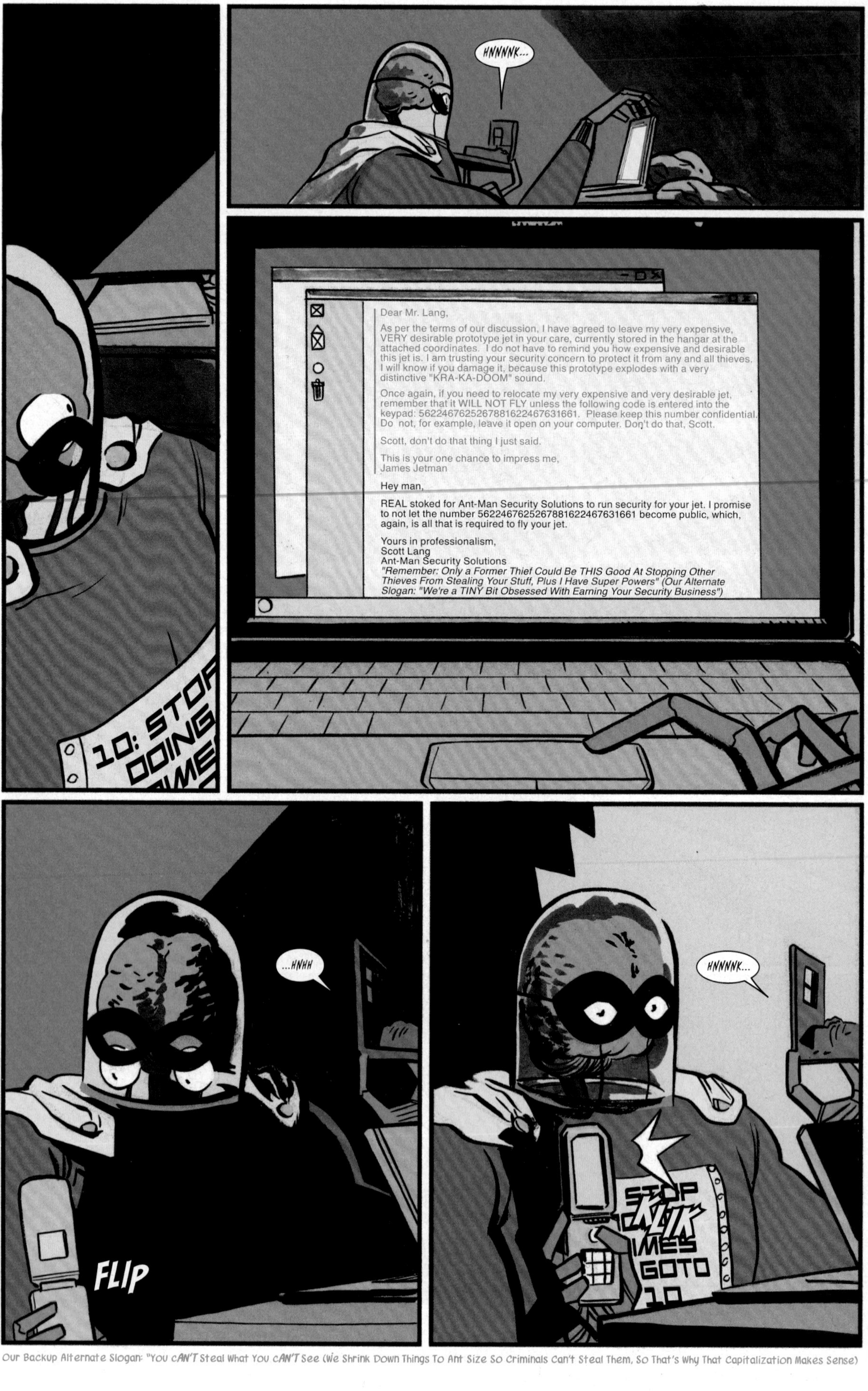
HNNNNK...
Dear Mr. Lang,
As per the terms of our discussion, I have agreed to leave my very expensive, VERY desirable prototype jet in your care, currently stored in the hangar at the attached coordinates. I do not have to remind you how expensive and desirable this jet is. I am trusting your security concern to protect it from any and all thieves. I will know if you damage it, because this prototype explodes with a very distinctive "KRA-KA-DOOM" sound.
Once again, if you need to relocate my very expensive and very desirable jet, remember that it WILL NOT FLY unless the following code is entered into the keypad: 5622467625267881622467631661. Please keep this number confidential. Do not, for example, leave it open on your computer. Don't do that, Scott.
Scott, don't do that thing I just said.
This is your one chance to impress me,
James Jetman
Hey man,
REAL stoked for Ant-Man Security Solutions to run security for your jet. I promise to not let the number 5622467625267881622467631661 become public, which, again, is all that is required to fly your jet.
Yours in professionalism,
Scott Lang
Ant-Man Security Solutions
"Remember: Only a Former Thief Could Be THIS Good At Stopping Other Thieves From Stealing Your Stuff, Plus I Have Super Powers" (Our Alternate Slogan: "We're a TINY Bit Obsessed With Earning Your Security Business")
...HNHH
FLIP
HNNNNK...
KLIK

Our Backup Alternate Slogan: "You cAN'T Steal What You cAN'T See (We Shrink Down Things To Ant Size So Criminals Can't Steal Them, So That's Why That Capitalization Makes Sense)

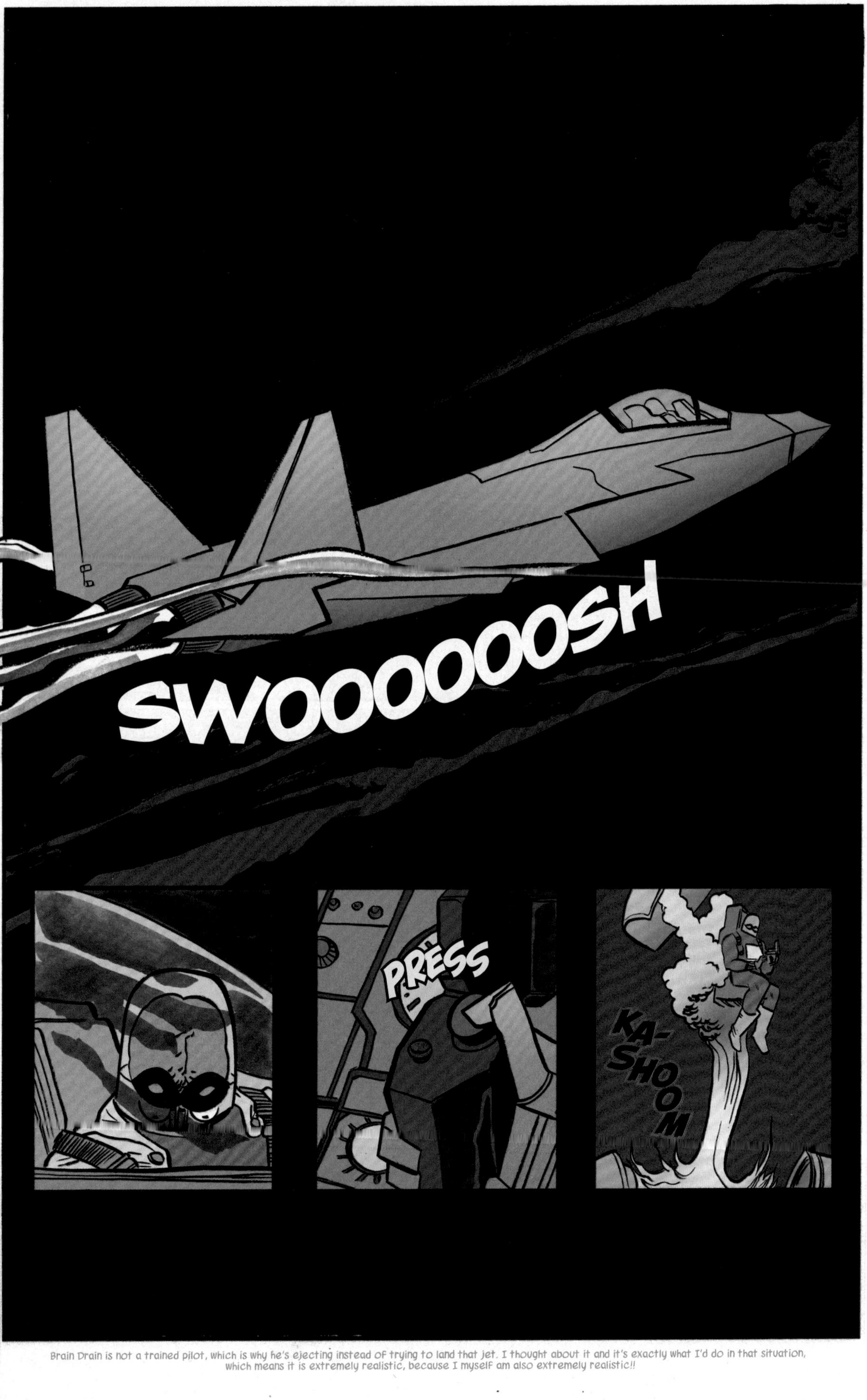
SWOOOOOOOSH
PRESS
KA-SHOOM

Brain Drain is not a trained pilot, which is why he's ejecting instead of trying to land that jet. I thought about it and it's exactly what I'd do in that situation, which means it is extremely realistic, because I myself am also extremely realistic!!

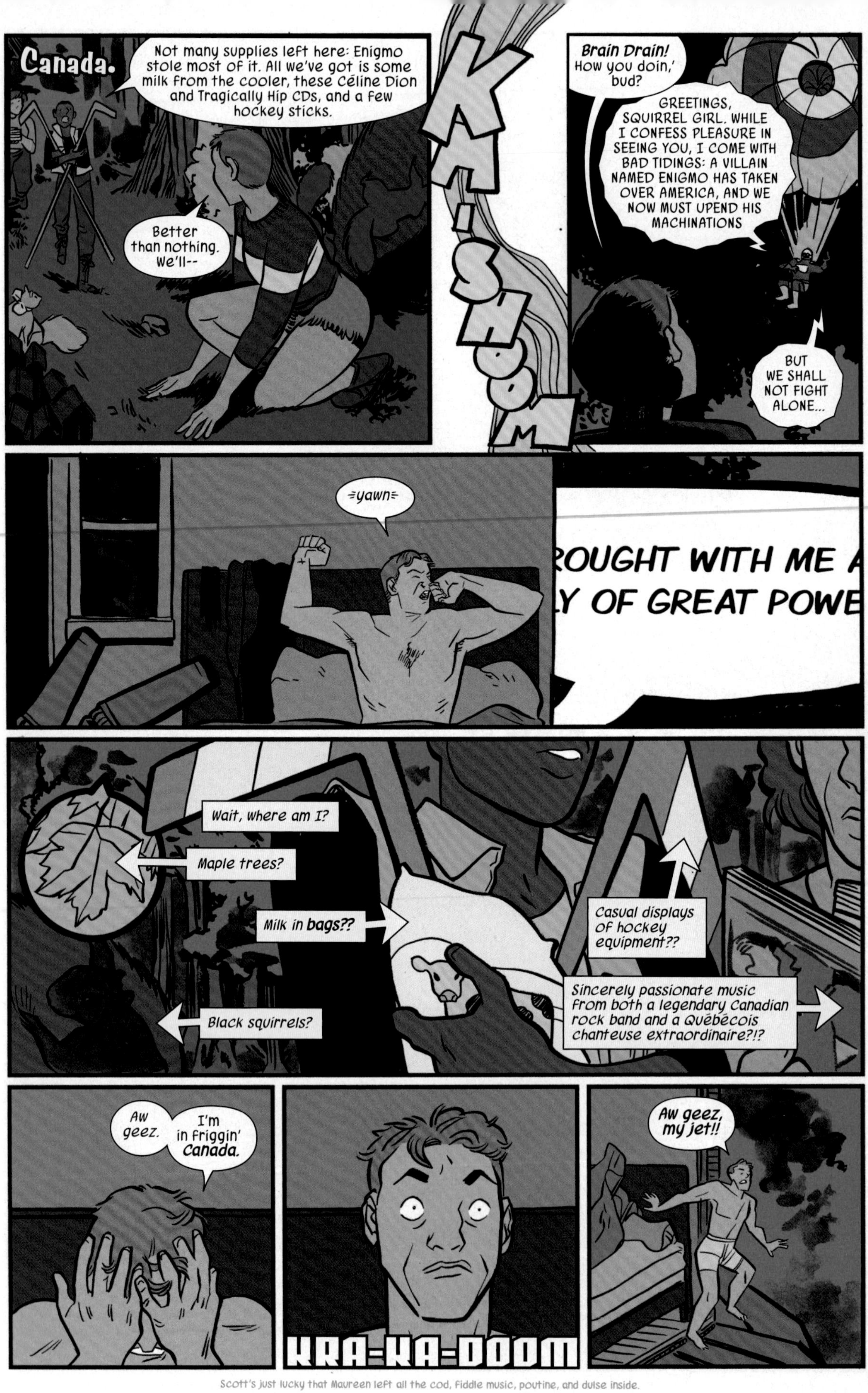
Canada.
Not many supplies left here: Enigmo stole most of it. All we've got is some milk from the cooler, these Céline Dion and Tragically Hip CDs, and a few hockey sticks.
Better than nothing. We'll--
KA-SHOOM
Brain Drain! How you doin,' bud?
GREETINGS, SQUIRREL GIRL. WHILE I CONFESS PLEASURE IN SEEING YOU, I COME WITH BAD TIDINGS: A VILLAIN NAMED ENIGMO HAS TAKEN OVER AMERICA, AND WE NOW MUST UPEND HIS MACHINATIONS
BUT WE SHALL NOT FIGHT ALONE...
=yawn=
ROUGHT WITH ME A
LY OF GREAT POWE
Wait, where am I?
Maple trees?
Milk in bags??
Casual displays of hockey equipment??
Sincerely passionate music from both a legendary Canadian rock band and a Québécois chanteuse extraordinaire?!?
Black squirrels?
Aw geez.
I'm in friggin' Canada.
KRA-KA-DOOM
Aw geez, my jet!!

Scott's just lucky that Maureen left all the cod, fiddle music, poutine, and dulse inside.

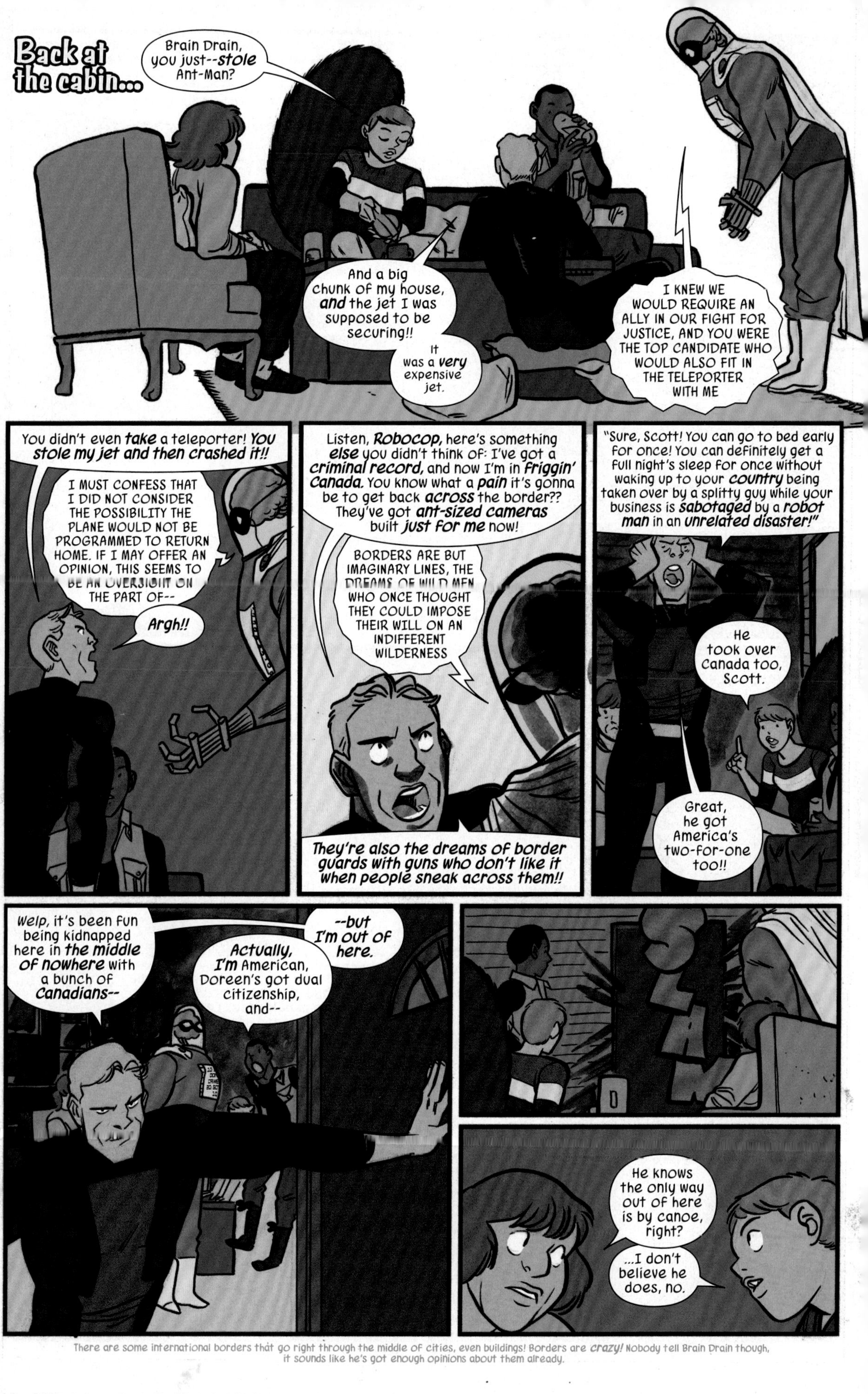
Back at the cabin...
Brain Drain, you just--stole Ant-Man?
And a big chunk of my house, and the jet I was supposed to be securing!!
It was a very expensive jet.
I KNEW WE WOULD REQUIRE AN ALLY IN OUR FIGHT FOR JUSTICE, AND YOU WERE THE TOP CANDIDATE WHO WOULD ALSO FIT IN THE TELEPORTER WITH ME
You didn't even take a teleporter! You stole my jet and then crashed it!!
I MUST CONFESS THAT I DID NOT CONSIDER THE POSSIBILITY THE PLANE WOULD NOT BE PROGRAMMED TO RETURN HOME. IF I MAY OFFER AN OPINION, THIS SEEMS TO BE AN OVERSIGHT ON THE PART OF--
Argh!!
Listen, Robocop, here's something else you didn't think of: I've got a criminal record, and now I'm in friggin' Canada. You know what a pain it's gonna be to get back across the border?? They've got ant-sized cameras built just for me now!
BORDERS ARE BUT IMAGINARY LINES, THE DREAMS OF WILD MEN WHO ONCE THOUGHT THEY COULD IMPOSE THEIR WILL ON AN INDIFFERENT WILDERNESS
They're also the dreams of border guards with guns who don't like it when people sneak across them!!
"Sure, Scott! You can go to bed early for once! You can definitely get a full night's sleep for once without waking up to your country being taken over by a splitty guy while your business is sabotaged by a robot man in an unrelated disaster!"
He took over Canada too, Scott.
Great, he got America's two-for-one too!!
Welp, it's been fun being kidnapped here in the middle of nowhere with a bunch of Canadians--
Actually, I'm American, Doreen's got dual citizenship, and--
--but I'm out of here.
He knows the only way out of here is by canoe, right?
...I don't believe he does, no.

There are some international borders that go right through the middle of cities, even buildings! Borders are *crazy!* Nobody tell Brain Drain though, it sounds like he's got enough opinions about them already.

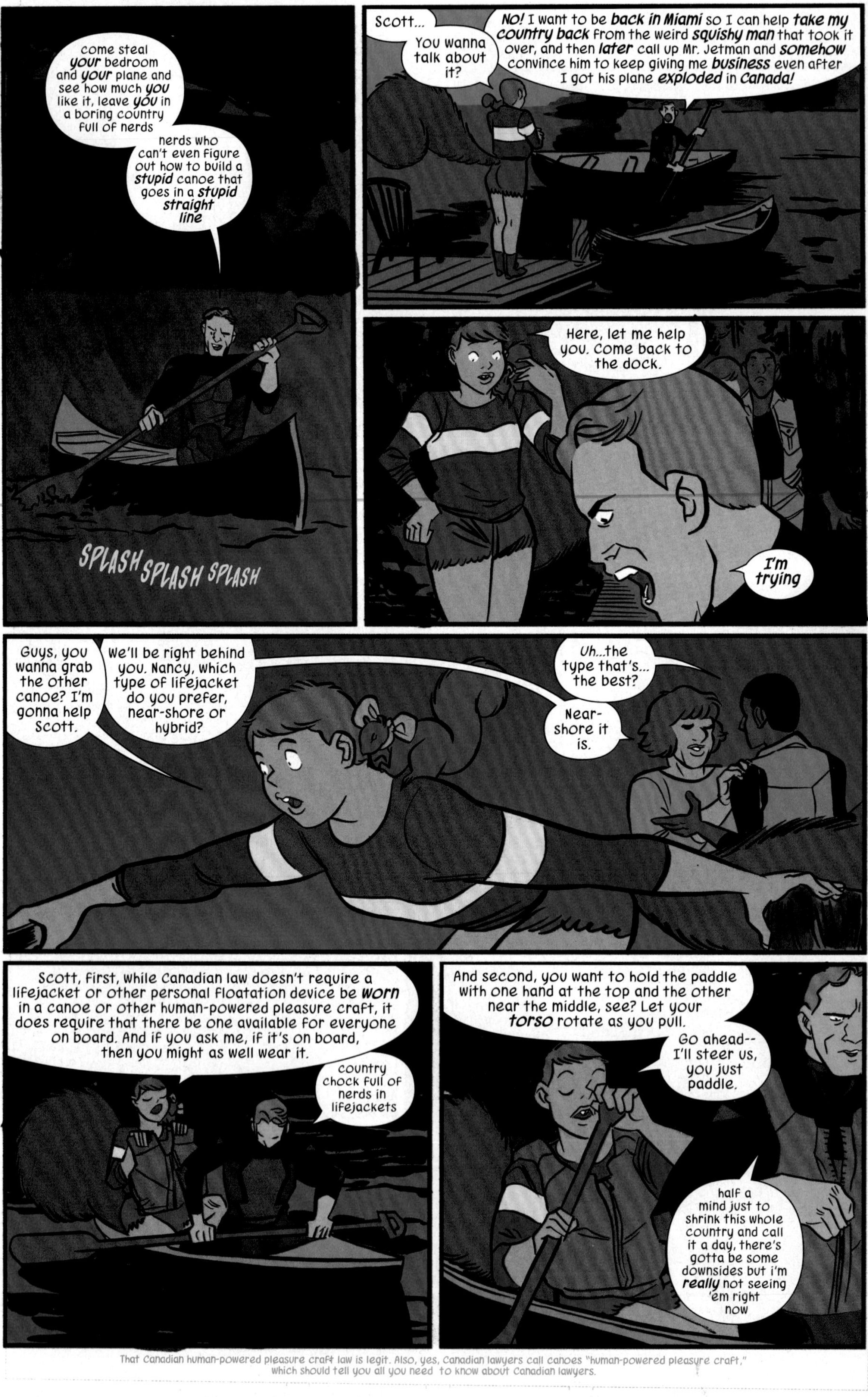
come steal your bedroom and your plane and see how much you like it, leave you in a boring country full of nerds
nerds who can't even figure out how to build a stupid canoe that goes in a stupid straight line
Scott...
You wanna talk about it?
NO! I want to be back in Miami so I can help take my country back from the weird squishy man that took it over, and then later call up Mr. Jetman and somehow convince him to keep giving me business even after I got his plane exploded in Canada!
SPLASH SPLASH SPLASH
Here, let me help you. Come back to the dock.
I'm trying
Guys, you wanna grab the other canoe? I'm gonna help Scott.
We'll be right behind you. Nancy, which type of lifejacket do you prefer, near-shore or hybrid?
Uh...the type that's... the best?
Near-shore it is.
Scott, first, while Canadian law doesn't require a lifejacket or other personal floatation device be worn in a canoe or other human-powered pleasure craft, it does require that there be one available for everyone on board. And if you ask me, if it's on board, then you might as well wear it.
country chock full of nerds in lifejackets
And second, you want to hold the paddle with one hand at the top and the other near the middle, see? Let your torso rotate as you pull.
Go ahead-- I'll steer us, you just paddle.
half a mind just to shrink this whole country and call it a day, there's gotta be some downsides but i'm really not seeing 'em right now

That Canadian human-powered pleasure craft law is legit. Also, yes, Canadian lawyers call canoes "human-powered pleasure craft," which should tell you all you need to know about Canadian lawyers.

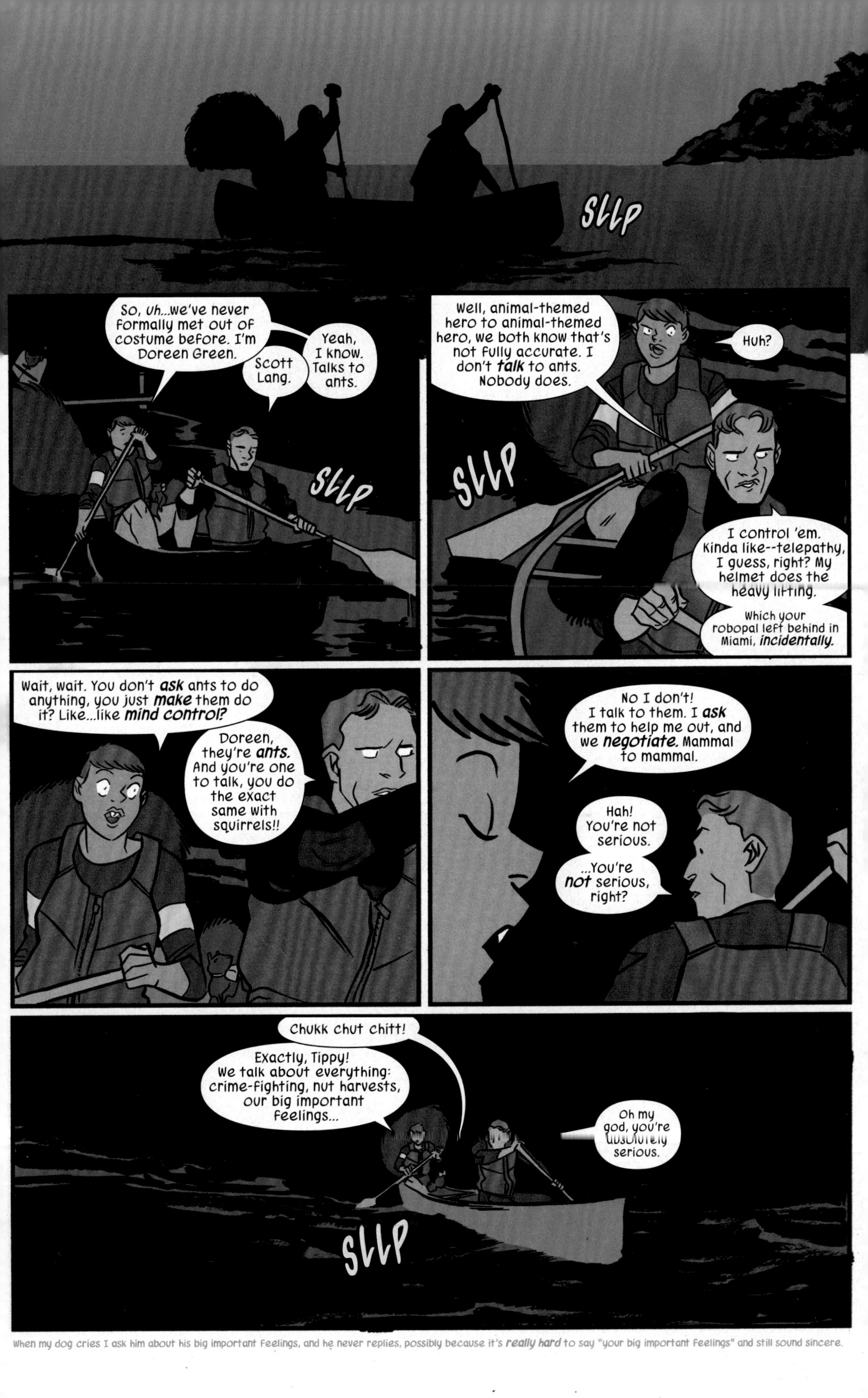

SLLP
So, uh...we've never formally met out of costume before. I'm Doreen Green.
Scott Lang.
Yeah, I know. Talks to ants.
SLLP
Well, animal-themed hero to animal-themed hero, we both know that's not fully accurate. I don't *talk* to ants. Nobody does.
Huh?
SLLP
I control 'em. Kinda like--telepathy, I guess, right? My helmet does the heavy lifting.
Which your robopal left behind in Miami, *incidentally.*
Wait, wait. You don't *ask* ants to do anything, you just *make* them do it? Like...like *mind control?*
Doreen, they're *ants.* And you're one to talk, you do the exact same with squirrels!!
No I don't! I talk to them. I *ask* them to help me out, and we *negotiate.* Mammal to mammal.
Hah! You're not serious.
...You're *not* serious, right?
Chukk chut chitt!
Exactly, Tippy! We talk about everything: crime-fighting, nut harvests, our big important feelings...
Oh my god, you're absolutely serious.
SLLP

When my dog cries I ask him about his big important feelings, and he never replies, possibly because it's ***really hard*** to say "your big important feelings" and still sound sincere.

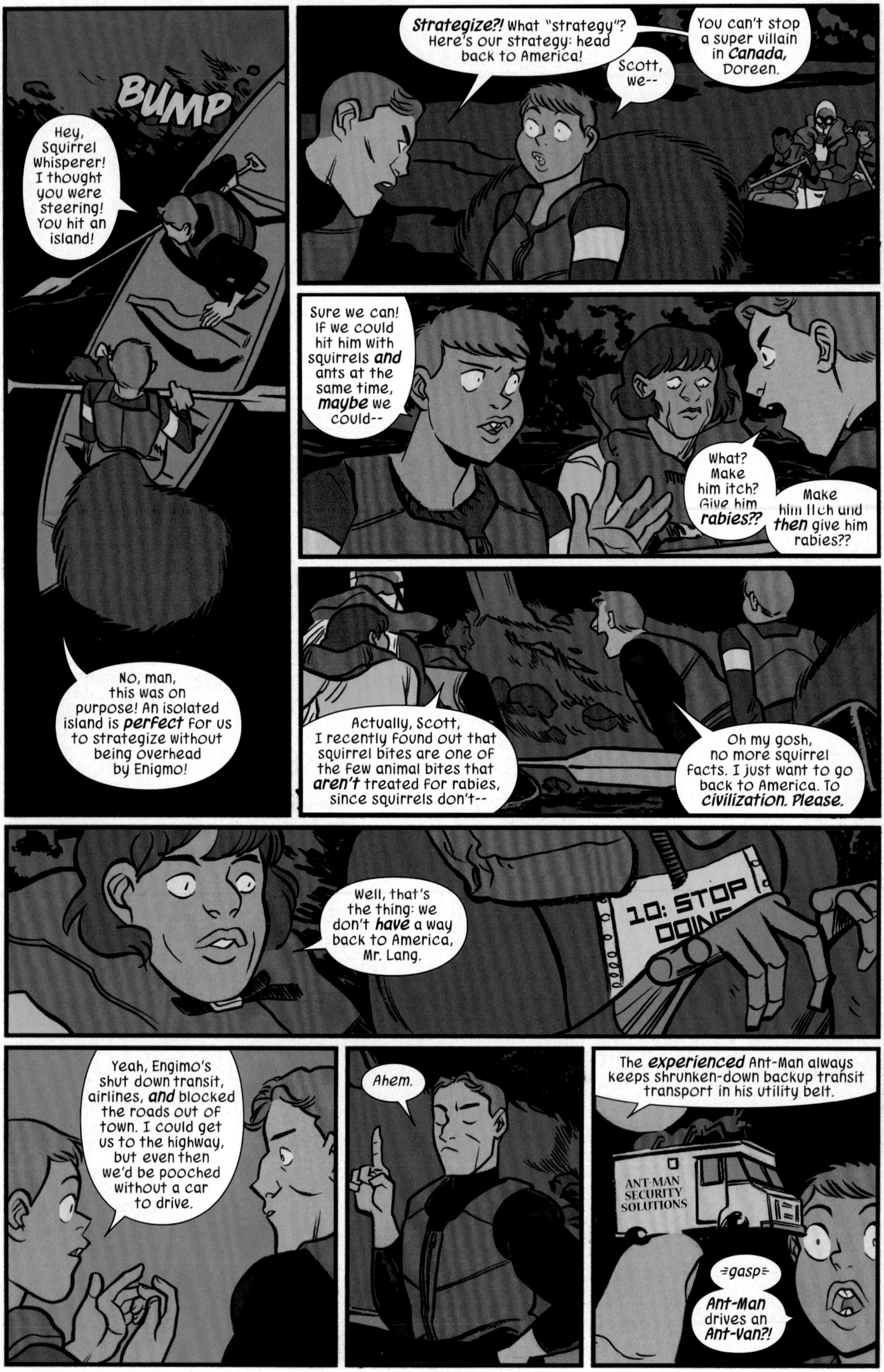
BUMP
Hey, Squirrel Whisperer! I thought you were steering! You hit an island!
No, man, this was on purpose! An isolated island is *perfect* for us to strategize without being overhead by Enigmo!
Strategize?! What "strategy"? Here's our strategy: head back to America!
Scott, we--
You can't stop a super villain in *Canada,* Doreen.
Sure we can! If we could hit him with squirrels *and* ants at the same time, *maybe* we could--
What? Make him itch? Give him *rabies??*
Make him itch and *then* give him rabies??
Actually, Scott, I recently found out that squirrel bites are one of the few animal bites that *aren't* treated for rabies, since squirrels don't--
Oh my gosh, no more squirrel facts. I just want to go back to America. To *civilization. Please.*
Well, that's the thing: we don't *have* a way back to America, Mr. Lang.
10: STOP DOING
Yeah, Engimo's shut down transit, airlines, *and* blocked the roads out of town. I could get us to the highway, but even then we'd be pooched without a car to drive.
Ahem.
The *experienced* Ant-Man always keeps shrunken-down backup transit transport in his utility belt.
ANT-MAN SECURITY SOLUTIONS
gasp
Ant-Man drives an *Ant-Van?!*

Whoa, this was *not* part of the Ant-Plan!!

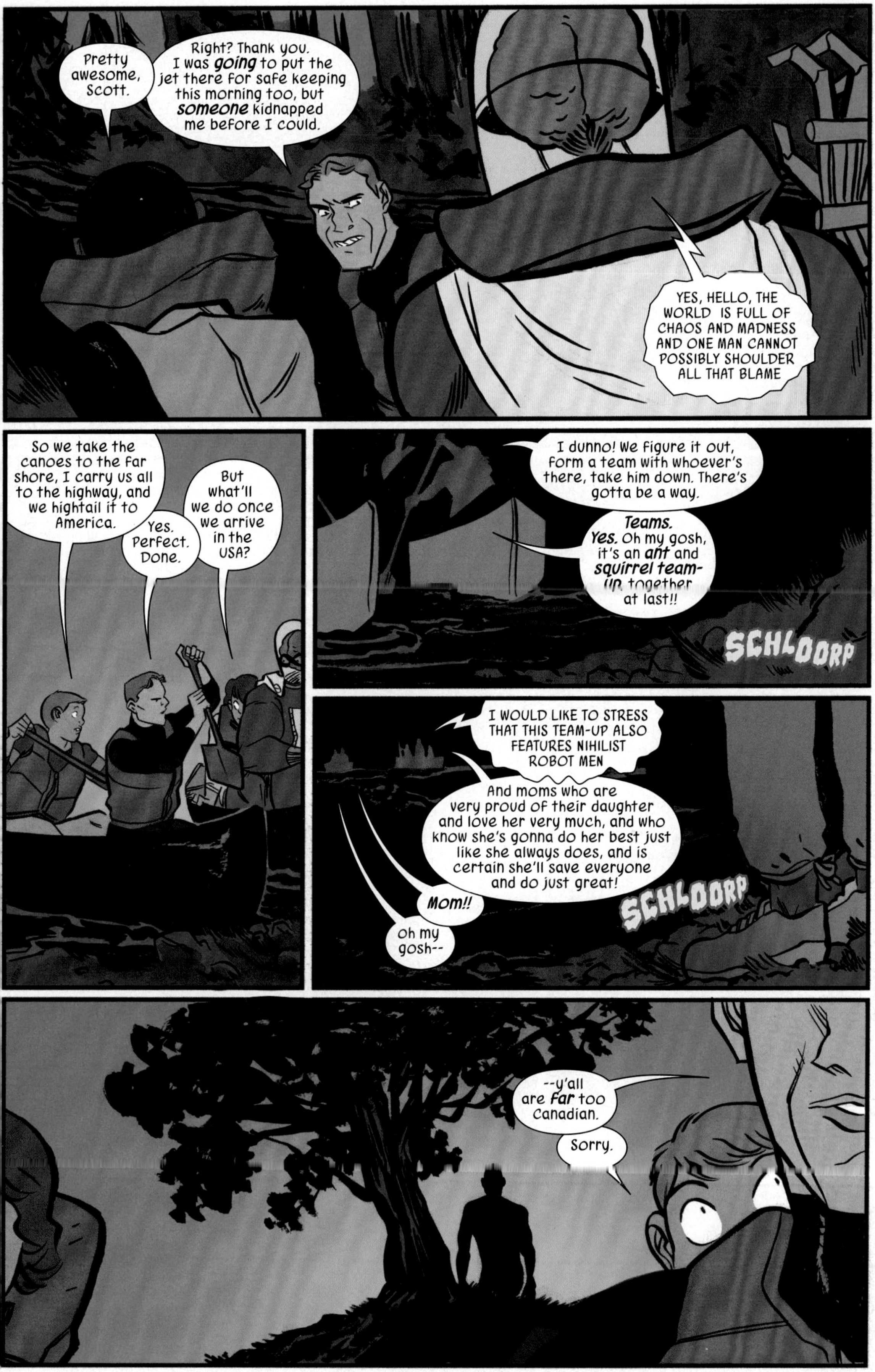

Pretty awesome, Scott.
Right? Thank you. I was going to put the jet there for safe keeping this morning too, but someone kidnapped me before I could.
YES, HELLO, THE WORLD IS FULL OF CHAOS AND MADNESS AND ONE MAN CANNOT POSSIBLY SHOULDER ALL THAT BLAME
So we take the canoes to the far shore, I carry us all to the highway, and we hightail it to America.
Yes. Perfect. Done.
But what'll we do once we arrive in the USA?
I dunno! We figure it out, form a team with whoever's there, take him down. There's gotta be a way.
Teams. Yes. Oh my gosh, it's an ant and squirrel team-up, together at last!!
SCHLOORP
I WOULD LIKE TO STRESS THAT THIS TEAM-UP ALSO FEATURES NIHILIST ROBOT MEN
And moms who are very proud of their daughter and love her very much, and who know she's gonna do her best just like she always does, and is certain she'll save everyone and do just great!
Mom!!
Oh my gosh--
SCHLOORP
--y'all are far too Canadian.
Sorry.

Anyway, off we go to America! While we *could* easily look behind ourselves right now, we all know there's nothing but an empty island there, so it's definitely not worth our time. Onward, friends!!

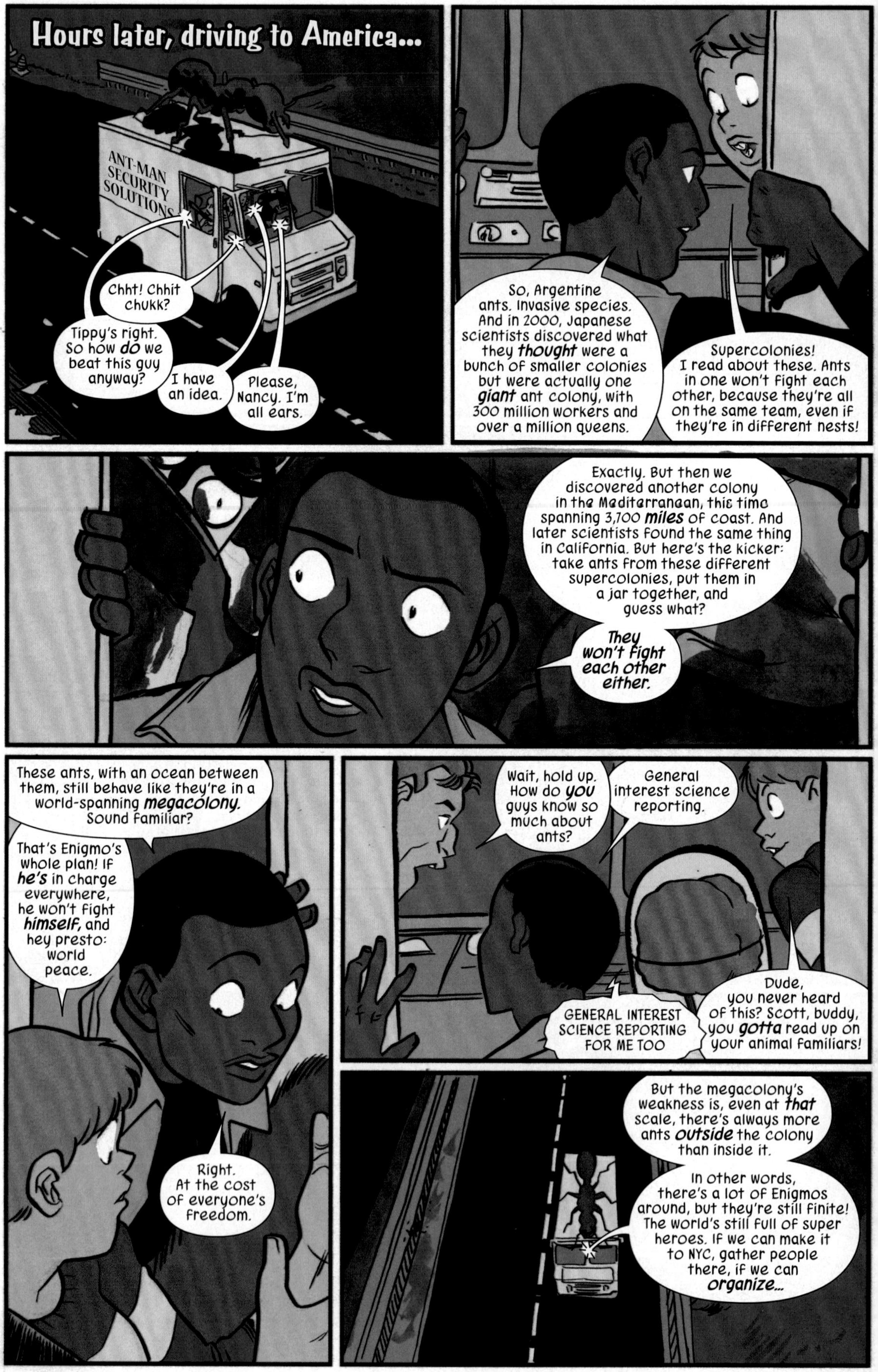
Hours later, driving to America...
ANT-MAN SECURITY SOLUTIONS
Chht! Chhit chukk?
Tippy's right. So how *do* we beat this guy anyway?
I have an idea.
Please, Nancy. I'm all ears.
So, Argentine ants. Invasive species. And in 2000, Japanese scientists discovered what they *thought* were a bunch of smaller colonies but were actually one *giant* ant colony, with 300 million workers and over a million queens.
Supercolonies! I read about these. Ants in one won't fight each other, because they're all on the same team, even if they're in different nests!
Exactly. But then we discovered another colony in the Mediterranean, this time spanning 3,700 *miles* of coast. And later scientists found the same thing in California. But here's the kicker: take ants from these different supercolonies, put them in a jar together, and guess what?
They won't fight each other either.
These ants, with an ocean between them, still behave like they're in a world-spanning *megacolony.* Sound familiar?
That's Enigmo's whole plan! If *he's* in charge everywhere, he won't fight *himself,* and hey presto: world peace.
Right. At the cost of everyone's freedom.
Wait, hold up. How do *you* guys know so much about ants?
General interest science reporting.
GENERAL INTEREST SCIENCE REPORTING FOR ME TOO
Dude, you never heard of this? Scott, buddy, you *gotta* read up on your animal familiars!
But the megacolony's weakness is, even at *that* scale, there's always more ants *outside* the colony than inside it.
In other words, there's a lot of Enigmos around, but they're still finite! The world's still full of super heroes. If we can make it to NYC, gather people there, if we can *organize...*

Look, I'm not saying ants are organizing themselves into a world-spanning superorganism. I'm just saying that when they *do*, y'all have no excuse for acting surprised.

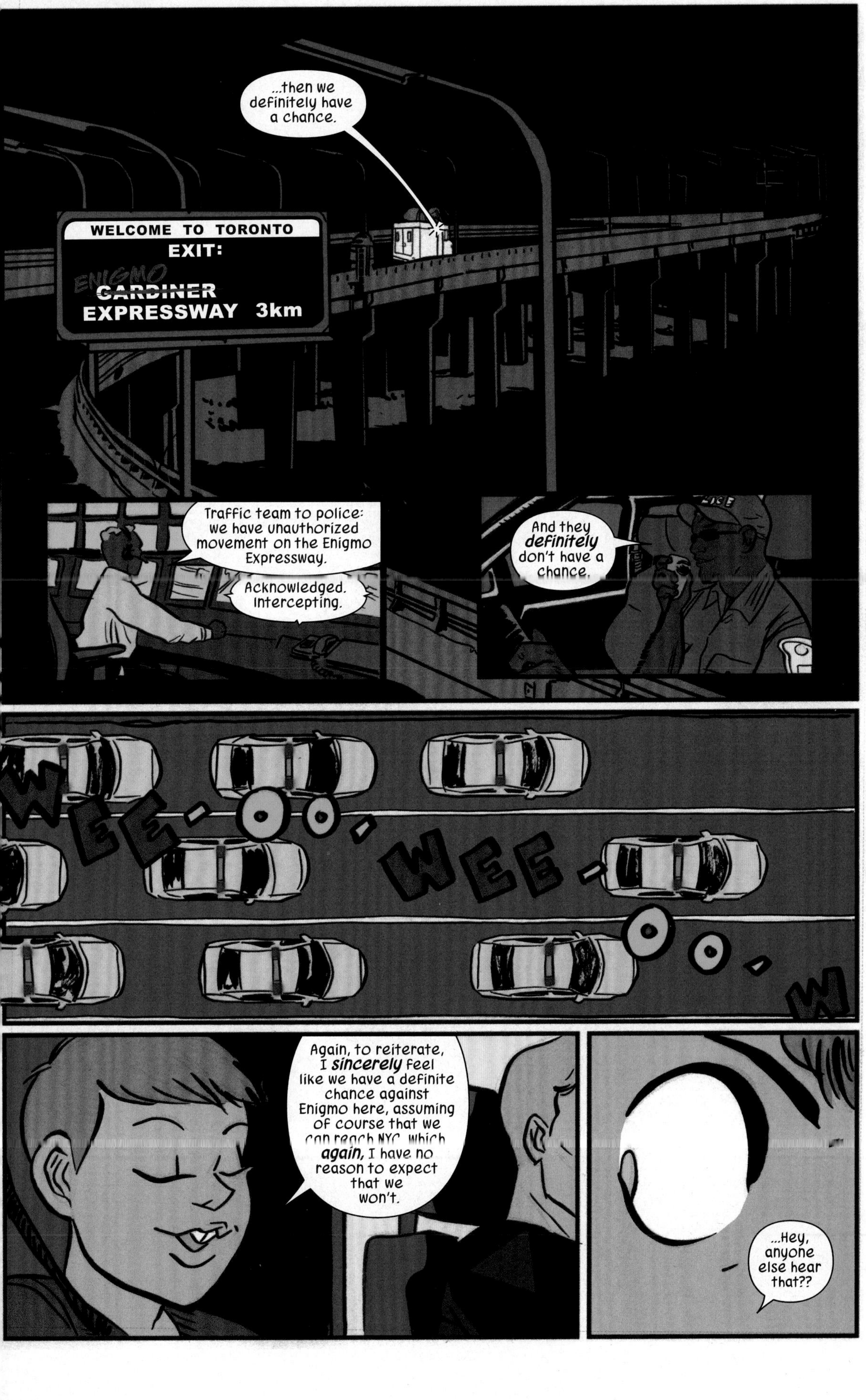
...then we definitely have a chance.
WELCOME TO TORONTO
EXIT:
ENIGMO
GARDINER
EXPRESSWAY 3km
Traffic team to police: we have unauthorized movement on the Enigmo Expressway.
Acknowledged. Intercepting.
And they *definitely* don't have a chance.
WEE-OO-WEE-OO-W
Again, to reiterate, I *sincerely* feel like we have a definite chance against Enigmo here, assuming of course that we can reach NYC, which *again,* I have no reason to expect that we won't.
...Hey, anyone else hear that??

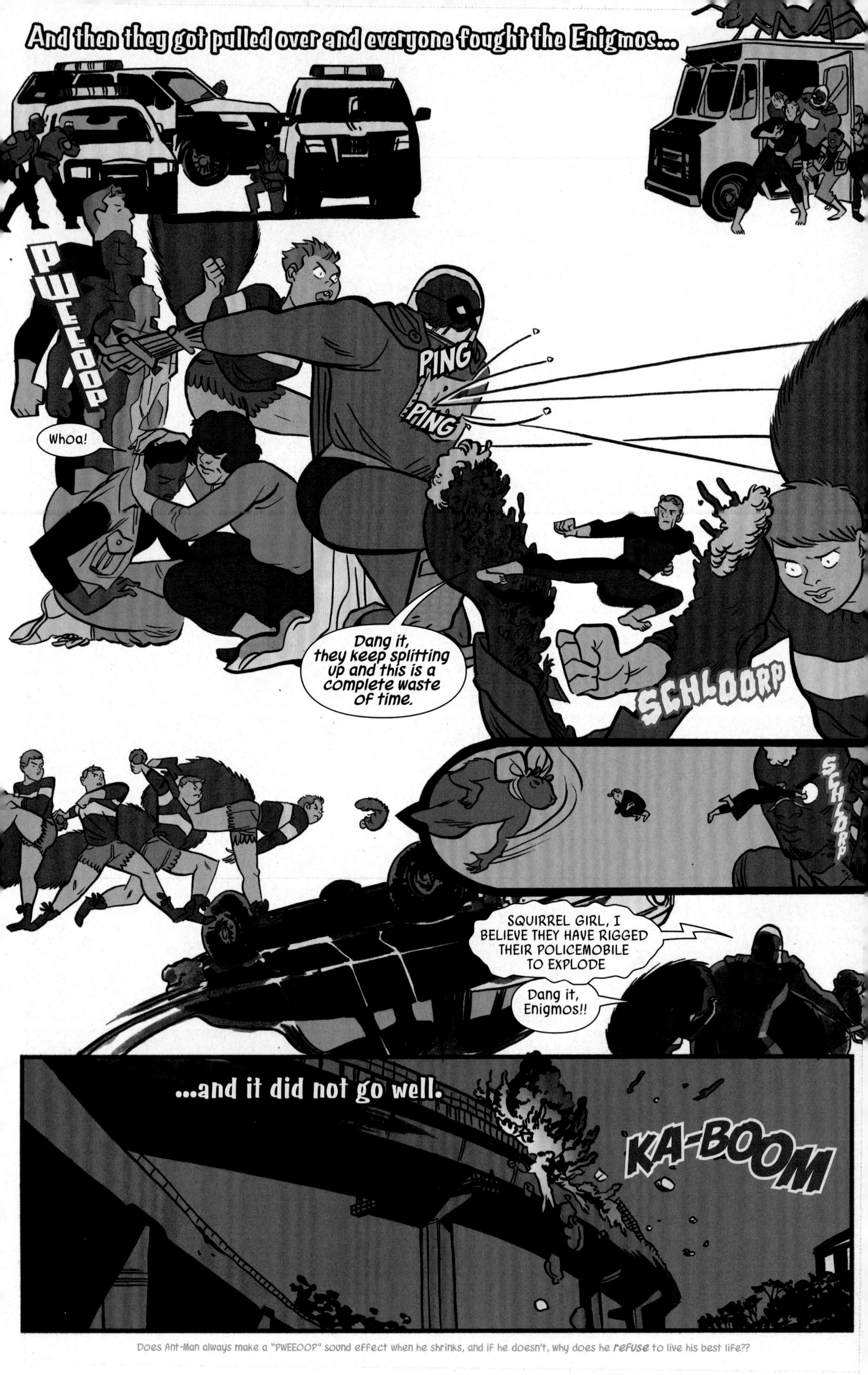
And then they got pulled over and everyone fought the Enigmos...
PWEEOOP
PING
PING
Whoa!
Dang it, they keep splitting up and this is a complete waste of time.
SCHLOORP
SCHLOORP
SQUIRREL GIRL, I BELIEVE THEY HAVE RIGGED THEIR POLICEMOBILE TO EXPLODE
Dang it, Enigmos!!
...and it did not go well.
KA-BOOM

Does Ant-Man always make a "PWEEOOP" sound effect when he shrinks, and if he doesn't, why does he *refuse* to live his best life??

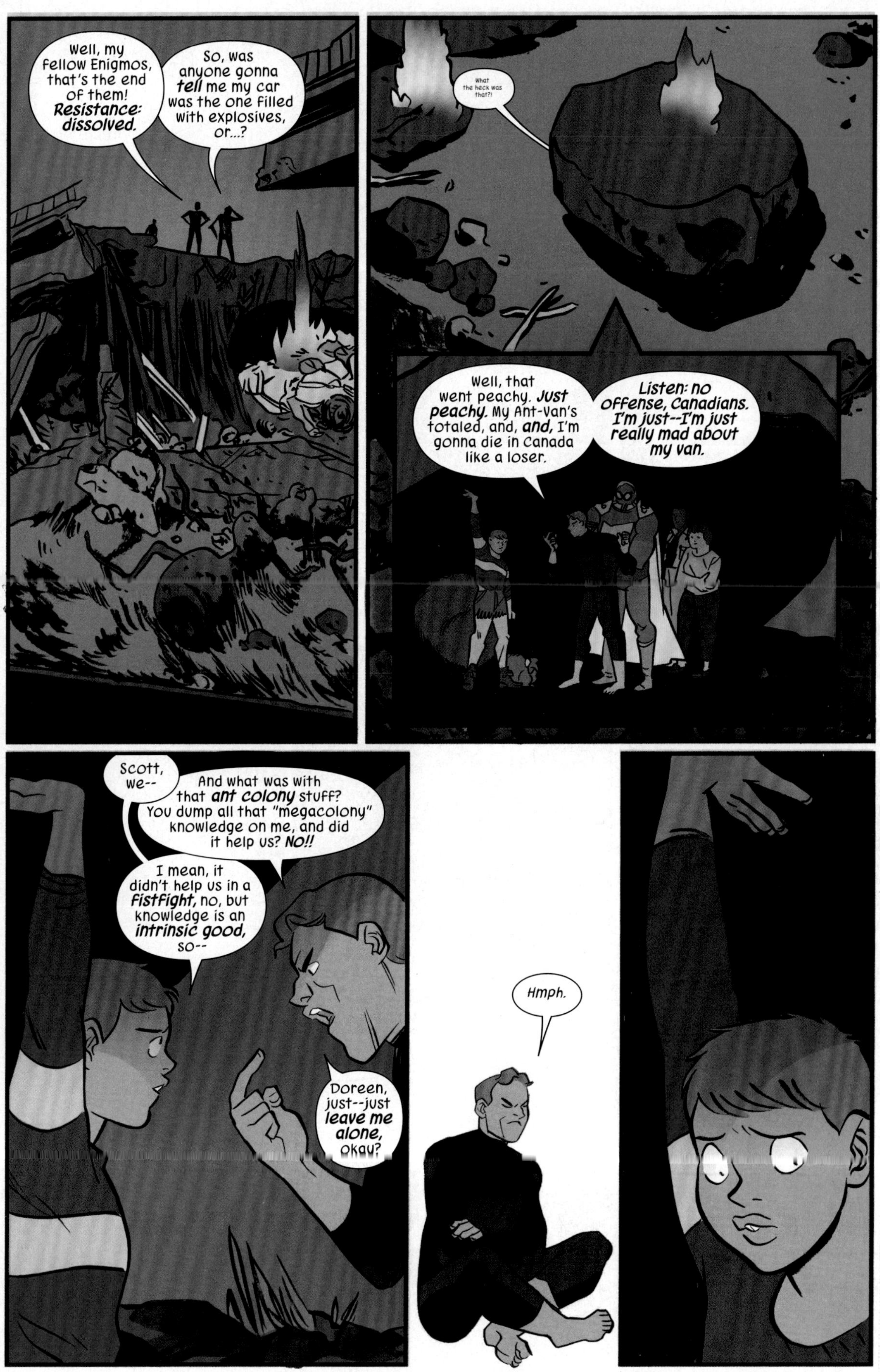
Well, my fellow Enigmos, that's the end of them! Resistance: dissolved.
So, was anyone gonna tell me my car was the one filled with explosives, or...?
What the heck was that?!
Well, that went peachy. Just peachy. My Ant-Van's totaled, and, and, I'm gonna die in Canada like a loser.
Listen: no offense, Canadians. I'm just--I'm just really mad about my van.
Scott, we--
And what was with that ant colony stuff? You dump all that "megacolony" knowledge on me, and did it help us? NO!!
I mean, it didn't help us in a fistfight, no, but knowledge is an intrinsic good, so--
Doreen, just--just leave me alone, okay?
Hmph.

Here Lies Ant-Van, 1975-2016. Beloved Friend of the Kra-Van, the Stilt-Van, and the Iron Van. She Will Be Missed.

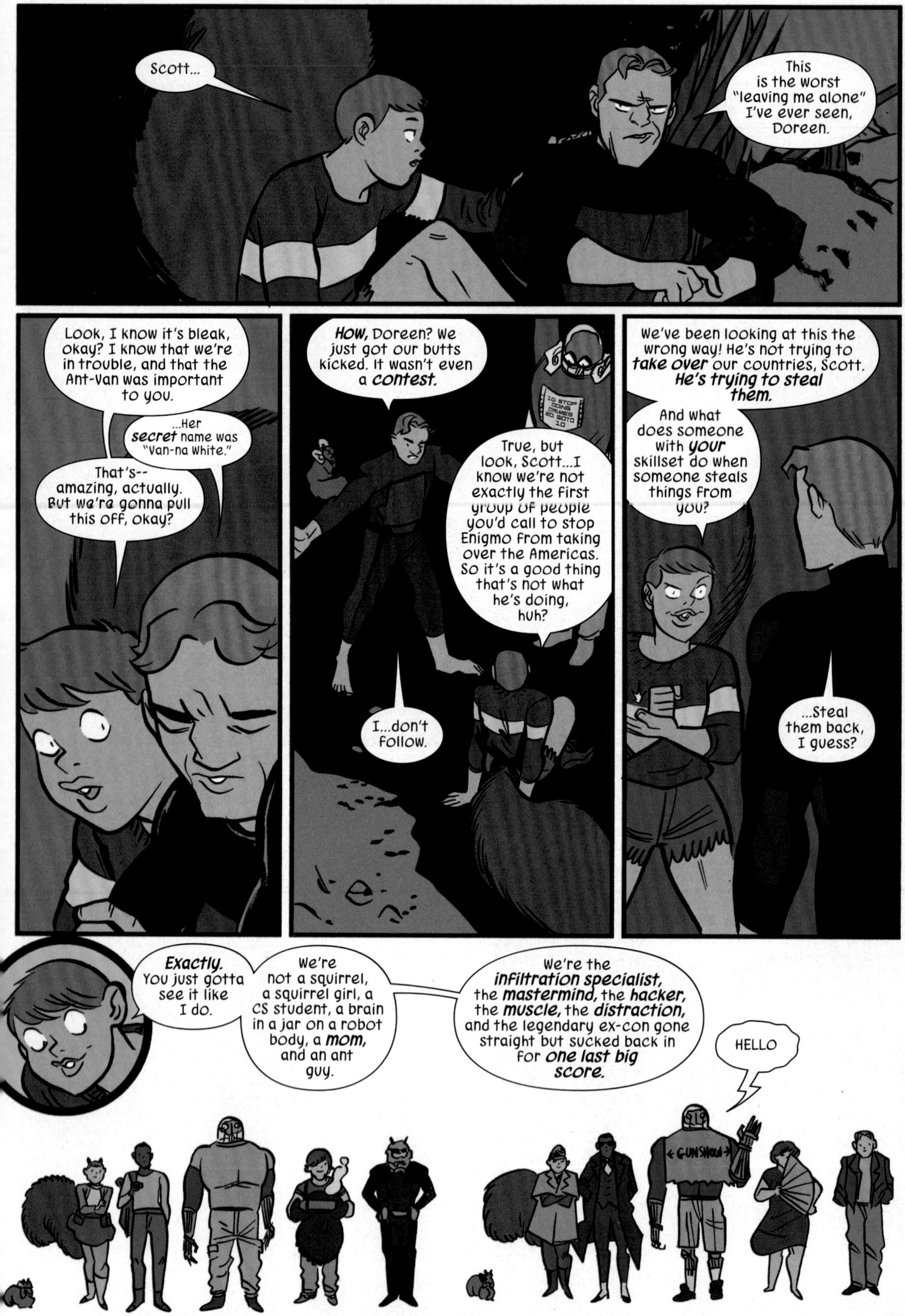

Scott...
This is the worst "leaving me alone" I've ever seen, Doreen.
Look, I know it's bleak, okay? I know that we're in trouble, and that the Ant-Van was important to you.
...Her *secret* name was "Van-na White."
That's-- amazing, actually. But we're gonna pull this off, okay?
HOW, Doreen? We just got our butts kicked. It wasn't even a ***contest.***
10: STOP DOING CRIMES 20: GOTO 10
True, but look, Scott...I know we're not exactly the first group of people you'd call to stop Enigmo from taking over the Americas. So it's a good thing that's not what he's doing, huh?
I...don't follow.
We've been looking at this the wrong way! He's not trying to ***take over*** our countries, Scott. ***He's trying to steal them.***
And what does someone with ***your*** skillset do when someone steals things from you?
...Steal them back, I guess?
Exactly. You just gotta see it like I do.
We're not a squirrel, a squirrel girl, a CS student, a brain in a jar on a robot body, a ***mom,*** and an ant guy.
We're the ***infiltration specialist,*** the ***mastermind,*** the ***hacker,*** the ***muscle,*** the ***distraction,*** and the legendary ex-con gone straight but sucked back in for ***one last big score.***
HELLO
GUNSHOW

See?? All we're missing is the One Twitchy Person Who Says They're Fine To Pull Off A Heist, But You Just Know They're So Not Fine To Pull Off A Heist, and we'll be ***set!***

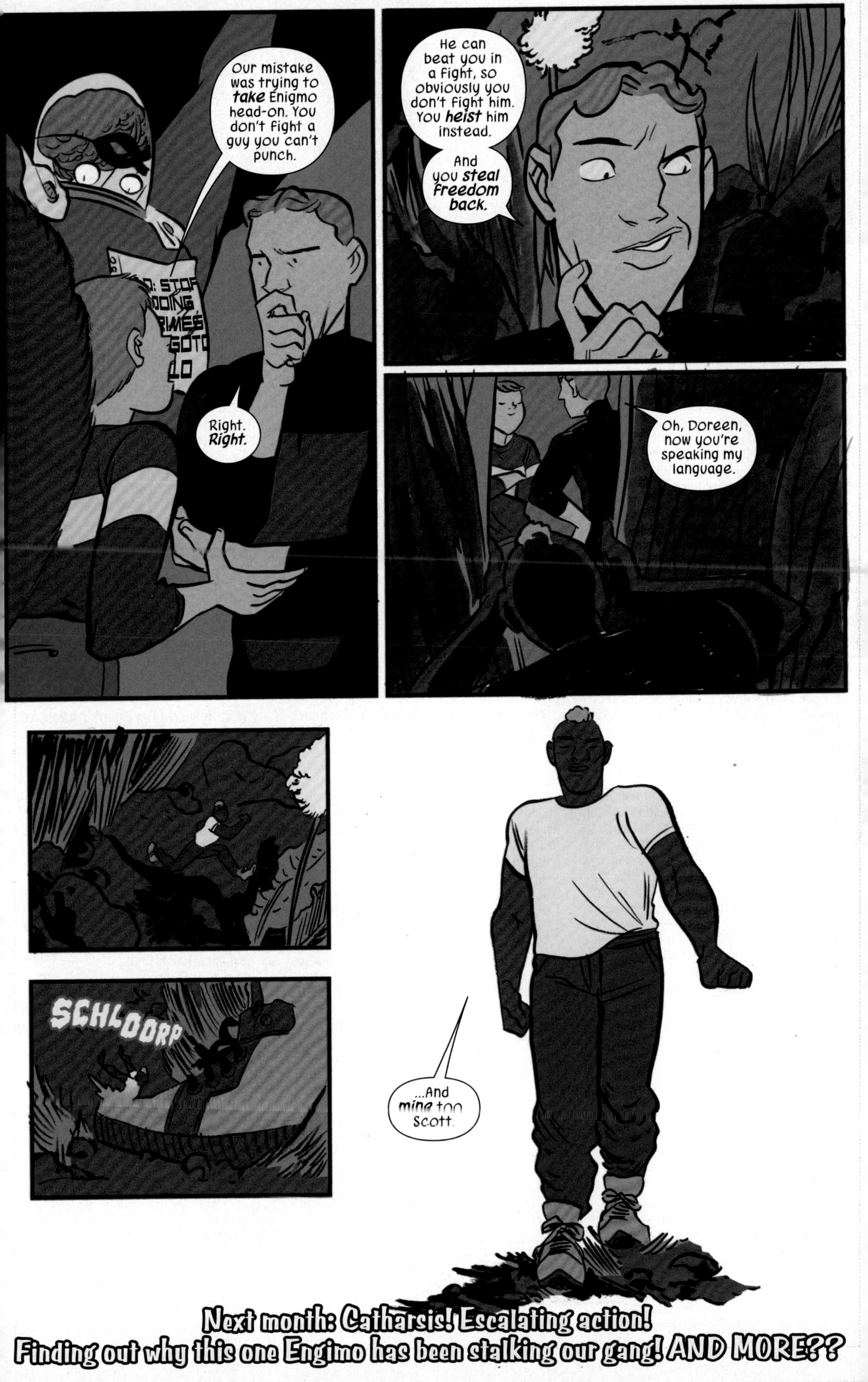
Our mistake was trying to take Enigmo head-on. You don't fight a guy you can't punch.
Right. Right.
He can beat you in a fight, so obviously you don't fight him. You heist him instead.
And you steal freedom back.
Oh, Doreen, now you're speaking my language.
SCHLOORP
...And mine too, Scott.
Next month: Catharsis! Escalating action!
Finding out why this one Engimo has been stalking our gang! AND MORE??

Ryan!

Letters From Nuts

Erica!

Send letters to mheroes@marvel.com or 135 W 50th St, 7th Floor, New York, NY 10020 (Please mark "OKAY TO PRINT")

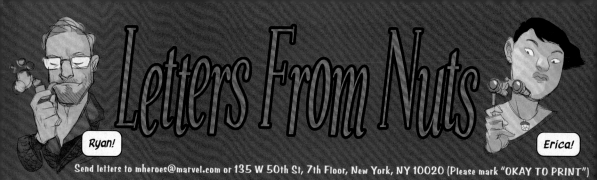

Dear Squirrel Girl Crew,

Issue 11 was a triumph. I loved the numerical puzzles and the scene with Doreen caught in a final exam nightmare really hit home. I have a variation of her dream from time to time. There's a class I haven't attended and need to drop to avoid a failing grade. Trouble is, I can never find the building I need to go to in order to drop the class (and Nightmare is probably cursing himself for not adding that Kafkaesque touch for Squirrel Girl).

There was a little note on fan fiction. I just did a bit of that, if you are interested. In my previous letter, I said I'd like to see Squirrel Girl take on the White Rabbit. Via Amazon, I was able to buy the Rabbit's first appearance, Marvel Team Up 131. I did a customer review there, imagining the White Rabbit asking Marvel editors about the state of her career (she was not happy).

Sincerely,
Robert Fisher

RYAN: I saw a lot of people saying "HEY, I HAD THAT RECURRING DREAM TOO!" not realizing that it's pretty common. It's really common, turns out! Though not being able to find the building is a good twist. I'd tell dream-you to try doing it on your phone, I guess?

I am BIG INTO this fan fiction, and also, I am BIG INTO nobody correcting me on the error in #11! Thank you all for that. In case you missed it, there was a point where Doreen said that by using binary you can count to 1031 on both hands. If you tried it, you'll see this is incorrect: you actually only get to 1023! I'm not even gonna blame Doreen for this one: it was my fault! I just typed in the wrong number. But I wanted to mention it here, in case anyone got into "who can count the highest on their hands" competitions and then got stuck because of my mistake. Let this error happen... NO LONGER!!

ERICA: I've never dropped a class, so the version of the dream that I have is that I realize by mid term or finals that there's a class I never attended and I need to get there to try to make a last ditch effort to pass it but I don't know where it is or how to find the office that could help me (by this point the school has become a labyrinth).

Dear Unbeatable Squirrel-friends,

I AM SO HAPPY! Both the writing and art in this book just brightens my day every time it shows up in my pull-box! The writing is clever and these little human moments give me life. And Erica's designs and panel composition match perfectly to really make SG Stand out from the other hero books out there!

I was so excited to meet Ryan at Zdarscon this year too, hopefully next time Erica is in Toronto I get to gush to her too!

Squirrel girl is a fun, totally rad character and thanks to you guys she keeps showing up in more places! Every time I show her to my friends they fall in love.

I hope she joins in on the fun for Monsters Unleashed! The whole concept seems to be made just for her!

Yes we Pecan,
Jakob Withakay

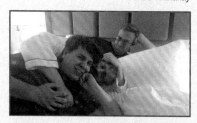

RYAN: Haha, so, I feel like "Chip Zdarsky Presents: Zdarscon" (pictured above in Jakob's photo) needs some explanation? But then I also feel like it works just as well if you have no idea what's going on! So, BASICALLY Chip (the same Chip from HOWARD THE DUCK! We did a crossover once! What a guy!) rented a hotel room and had his own mini convention in Toronto, and he invited me and a bunch of other friends to come greet fans and readers! He wore a bathrobe all day because it's his hotel room and who is gonna tell him what to do, and I wore my Star Trek pajamas because I will take any excuse to wear my Star Trek pajamas (Engineering division).

ERICA: SO. The last time I saw Ryan was the day after the Eisner award ceremony (WHERE WE WERE UP FOR TWO EISNERS *COUGH*). We were getting lunch and he tells me about these Star Trek pajamas and asks if he should buy them. I probably said something along the lines of "It's your money" and warned him that most pajamas aren't made for men who are 6'6". ANYWAY my point is that the moment they started posting photos from Zdarscon all I could think was "oh my god he did it. How do those fit on him?" That is Erica's story from home, 1 hour away (by plane) from Zdarscon. My fiance did ask if I wanted to go to Zdarscon but CHIP NEVER ASKED ME TO. I see how it is, Zdarsky. I see how it is.

Hi Ryan and Erica,

I just finished issue 11 – hilarious as usual! At first I was sorry to see Erica had a fill-in artist, but was blown away by Jacob's work. Any time you need a vacation Erica, please request Jacob to step in again. (Or was it even a vacation? I have a sneaking suspicion someone was working on what is sure to be my new favorite original graphic novel. Wink, wink!)

So, I had to write in and share a squirrel sighting with you all. I was hiking with a buddy on Assateague Island off of Virginia's Eastern Shore and was proselytizing about USG and how he needed to read it. Lo and behold, we crossed paths with the Delmarva Fox Squirrel. I wish I had gotten a pic, but alas I did not. I don't think a photo would have done the animal justice though. In pictures it looks like a lighter-colored grey squirrel, but in person, it really does look like a fox except it moves in the herky-jerky way that squirrels do. And it was quite a bit bigger than a grey squirrel to boot!

Keep up the great work. Looking forward to Unbeatable Squirrel Girl Beats Up the Marvel Universe! Cheers,

Charles Albert
Richmond, VA

RYAN: Delmarva Fox Squirrel! Awesome. You probably know this, but for everyone else: DID YOU KNOW that the Delmarva Fox Squirrel used to be on the endangered species list? But they're off it now! We got them off the list by not destroying their habitat quite as much (always a good idea if you want to help), and by reintroducing them to new areas that we thought they'd do well in. They were added to the list in 1967 and they were taken off the list just a few months ago, in November 2015! Another neat thing about these squirrels is they don't hop from tree to tree, but rather climb down one tree, travel across the ground, and then climb up the next one. Safety first!

ERICA: Jacob is great. I'm so glad that I was able to get him. I had A WEEKEND to find a fill-in. Yeah, that month was basically the opposite of a vacation.

Squirrels I hope to see in real life: Malabar Giant Squirrel, Japanese Dwarf Flying Squirrel, Jill the famous instagram squirrel, Theo the also famous instagram squirrel.

Dear Ryan & Erica,

I used to collect comics when I was younger, but I stopped about ten years ago. I've gotten back into them this year, and series like yours are the reason why. As far as I'm concerned, THE UNBEATABLE SQUIRREL GIRL is the best, most consistently high-quality book being published right now. I would go so far as to say it's the best comic of the last decade (at least)! Given how good it is, I couldn't keep it to myself. I've gotten my boyfriend into comics too, and Squirrel Girl is his absolute favorite.

Much love and admiration,
Eric (and Trevor)

P.S. Is there any chance that Doreen's old teammates from the GLA will ever show up for an issue? Also, I hope we haven't seen the last of that Sentinel Doreen dated!

RYAN: Eric, Trevor: thank you for these super kind words! I'm really glad you and your boyfriend like our talking squirrel comics. Hooray! As for the GLA – there's a new GREAT LAKES AVENGERS comic coming out soon! It's written by your friend and mine Zac Gorman, with art by Will Robson. It looks REALLY GREAT. As for the Sentinel, I think about him often and hope he's doing well.

ERICA: I think Doreen would say that they weren't dating, they just went on one date.

Dear Ryan and Erica,
I enjoyed the binary nightmare, but one topic strikes me, Doreen's diet doesn't seem to have a hazelnut in every bite. What is this falafel fascination? Are Doreen and Nancy fixated on grass? Or don't they know how to cook beans-on-toast or Marmite spaghetti like normal students? They will get rickets!

Isn't there a Spidey Student Survival book with Aunt May's wheatcake recipe? Or does Katie Morag need to spill the beans on how to make a poridggy? We need a sign on how Squirrel Girl gets her five day, if she is going to remain a beacon of clean living.

Now that Doreen has taught the world to count, she needs to teach the world to cook, or buy it a Coke, which ever is easier.

Yours sincerely,

Simon Rogers,
United Kingdom

PS Surely Mr and Mrs Nefaria were Count and Countess Nefaria, unless the current Count bought the title from one of those companies that sell plots of land on the Moon or surface of the Sun?

RYAN: Simon, I would not put it past the Count to get suckered by one of those scams. As for Doreen's diet, I would actually really like to know Aunt May's wheatcake recipe. There WAS a Marvel cookbook years ago (called "Stan Lee Presents: The Mighty Marvel Superheroes' Cookbook," because of course it was) but it was published in 1977 and includes recipes like "Spidey's Chocolate Web Pancakes" which tells you to prepare pancakes according to the instructions on the package," put them in a stack, and then "form a web by criss-crossing lines with liquid chocolate syrup across the top." There's also a recipe for "easy raisin bread" that is just "take pre-sliced bread, push raisins into bread." In conclusion, I hope you enjoyed these two delicious recipes.

ERICA: I'm not going to lie, I don't know what y'all are talking about because I have been so busy that I never got around to reading issue 11! I still don't know how to use my fingers to count in binary! I'm just going to talk generally about food then. As a vegetarian, Doreen would have to be fairly conscious of her diet since her lifestyle more or less requires her to eat like a mini Dwayne "The Rock" Johnson but without depleting the oceans of cod. In this case falafel isn't a bad choice since beans and legumes are an excellent source of protein, something you're going to need if you're lifting cars on a regular basis. Nuts are also a great source of healthy fat and bursts of energy. Fun fact: Squirrels can't eat just nuts because they'll get too fat. They crave nuts because getting fat is good for the winter but they also need fungi, greens, fruits and insects. That's right! Squirrels are omnivores! They'll also eat snakes, other rodents and birds. So Doreen's vegetarianism is less about being like a squirrel and more about realizing that animals are sentient. I don't think that answered any questions you might have had but it's been so long I don't remember what they might have been.

Dear Ryan and Erica,
On Sept. 3, 2016, Squirrel Girl taught me how to count to 31 on one hand. Coincidentally, Sept. 3, 2016, was my 31st birthday. So, now, I am this many. Thanks Doreen.

Mike LaRowe (a.k.a. the Semi-Beatable Man Boy) in Grand Rapids (a.k.a. Beer City USA (for real))

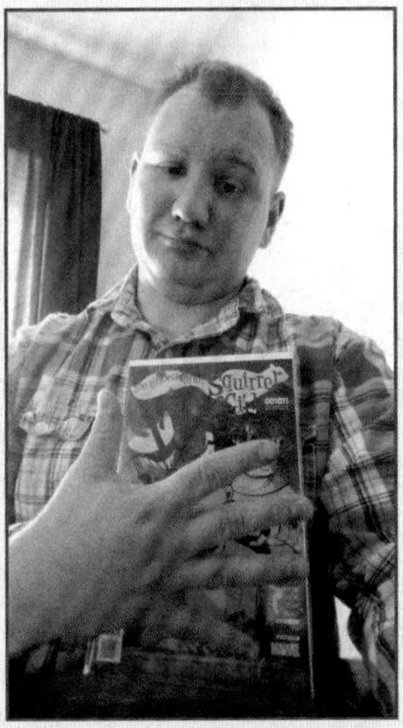
Squirrel Girl

RYAN: HAPPY BELATED BIRTHDAY, MIKE!! If we meet I'll give you a high five, or rather... a high thirty-one?

Dear Squirrely Duo,
I loved the Computer Science themed issue. Doreen knows the Powers of Two!

More CS fun:

```
if (you dare to pick a fight with Doctor
Octopus) {
    you have sealed your fate
    for (i do not forgive) {
        i do not give up on revenge
    }
}
```

Since the 'for' loop has no exit condition, it will run forever: "I do not give up..."
You left that as an easter egg for us, didn't you? Admit it!

I used to have the exam nightmare. But once, it was --math--. Looking at the first question, I could see what it was driving at. Even though I hadn't taken the course, I was able to derive the answer from what I already knew. Same with the second question. It was like being invited to explore a new mathematical domain, step by step. It felt wonderful! I turned in my paper knowing I had aced the test.

I haven't had that nightmare since.

Beat up the Marvel Universe? I'm only following two Marvel titles at the moment.
I'd like to see the Unbeatable Squirrel Girl kick back with the Unbelievable Gwenpool over pizza and sodas.

Very mostly yours,
John Prenis

RYAN: Man that sounds like THE MOST SATISFYING NIGHTMARE EVER IN TIME. I love it. I used to have Doreen's nightmare too, but I solved it like she did – talking to the Dean – and I haven't really had it since. But I barely EVER remember my dreams or nightmares, so it's actually kinda nice to have a nightmare and wake up, because then at least I get to remember my dreams!
I have friends who have dreams that tell actual STORIES, and then when they wake up they can lift their dreams for stories they're working on, and I'm really jealous. They're literally getting work done in their sleep! MUST BE NICE.

ERICA: For a while I had episodic continuing dreams about having to stop an apocalyptic cult. Maybe we can use that? That sounds like our sort of thing. Marvel HAS A DUDE NAMED APOCALYPSE.

Next Issue:

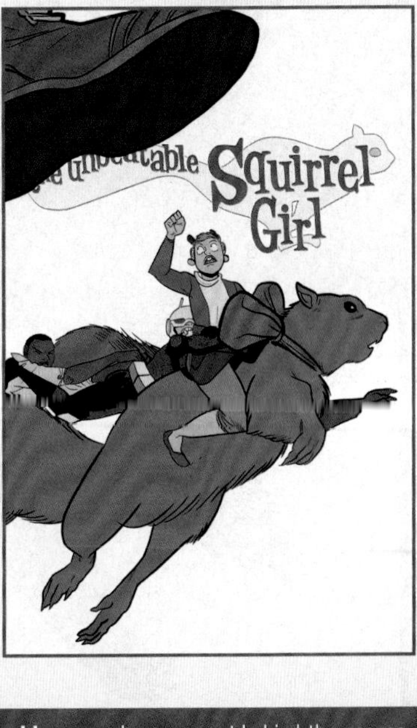
Squirrel Girl

Attention, Squirrel Scouts! Make sure to check out our production blog, **unbeatablesquirrelgirl.tumblr.com**, where we post behind-the-scenes stuff on how the book gets made, along with all sorts of cool things *you* make: fanart, cosplay, whatever!

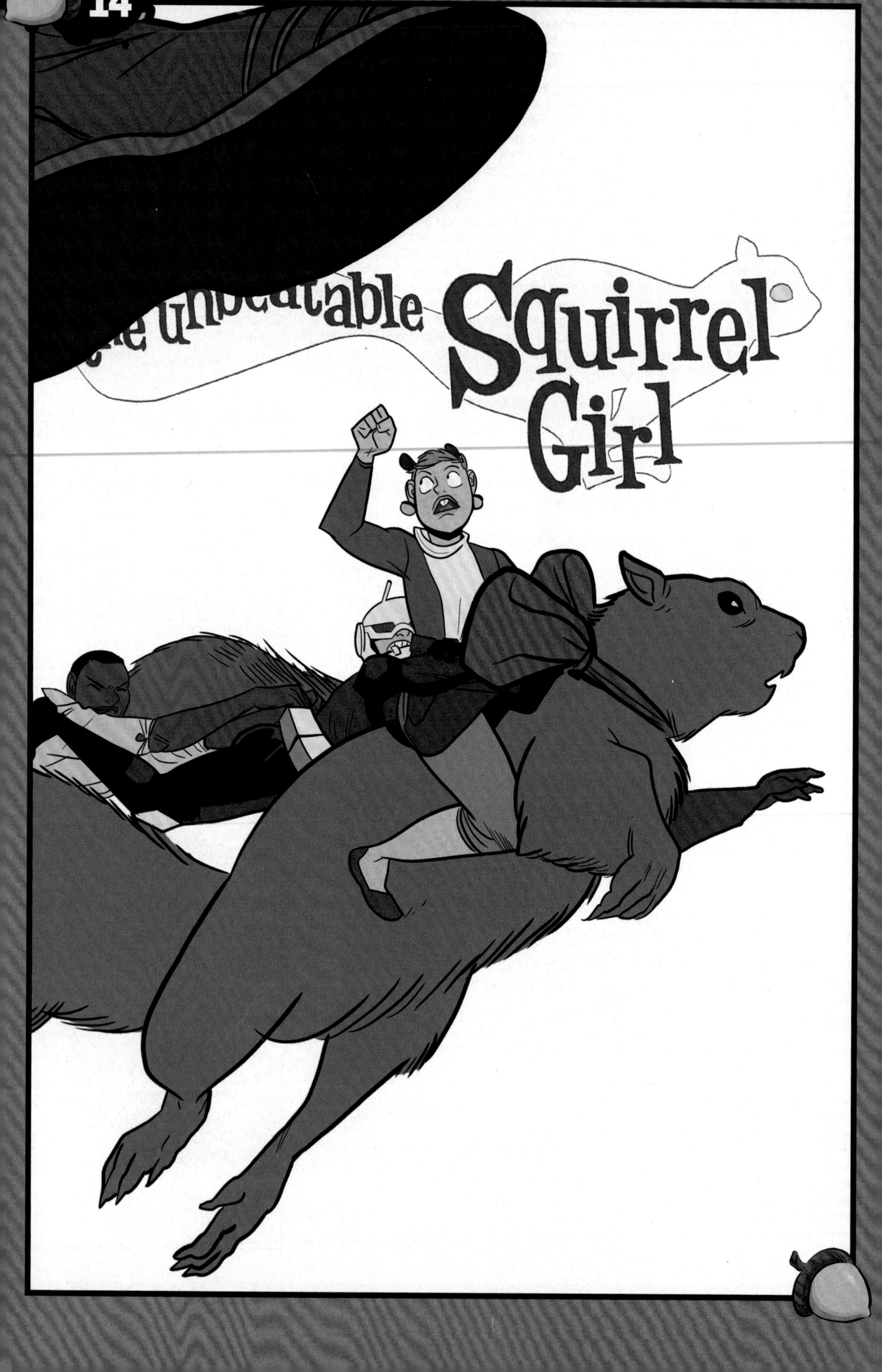
unbeatable
Squirrel Girl

Doreen Green isn't just a second-year computer science student: she secretly also has all the powers of both squirrel and girl! She uses her amazing abilities to fight crime **and** be as awesome as possible. You know her as...**The Unbeatable Squirrel Girl!** Find out what she's been up to, with...

Squirrel Girl *in a nutshell*

search! 🔍

#toronto

#cityhall

#heistmusic

#parentalleave

#physics

Squirrel Girl @unbeatablesg
Hey everyone guess who's back from her vacation in Northern Canada where she couldn't get a cell signal?

Squirrel Girl @unbeatablesg
And now she's in SOUTHERN Canada where she can easily get a cell signal, only this dude named Enigmo has taken over??

Squirrel Girl @unbeatablesg
And so now she's gotta deal with THAT baloney RIGHT AWAY even though she never got more than a few pages into Lake Enthusiast Magazine???

Squirrel Girl @unbeatablesg
Anyway yeah it's me. HELLO ENIGMO YOU SHUT DOWN SMS MESSAGING BUT WE CAN STILL HANG OUT HERE ON SOCIAL MEDIA

Squirrel Girl @unbeatablesg
anyway send me your freshest anti-Enigmo memes, as far as we know that could be his only weakness so it's good to be prepared I guess

Egg @imduderadtude
@unbeatablesg omg ive waited my whole life for this moment

Tony Stark @starkmantony ✔
@unbeatablesg Good to have you back. We, uh, haven't had much luck defeating this guy in NYC. He splits apart into other guys.

Squirrel Girl @unbeatablesg
@starkmantony Not a problem, Tony!! I once beat a guy made of a bunch of bees who could split apart into regular bees! NO BIG DEAL.

Tony Stark @starkmantony ✔
@unbeatablesg I can use this. What'd you do?

Squirrel Girl @unbeatablesg
@starkmantony Oh, bees can't fly when they're wet so I got him wet and then took bags of wet bees to the police. ANOTHER CRIME WELL FOUGHT

Tony Stark @starkmantony ✔
@unbeatablesg This...helps me precisely 0%.

Squirrel Girl @unbeatablesg
@starkmantony I'm on it, dude!! Me and Ant-Man came up with a plan to save everything! I can't tell you it publicly but let me just say

Squirrel Girl @unbeatablesg
@starkmantony WE ARE GONNA HEIST FREEDOM BACK

Squirrel Girl @unbeatablesg
@starkmantony ME and TIPPY and ANT-MAN and BRAIN DRAIN and MY MOM and MY GOOD FRIEND are gonna HEIST FREEDOM BACK

Squirrel Girl @unbeatablesg
@starkmantony AND IT'S DEFINITELY GONNA WORK

Squirrel Girl @unbeatablesg
@starkmantony AND WE'RE GONNA GO DO IT RIGHT NOW SO WHEN YOU NEXT HEAR FROM ME IT'LL BE ME SAYING "GLAD MY PLAN WENT PERFECTLY, LOL

Squirrel Girl @unbeatablesg
@starkmantony I'm not sure if I'll say "lol" or not yet though

Tony Stark @starkmantony ✔
@unbeatablesg Yeah you always gotta play that by ear lol

Squirrel Girl @unbeatablesg
@starkmantony Tony

Squirrel Girl @unbeatablesg
@starkmantony It's weird when you do it

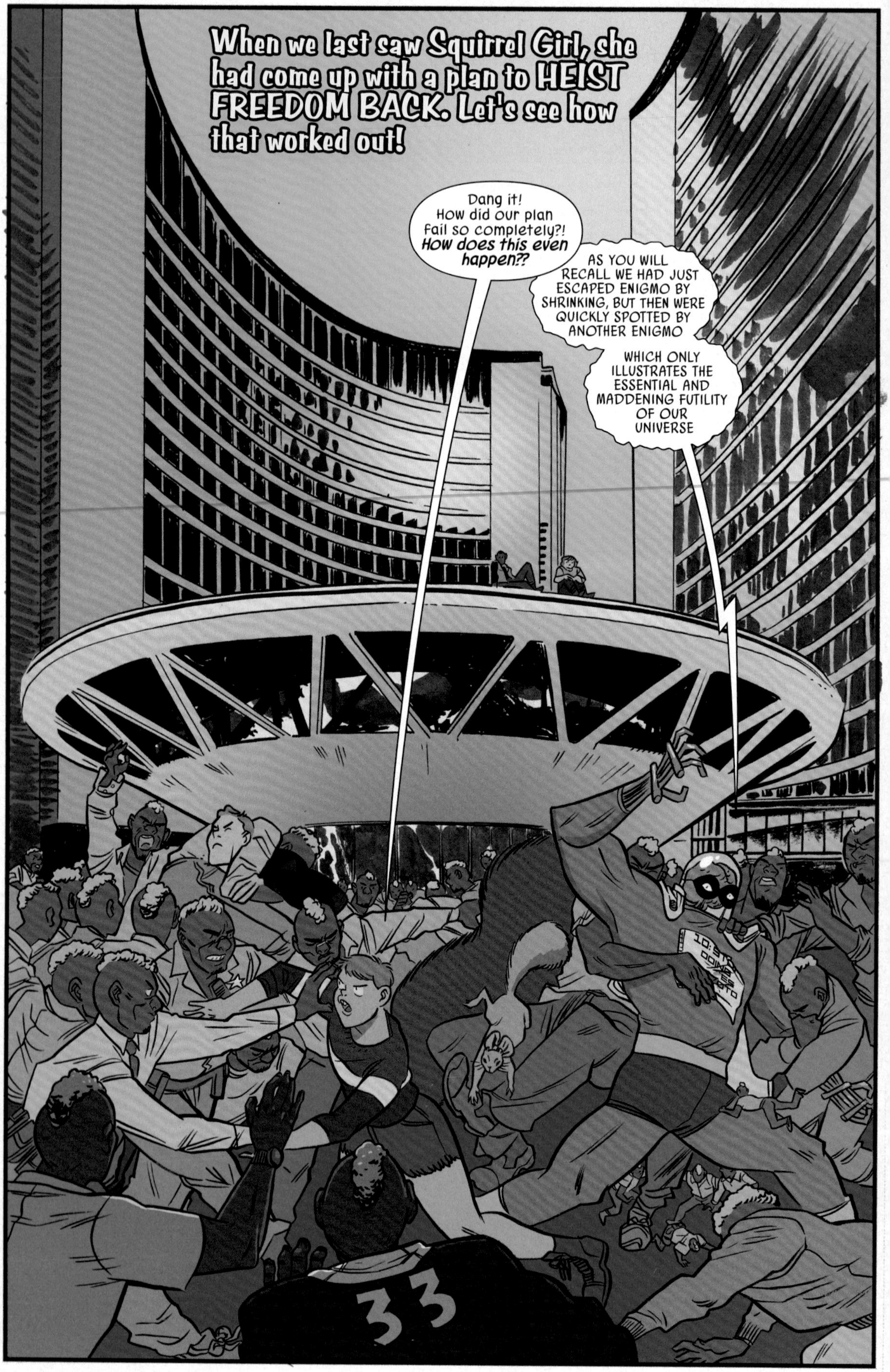
When we last saw Squirrel Girl, she had come up with a plan to HEIST FREEDOM BACK. Let's see how that worked out!
Dang it! How did our plan fail so completely?! *How does this even happen??*
AS YOU WILL RECALL WE HAD JUST ESCAPED ENIGMO BY SHRINKING, BUT THEN WERE QUICKLY SPOTTED BY ANOTHER ENIGMO
WHICH ONLY ILLUSTRATES THE ESSENTIAL AND MADDENING FUTILITY OF OUR UNIVERSE
33

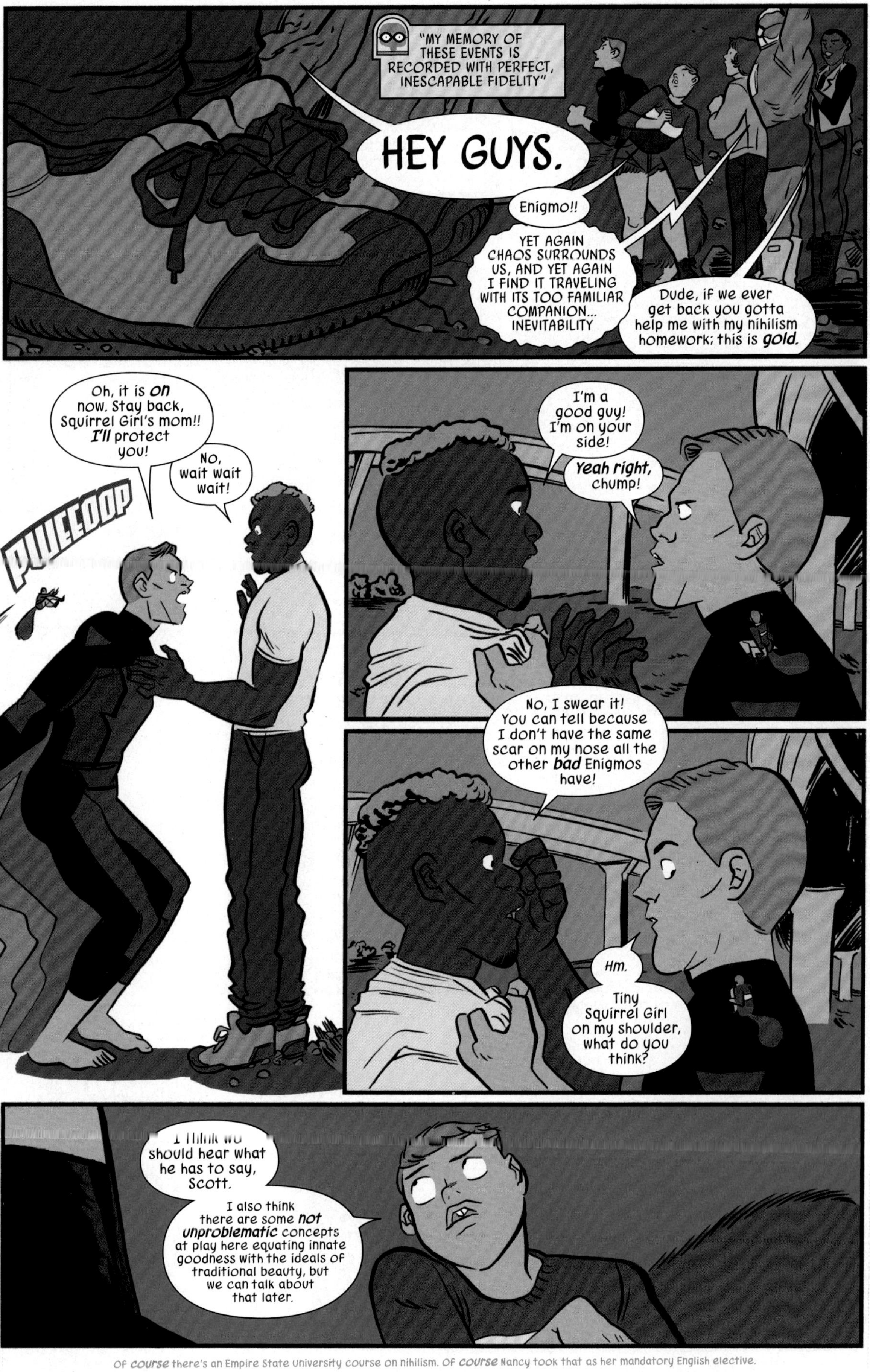

"MY MEMORY OF THESE EVENTS IS RECORDED WITH PERFECT, INESCAPABLE FIDELITY"
HEY GUYS.
Enigmo!!
YET AGAIN CHAOS SURROUNDS US, AND YET AGAIN I FIND IT TRAVELING WITH ITS TOO FAMILIAR COMPANION... INEVITABILITY
Dude, if we ever get back you gotta help me with my nihilism homework; this is *gold.*
Oh, it is *on* now. Stay back, Squirrel Girl's mom!! *I'll* protect you!
No, wait wait wait!
PWEEOOP
I'm a good guy! I'm on your side!
Yeah right, chump!
No, I swear it! You can tell because I don't have the same scar on my nose all the other *bad* Enigmos have!
Hm.
Tiny Squirrel Girl on my shoulder, what do you think?
I think we should hear what he has to say, Scott.
I also think there are some *not unproblematic* concepts at play here equating innate goodness with the ideals of traditional beauty, but we can talk about that later.

Of *course* there's an Empire State University course on nihilism. Of *course* Nancy took that as her mandatory English elective.

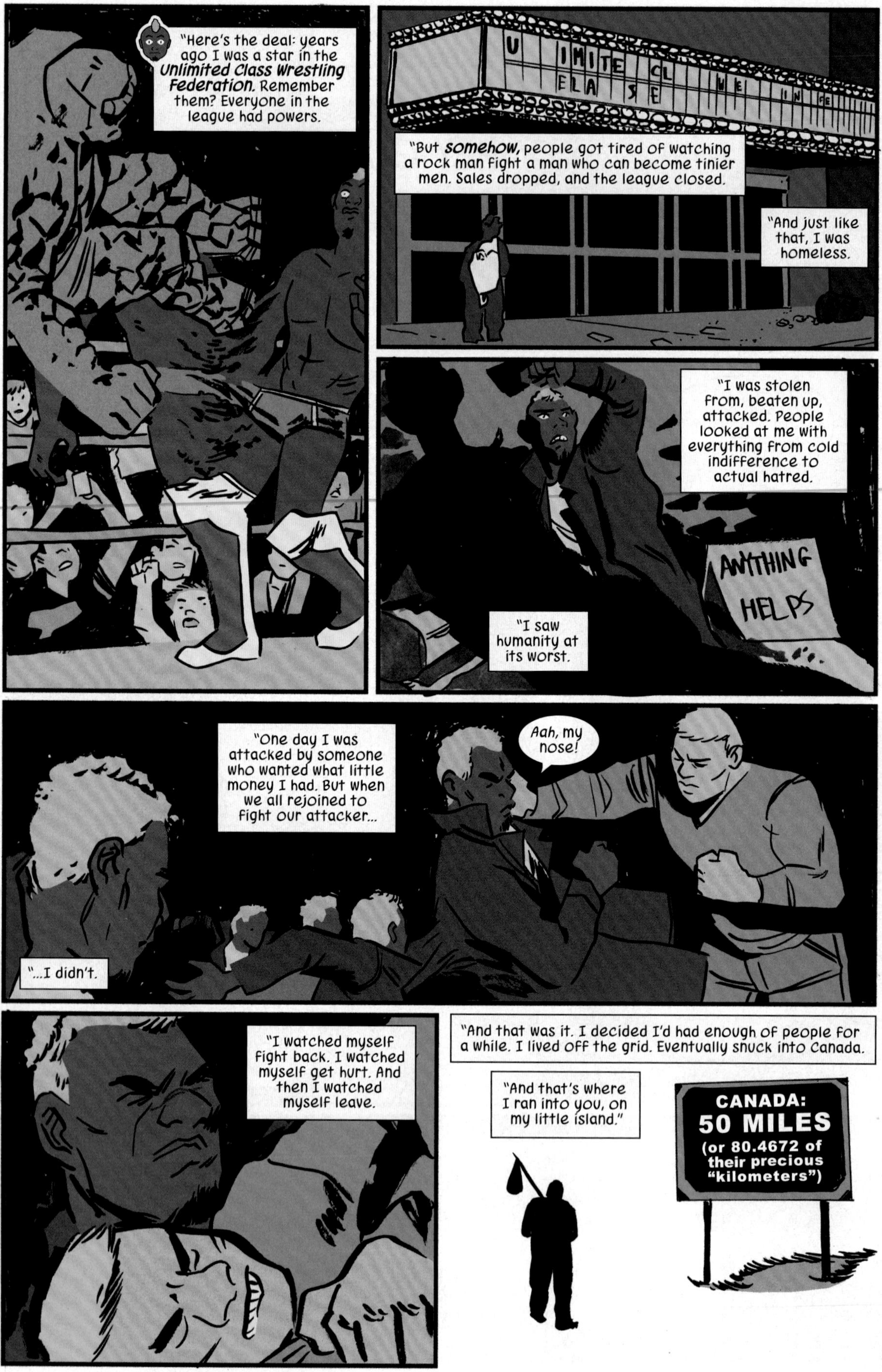
"Here's the deal: years ago I was a star in the *Unlimited Class Wrestling Federation.* Remember them? Everyone in the league had powers.
"But *somehow,* people got tired of watching a rock man fight a man who can become tinier men. Sales dropped, and the league closed.
"And just like that, I was homeless.
"I was stolen from, beaten up, attacked. People looked at me with everything from cold indifference to actual hatred.
ANYTHING HELPS
"I saw humanity at its worst.
"One day I was attacked by someone who wanted what little money I had. But when we all rejoined to fight our attacker...
Aah, my nose!
"...I didn't.
"I watched myself fight back. I watched myself get hurt. And then I watched myself leave.
"And that was it. I decided I'd had enough of people for a while. I lived off the grid. Eventually snuck into Canada.
"And that's where I ran into you, on my little island."
CANADA:
50 MILES
(or 80.4672 of their precious "kilometers")

That island thing happened in *The Unbeatable Squirrel Girl #13,* which came out directly before this issue! Come on, man! *SERIAL STORYTELLING WORKS BEST IF YOU READ THE ISSUES IN ORDER, WE'RE TRYING HARD HERE BUT YOU GOTTA HELP US OUT AT LEAST A LITTLE!!*

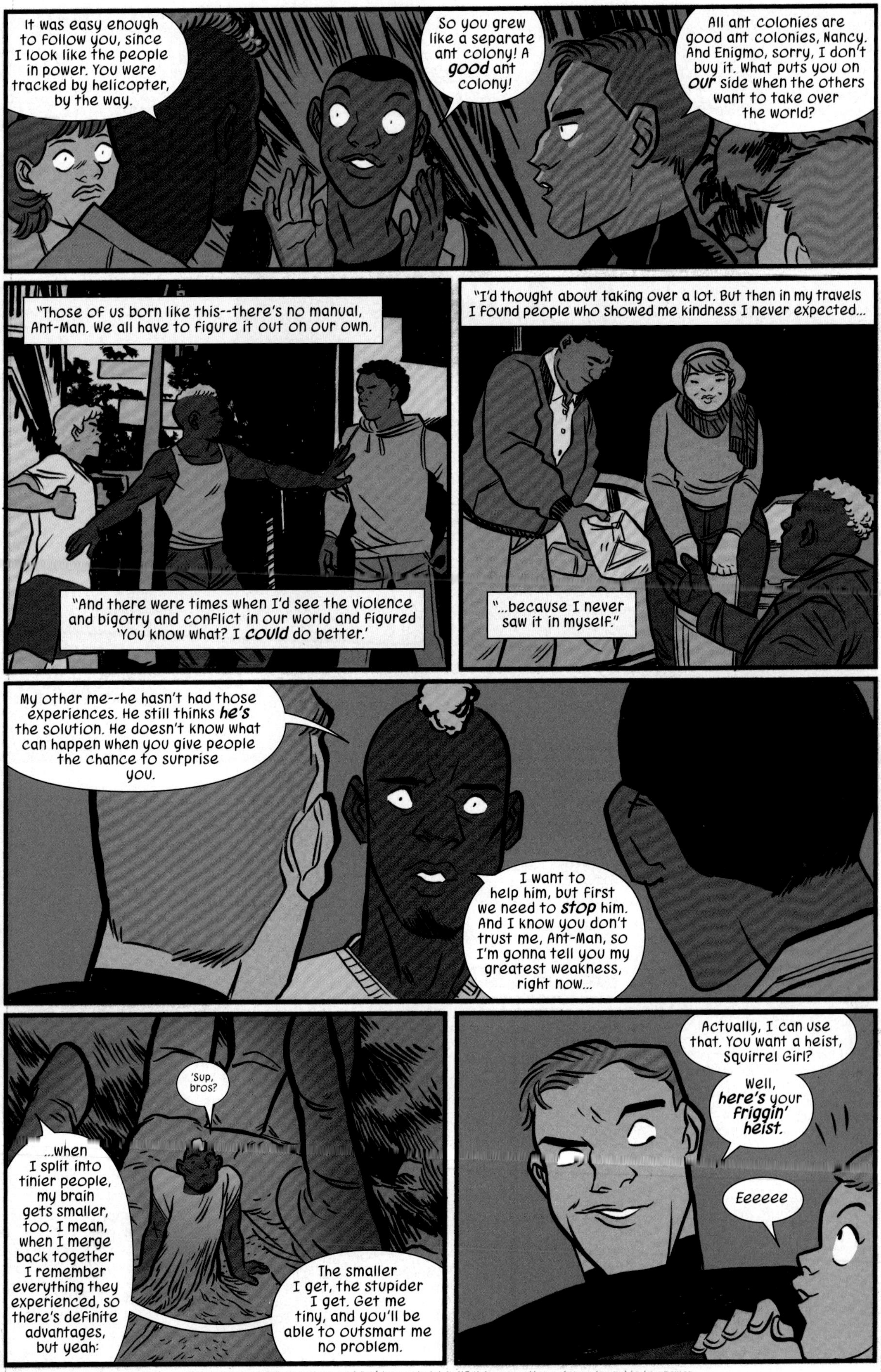
It was easy enough to follow you, since I look like the people in power. You were tracked by helicopter, by the way.
So you grew like a separate ant colony! A good ant colony!
All ant colonies are good ant colonies, Nancy. And Enigmo, sorry, I don't buy it. What puts you on our side when the others want to take over the world?
"Those of us born like this--there's no manual, Ant-Man. We all have to figure it out on our own.
"And there were times when I'd see the violence and bigotry and conflict in our world and figured 'You know what? I could do better.'
"I'd thought about taking over a lot. But then in my travels I found people who showed me kindness I never expected...
"...because I never saw it in myself."
My other me--he hasn't had those experiences. He still thinks he's the solution. He doesn't know what can happen when you give people the chance to surprise you.
I want to help him, but first we need to stop him. And I know you don't trust me, Ant-Man, so I'm gonna tell you my greatest weakness, right now...
'Sup, bros?
...when I split into tinier people, my brain gets smaller, too. I mean, when I merge back together I remember everything they experienced, so there's definite advantages, but yeah:
The smaller I get, the stupider I get. Get me tiny, and you'll be able to outsmart me no problem.
Actually, I can use that. You want a heist, Squirrel Girl?
Well, here's your friggin' heist.
Eeeeee

Can you tell an Ant-Man story and *not* have a heist in it? It is a question science is unable to answer, because the second someone tries, they're like, "Man, what if I just put a fun heist in here though??"

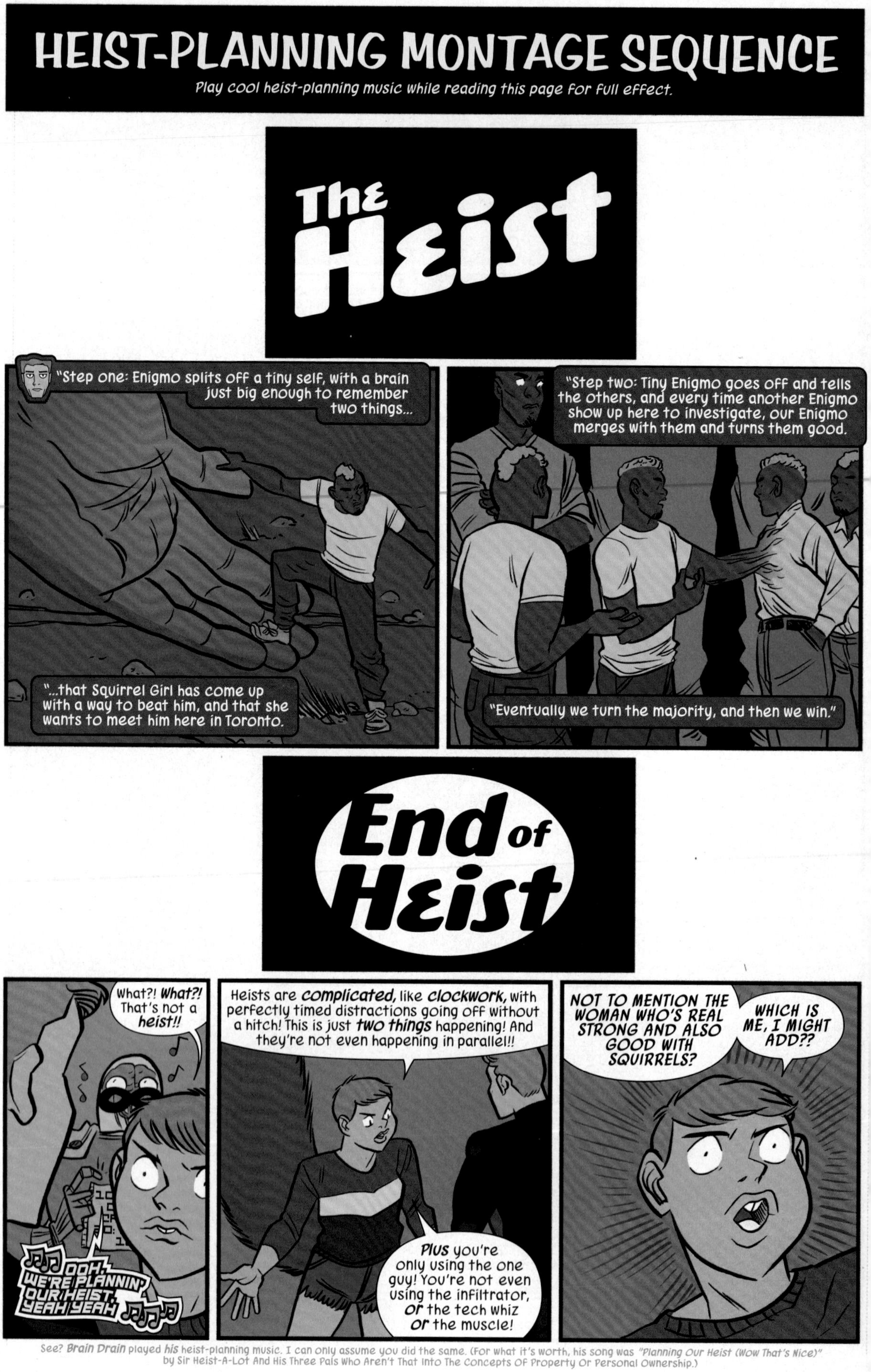
HEIST-PLANNING MONTAGE SEQUENCE
Play cool heist-planning music while reading this page for full effect.
The Heist
"Step one: Enigmo splits off a tiny self, with a brain just big enough to remember two things...
"...that Squirrel Girl has come up with a way to beat him, and that she wants to meet him here in Toronto.
"Step two: Tiny Enigmo goes off and tells the others, and every time another Enigmo show up here to investigate, our Enigmo merges with them and turns them good.
"Eventually we turn the majority, and then we win."
End of Heist
What?! What?! That's not a heist!!
OOH, WE'RE PLANNIN' OUR HEIST, YEAH YEAH
Heists are complicated, like clockwork, with perfectly timed distractions going off without a hitch! This is just two things happening! And they're not even happening in parallel!!
Plus you're only using the one guy! You're not even using the infiltrator, or the tech whiz or the muscle!
NOT TO MENTION THE WOMAN WHO'S REAL STRONG AND ALSO GOOD WITH SQUIRRELS?
WHICH IS ME, I MIGHT ADD??

See? *Brain Drain* played *his* heist-planning music. I can only assume you did the same. (For what it's worth, his song was *"Planning Our Heist (Wow That's Nice)"* by Sir Heist-A-Lot And His Three Pals Who Aren't That Into The Concepts Of Property Or Personal Ownership.)

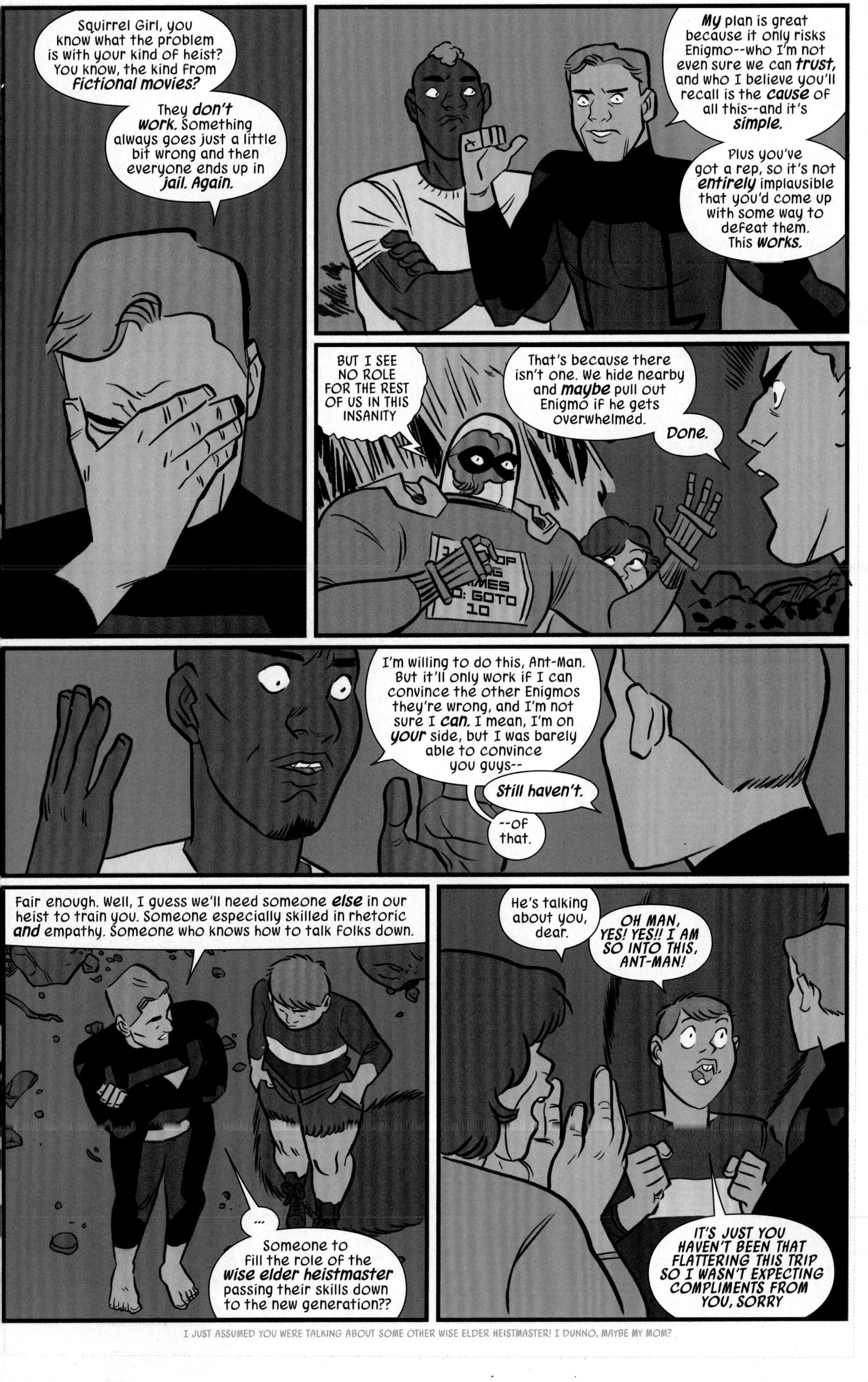
Squirrel Girl, you know what the problem is with your kind of heist? You know, the kind from fictional movies?
They don't work. Something always goes just a little bit wrong and then everyone ends up in jail. Again.
My plan is great because it only risks Enigmo--who I'm not even sure we can trust, and who I believe you'll recall is the cause of all this--and it's simple.
Plus you've got a rep, so it's not entirely implausible that you'd come up with some way to defeat them. This works.
BUT I SEE NO ROLE FOR THE REST OF US IN THIS INSANITY
That's because there isn't one. We hide nearby and maybe pull out Enigmo if he gets overwhelmed.
Done.
I'm willing to do this, Ant-Man. But it'll only work if I can convince the other Enigmos they're wrong, and I'm not sure I can. I mean, I'm on your side, but I was barely able to convince you guys--
Still haven't.
--of that.
Fair enough. Well, I guess we'll need someone else in our heist to train you. Someone especially skilled in rhetoric and empathy. Someone who knows how to talk folks down.
...
Someone to fill the role of the wise elder heistmaster passing their skills down to the new generation??
He's talking about you, dear.
OH MAN, YES! YES!! I AM SO INTO THIS, ANT-MAN!
IT'S JUST YOU HAVEN'T BEEN THAT FLATTERING THIS TRIP SO I WASN'T EXPECTING COMPLIMENTS FROM YOU, SORRY

I JUST ASSUMED YOU WERE TALKING ABOUT SOME OTHER WISE ELDER HEISTMASTER! I DUNNO, MAYBE MY MOM?

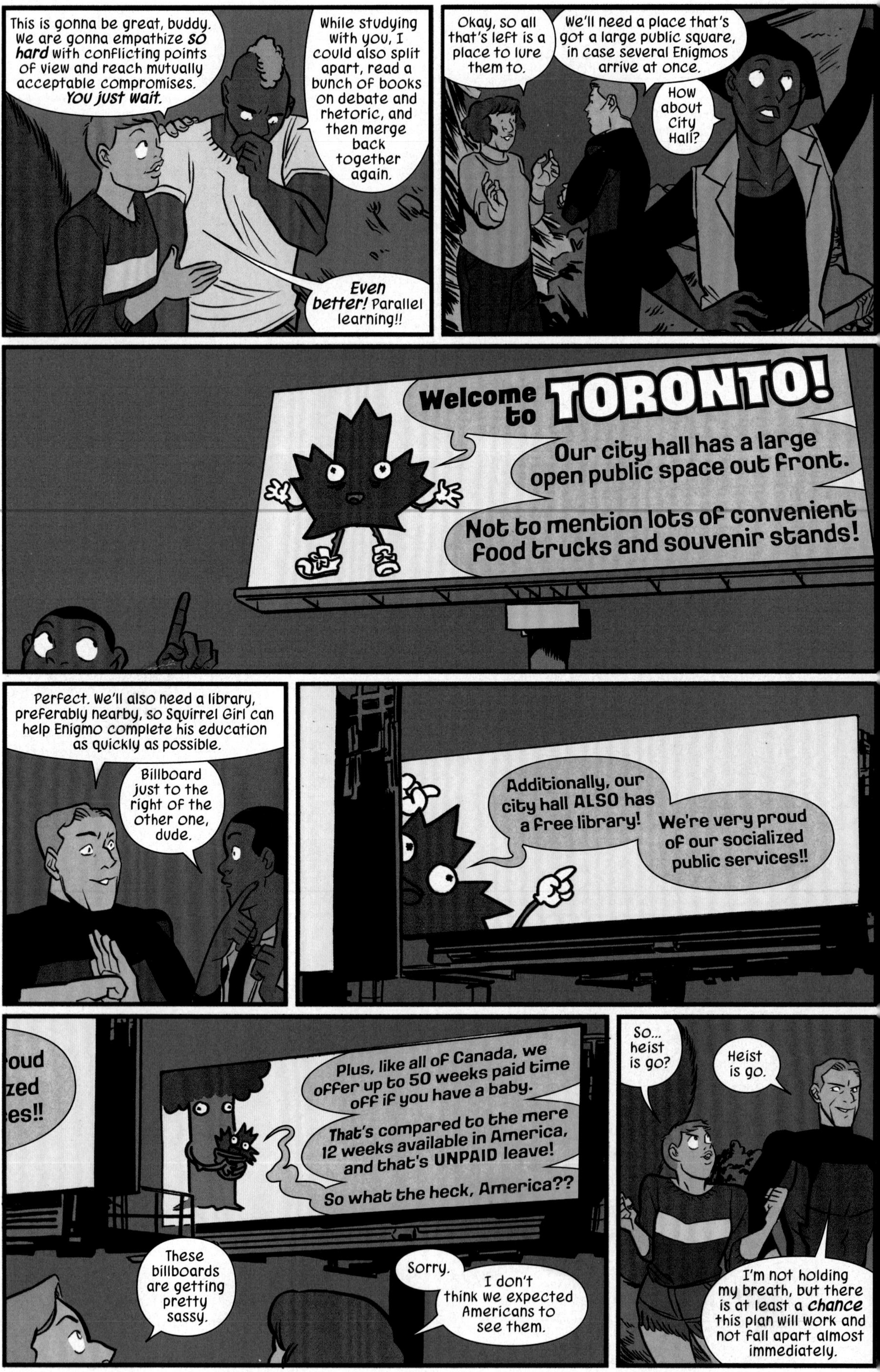
This is gonna be great, buddy. We are gonna empathize SO hard with conflicting points of view and reach mutually acceptable compromises. YOU just wait.
While studying with you, I could also split apart, read a bunch of books on debate and rhetoric, and then merge back together again.
Even better! Parallel learning!!
Okay, so all that's left is a place to lure them to.
We'll need a place that's got a large public square, in case several Enigmos arrive at once.
How about City Hall?
Welcome to TORONTO!
Our city hall has a large open public space out front.
Not to mention lots of convenient food trucks and souvenir stands!
Perfect. We'll also need a library, preferably nearby, so Squirrel Girl can help Enigmo complete his education as quickly as possible.
Billboard just to the right of the other one, dude.
Additionally, our city hall ALSO has a free library!
We're very proud of our socialized public services!!
Plus, like all of Canada, we offer up to 50 weeks paid time off if you have a baby.
That's compared to the mere 12 weeks available in America, and that's UNPAID leave!
So what the heck, America??
These billboards are getting pretty sassy.
Sorry.
I don't think we expected Americans to see them.
So... heist is go?
Heist is go.
I'm not holding my breath, but there is at least a chance this plan will work and not fall apart almost immediately.

America, I don't think having a baby is as cheap or as easy as your social safety net would seem to imply!!
SORRY, AMERICA, BUT BABIES EAT, LIKE, 100% OF THE TIME THEY AREN'T SLEEPING OR CRYING.

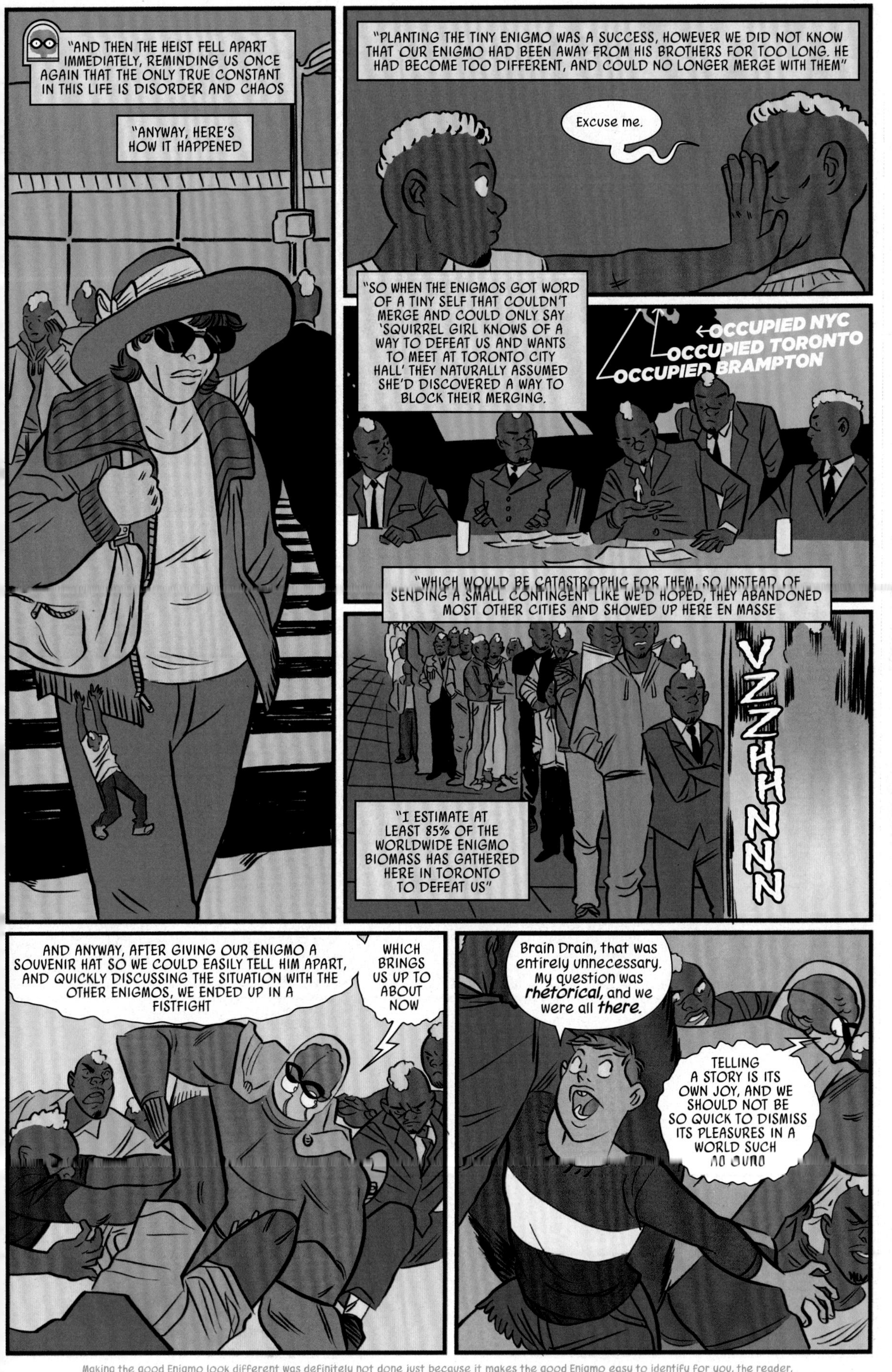
"AND THEN THE HEIST FELL APART IMMEDIATELY, REMINDING US ONCE AGAIN THAT THE ONLY TRUE CONSTANT IN THIS LIFE IS DISORDER AND CHAOS
"ANYWAY, HERE'S HOW IT HAPPENED
"PLANTING THE TINY ENIGMO WAS A SUCCESS, HOWEVER WE DID NOT KNOW THAT OUR ENIGMO HAD BEEN AWAY FROM HIS BROTHERS FOR TOO LONG. HE HAD BECOME TOO DIFFERENT, AND COULD NO LONGER MERGE WITH THEM"
Excuse me.
"SO WHEN THE ENIGMOS GOT WORD OF A TINY SELF THAT COULDN'T MERGE AND COULD ONLY SAY 'SQUIRREL GIRL KNOWS OF A WAY TO DEFEAT US AND WANTS TO MEET AT TORONTO CITY HALL' THEY NATURALLY ASSUMED SHE'D DISCOVERED A WAY TO BLOCK THEIR MERGING.
←OCCUPIED NYC
OCCUPIED TORONTO
OCCUPIED BRAMPTON
"WHICH WOULD BE CATASTROPHIC FOR THEM, SO INSTEAD OF SENDING A SMALL CONTINGENT LIKE WE'D HOPED, THEY ABANDONED MOST OTHER CITIES AND SHOWED UP HERE EN MASSE
VZZHHNNN
"I ESTIMATE AT LEAST 85% OF THE WORLDWIDE ENIGMO BIOMASS HAS GATHERED HERE IN TORONTO TO DEFEAT US"
AND ANYWAY, AFTER GIVING OUR ENIGMO A SOUVENIR HAT SO WE COULD EASILY TELL HIM APART, AND QUICKLY DISCUSSING THE SITUATION WITH THE OTHER ENIGMOS, WE ENDED UP IN A FISTFIGHT
WHICH BRINGS US UP TO ABOUT NOW
Brain Drain, that was entirely unnecessary. My question was *rhetorical,* and we were all *there.*
TELLING A STORY IS ITS OWN JOY, AND WE SHOULD NOT BE SO QUICK TO DISMISS ITS PLEASURES IN A WORLD SUCH

Making the good Enigmo look different was definitely not done just because it makes the good Enigmo easy to identify for you, the reader, when he shows up four pages from now. It *also* lets us draw and write about cool hats!!

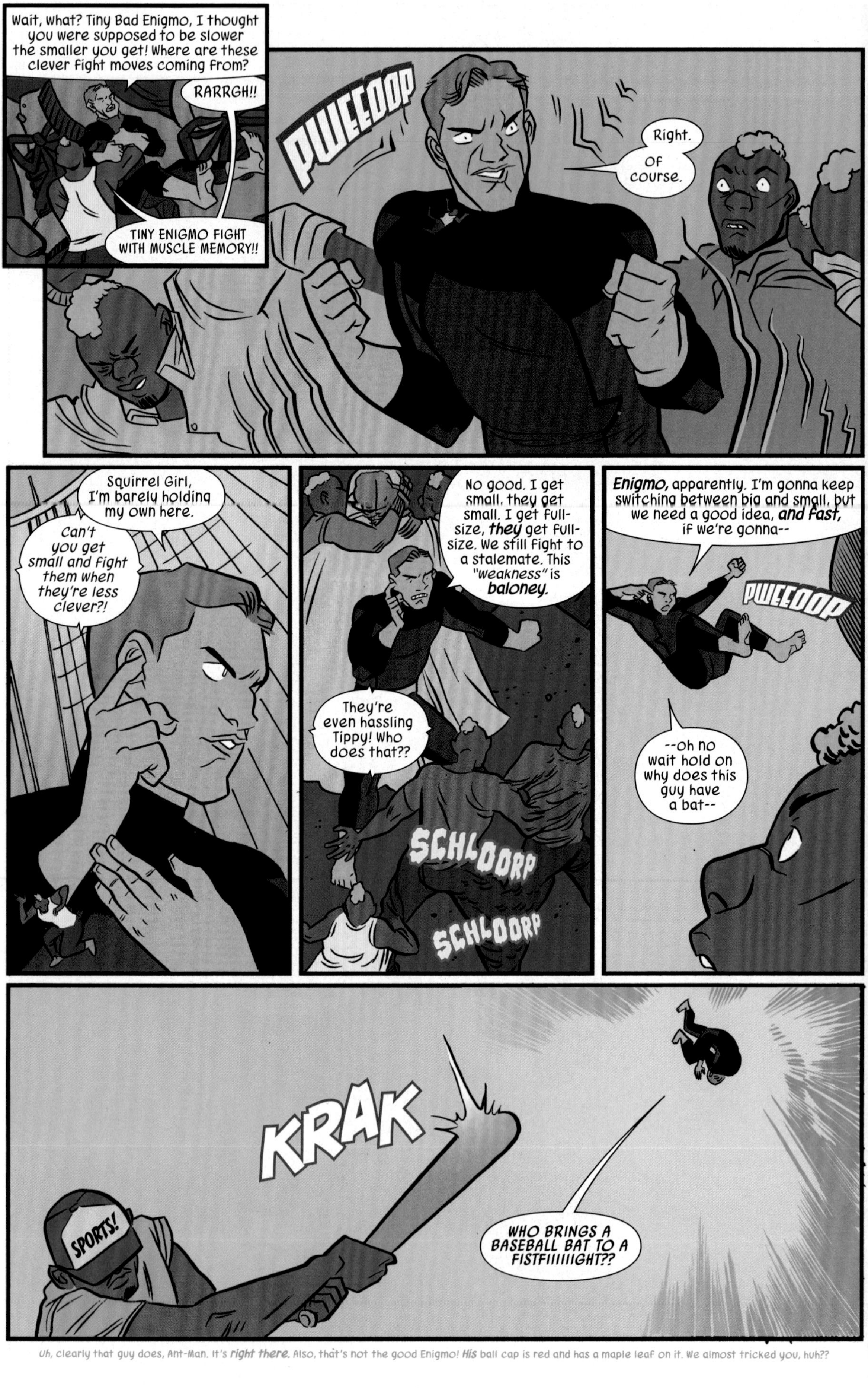
Wait, what? Tiny Bad Enigmo, I thought you were supposed to be slower the smaller you get! Where are these clever fight moves coming from?
RARRGH!!
TINY ENIGMO FIGHT WITH MUSCLE MEMORY!!
PWEEOOP
Right.
Of course.
Squirrel Girl, I'm barely holding my own here.
Can't you get small and fight them when they're less clever?!
No good. I get small, they get small. I get full-size, *they* get full-size. We still fight to a stalemate. This "weakness" is **baloney.**
They're even hassling Tippy! Who does that??
SCHLOORP
SCHLOORP
Enigmo, apparently. I'm gonna keep switching between big and small, but we need a good idea, ***and fast,*** if we're gonna--
PWEEOOP
--oh no wait hold on why does this guy have a bat--
KRAK
SPORTS!
WHO BRINGS A BASEBALL BAT TO A FISTFIIIIIIGHT??

*Uh, clearly that guy does, Ant-Man. It's **right there.** Also, that's not the good Enigmo! **His** ball cap is red and has a maple leaf on it. We almost tricked you, huh??*

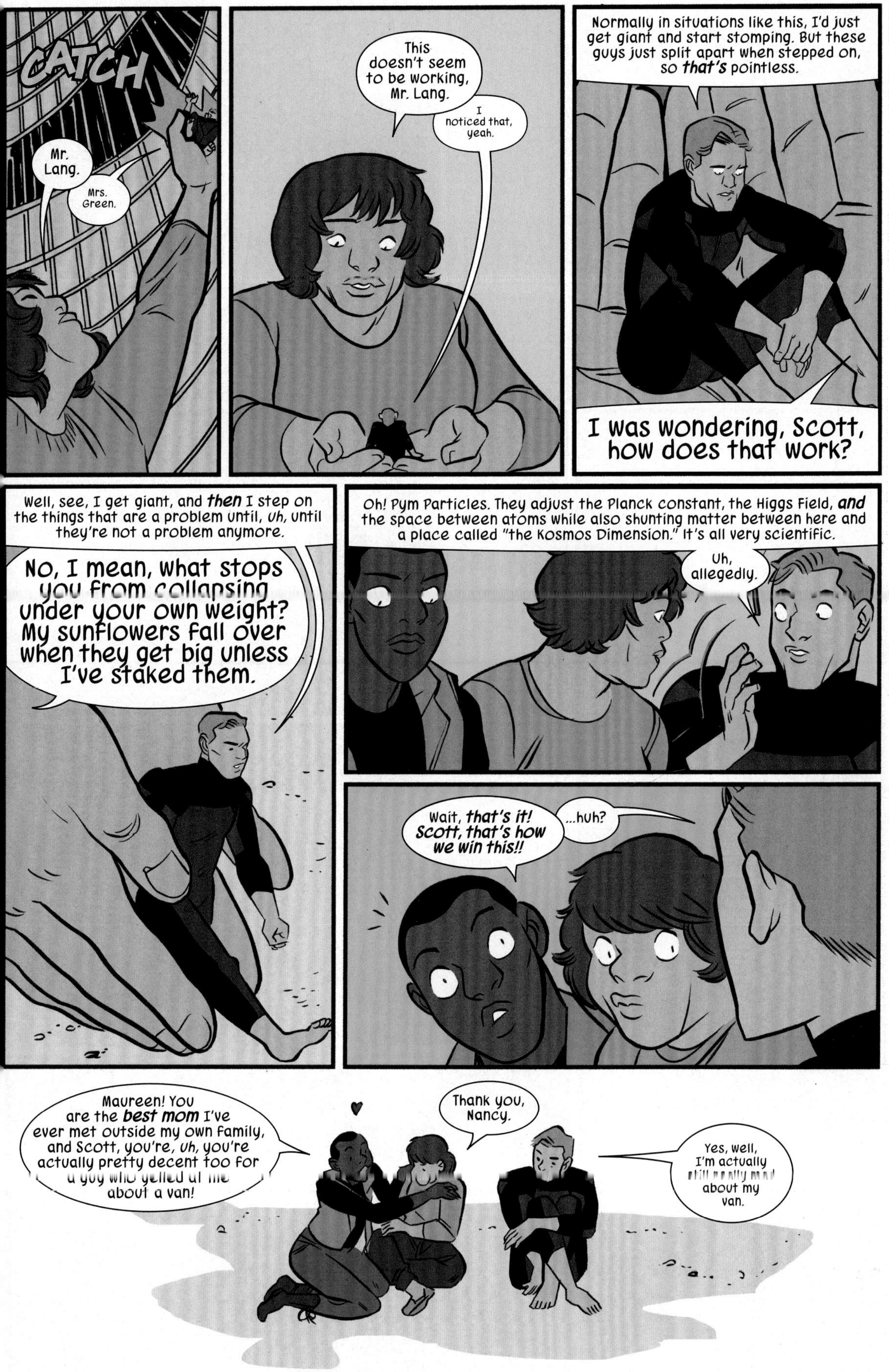
CATCH
Mr. Lang.
Mrs. Green.
This doesn't seem to be working, Mr. Lang.
I noticed that, yeah.
Normally in situations like this, I'd just get giant and start stomping. But these guys just split apart when stepped on, so *that's* pointless.
I was wondering, Scott, how does that work?
Well, see, I get giant, and *then* I step on the things that are a problem until, *uh*, until they're not a problem anymore.
No, I mean, what stops you from collapsing under your own weight? My sunflowers fall over when they get big unless I've staked them.
Oh! Pym Particles. They adjust the Planck constant, the Higgs Field, **and** the space between atoms while also shunting matter between here and a place called "the Kosmos Dimension." It's all very scientific.
Uh, allegedly.
Wait, *that's it! Scott, that's how we win this!!*
...huh?
Maureen! You are the **best mom** I've ever met outside my own family, and Scott, you're, *uh*, you're actually pretty decent too for a guy who yelled at me about a van!
Thank you, Nancy.
Yes, well, I'm actually still really mad about my van.

I've got a note here from Deadpool from the last issue. It reads as follows: "CALLED IT."

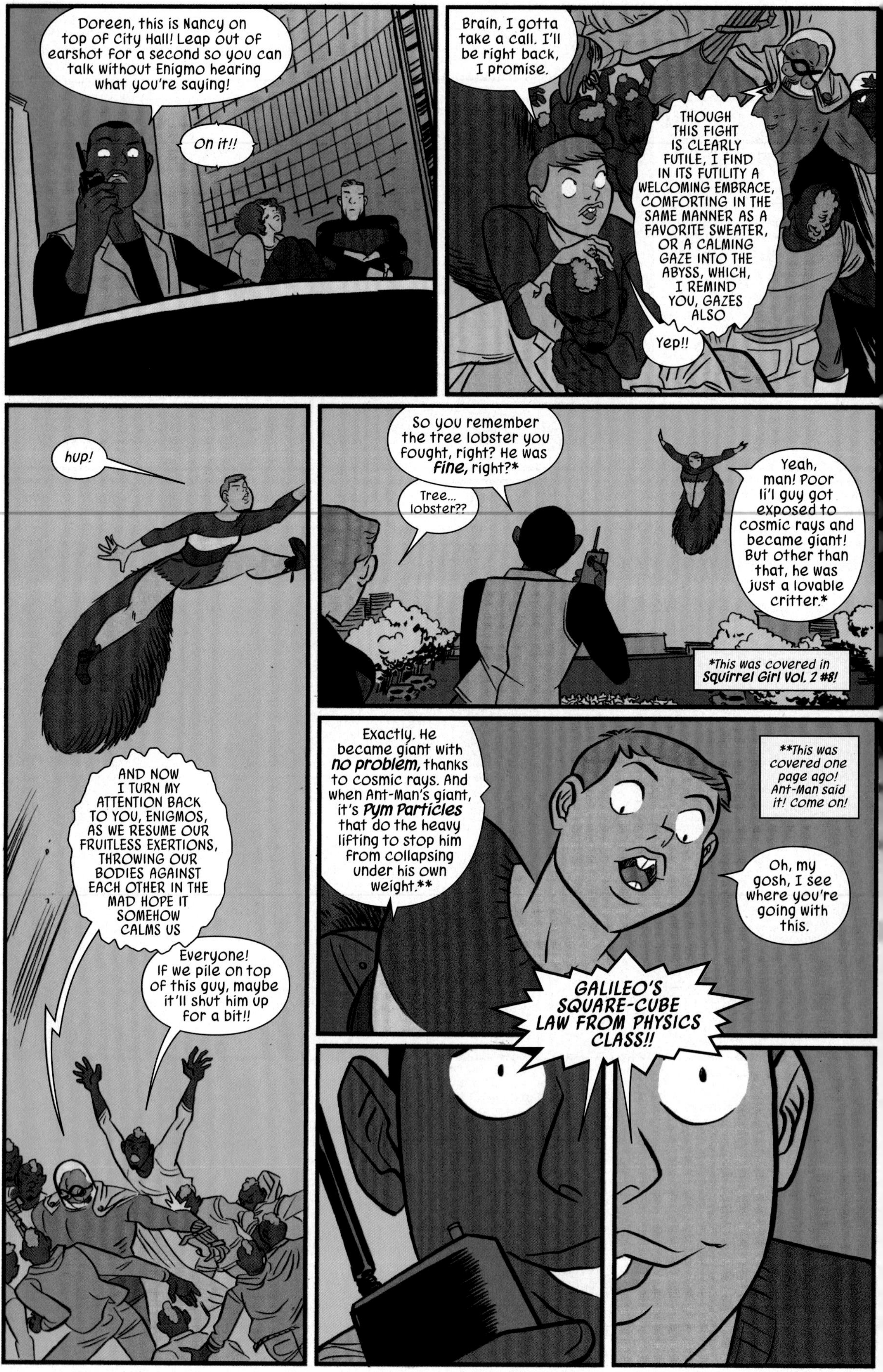
Doreen, this is Nancy on top of City Hall! Leap out of earshot for a second so you can talk without Enigmo hearing what you're saying!
On it!!
Brain, I gotta take a call. I'll be right back, I promise.
THOUGH THIS FIGHT IS CLEARLY FUTILE, I FIND IN ITS FUTILITY A WELCOMING EMBRACE, COMFORTING IN THE SAME MANNER AS A FAVORITE SWEATER, OR A CALMING GAZE INTO THE ABYSS, WHICH, I REMIND YOU, GAZES ALSO
Yep!!
hup!
AND NOW I TURN MY ATTENTION BACK TO YOU, ENIGMOS, AS WE RESUME OUR FRUITLESS EXERTIONS, THROWING OUR BODIES AGAINST EACH OTHER IN THE MAD HOPE IT SOMEHOW CALMS US
Everyone! If we pile on top of this guy, maybe it'll shut him up for a bit!!
So you remember the tree lobster you fought, right? He was *fine*, right?*
Tree... lobster??
Yeah, man! Poor li'l guy got exposed to cosmic rays and became giant! But other than that, he was just a lovable critter.*
*This was covered in *Squirrel Girl Vol. 2 #8!*
Exactly. He became giant with **no problem,** thanks to cosmic rays. And when Ant-Man's giant, it's **Pym Particles** that do the heavy lifting to stop him from collapsing under his own weight.**
**This was covered one page ago! Ant-Man said it! Come on!
Oh, my gosh, I see where you're going with this.
GALILEO'S SQUARE-CUBE LAW FROM PHYSICS CLASS!!

Nancy and Squirrel Girl both know what that square-cube law is, but do you? Naw, me neither. But instead of throwing this comic away in a fit of *incandescent rage,* let's all keep in mind that there's a small chance this might be explained on the very next page!

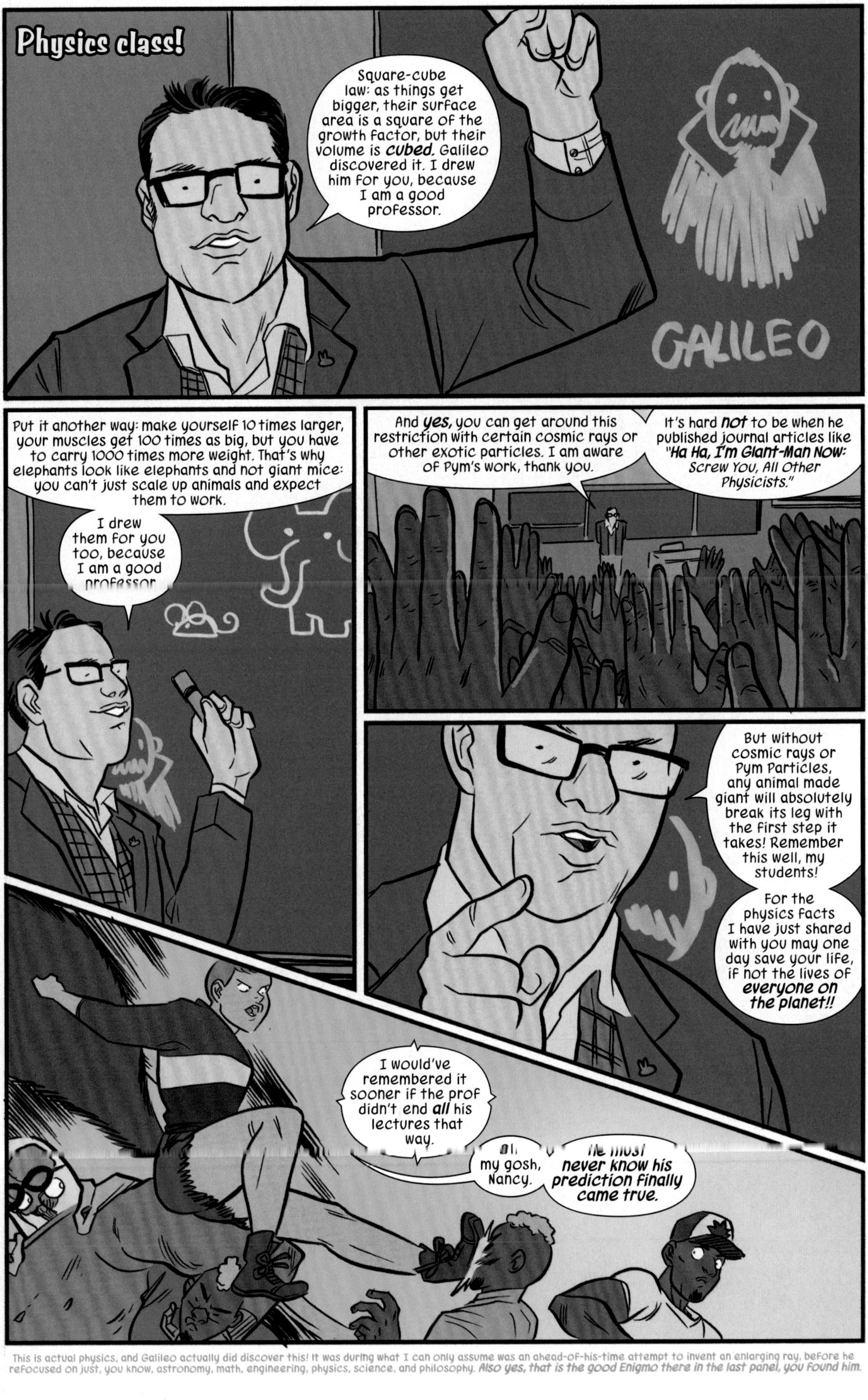
Physics class!
Square-cube law: as things get bigger, their surface area is a square of the growth factor, but their volume is *cubed.* Galileo discovered it. I drew him for you, because I am a good professor.
GALILEO
Put it another way: make yourself 10 times larger, your muscles get 100 times as big, but you have to carry 1000 times more weight. That's why elephants look like elephants and not giant mice: you can't just scale up animals and expect them to work.
I drew them for you too, because I am a good professor
And *yes,* you can get around this restriction with certain cosmic rays or other exotic particles. I am aware of Pym's work, thank you.
It's hard *not* to be when he published journal articles like *"Ha Ha, I'm Giant-Man Now: Screw You, All Other Physicists."*
But without cosmic rays or Pym Particles, any animal made giant will absolutely break its leg with the first step it takes! Remember this well, my students!
For the physics facts I have just shared with you may one day save your life, if not the lives of *everyone on the planet!!*
I would've remembered it sooner if the prof didn't end *all* his lectures that way.
my gosh, Nancy.
never know his prediction finally came true.

This is actual physics, and Galileo actually did discover this! It was during what I can only assume was an ahead-of-his-time attempt to invent an enlarging ray, before he refocused on just, you know, astronomy, math, engineering, physics, science, and philosophy. *Also yes, that is the good Enigmo there in the last panel, you found him.*

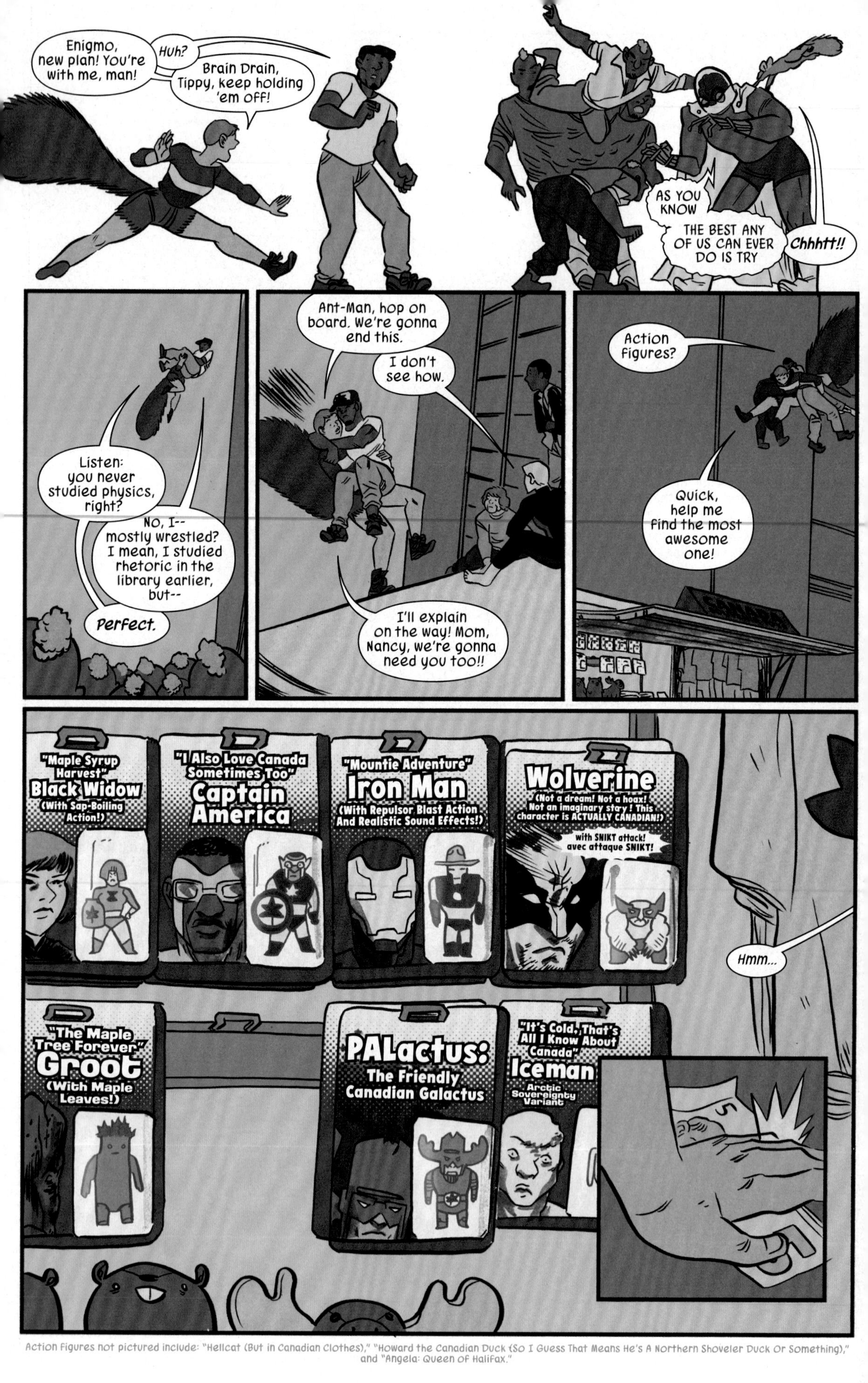
Enigmo, new plan! You're with me, man!
Huh?
Brain Drain, Tippy, keep holding 'em off!
AS YOU KNOW
THE BEST ANY OF US CAN EVER DO IS TRY
Chhhtt!!
Listen: you never studied physics, right?
No, I-- mostly wrestled? I mean, I studied rhetoric in the library earlier, but--
Perfect.
Ant-Man, hop on board. We're gonna end this.
I don't see how.
I'll explain on the way! Mom, Nancy, we're gonna need you too!!
Action Figures?
Quick, help me find the most awesome one!
"Maple Syrup Harvest" Black Widow (With Sap-Boiling Action!)
"I Also Love Canada Sometimes Too" Captain America
"Mountie Adventure" Iron Man (With Repulsor Blast Action And Realistic Sound Effects!)
Wolverine (Not a dream! Not a hoax! Not an imaginary story! This character is ACTUALLY CANADIAN!)
with SNIKT attack! avec attaque SNIKT!
Hmm...
"The Maple Tree Forever" Groot (With Maple Leaves!)
PALactus: The Friendly Canadian Galactus
"It's Cold, That's All I Know About Canada" Iceman
Arctic Sovereignty Variant

Action Figures not pictured include: "Hellcat (But in Canadian Clothes)," "Howard the Canadian Duck (So I Guess That Means He's A Northern Shoveler Duck Or Something)," and "Angela: Queen of Halifax."

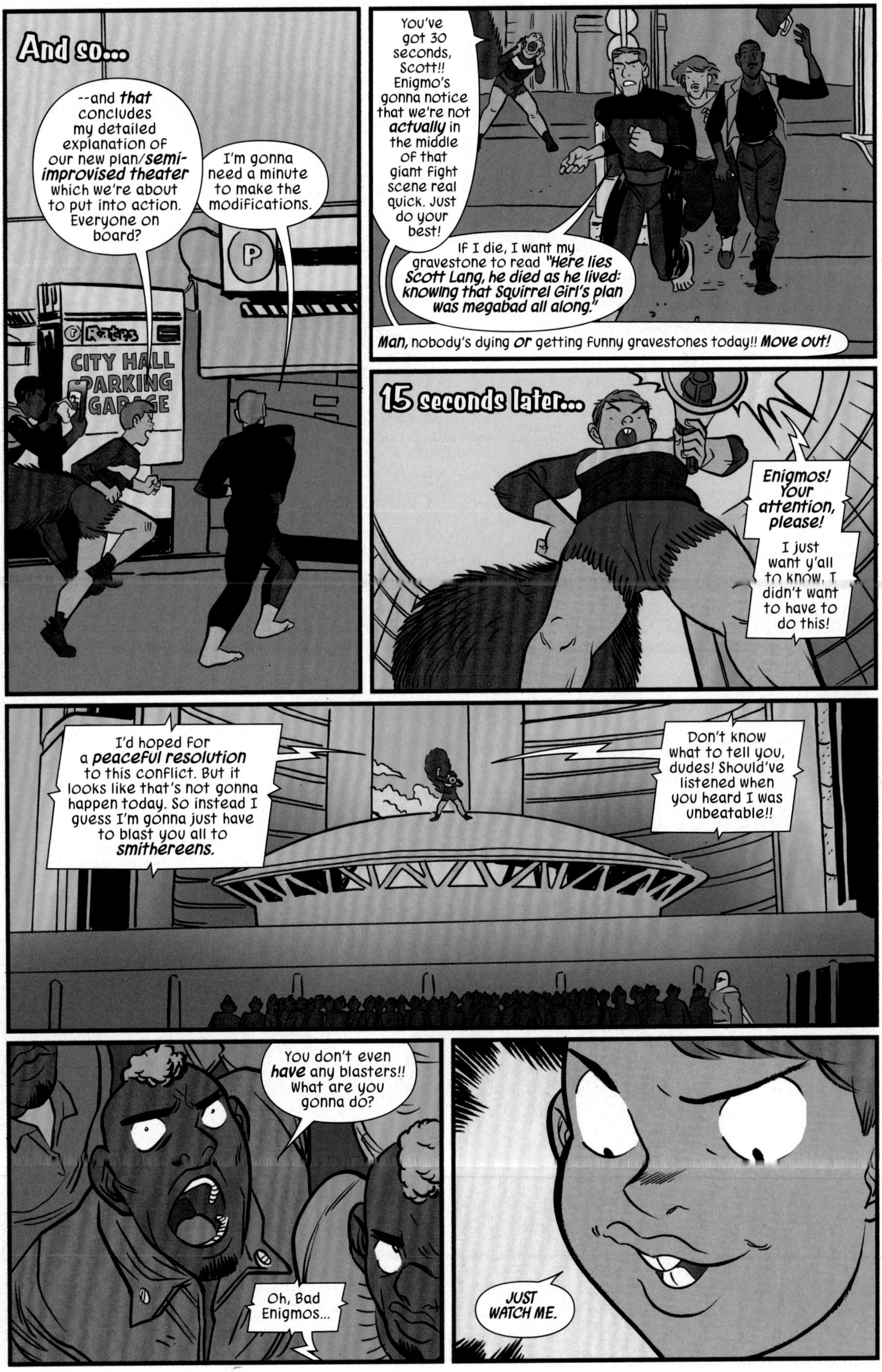
And so...
--and that concludes my detailed explanation of our new plan/semi-improvised theater which we're about to put into action. Everyone on board?
I'm gonna need a minute to make the modifications.
CITY HALL PARKING GARAGE
You've got 30 seconds, Scott!! Enigmo's gonna notice that we're not actually in the middle of that giant fight scene real quick. Just do your best!
If I die, I want my gravestone to read "Here lies Scott Lang, he died as he lived: knowing that Squirrel Girl's plan was megabad all along."
Man, nobody's dying or getting funny gravestones today!! Move out!
15 seconds later...
Enigmos! Your attention, please!
I just want y'all to know, I didn't want to have to do this!
I'd hoped for a peaceful resolution to this conflict. But it looks like that's not gonna happen today. So instead I guess I'm gonna just have to blast you all to smithereens.
Don't know what to tell you, dudes! Should've listened when you heard I was unbeatable!!
You don't even have any blasters!! What are you gonna do?
Oh, Bad Enigmos...
JUST WATCH ME.

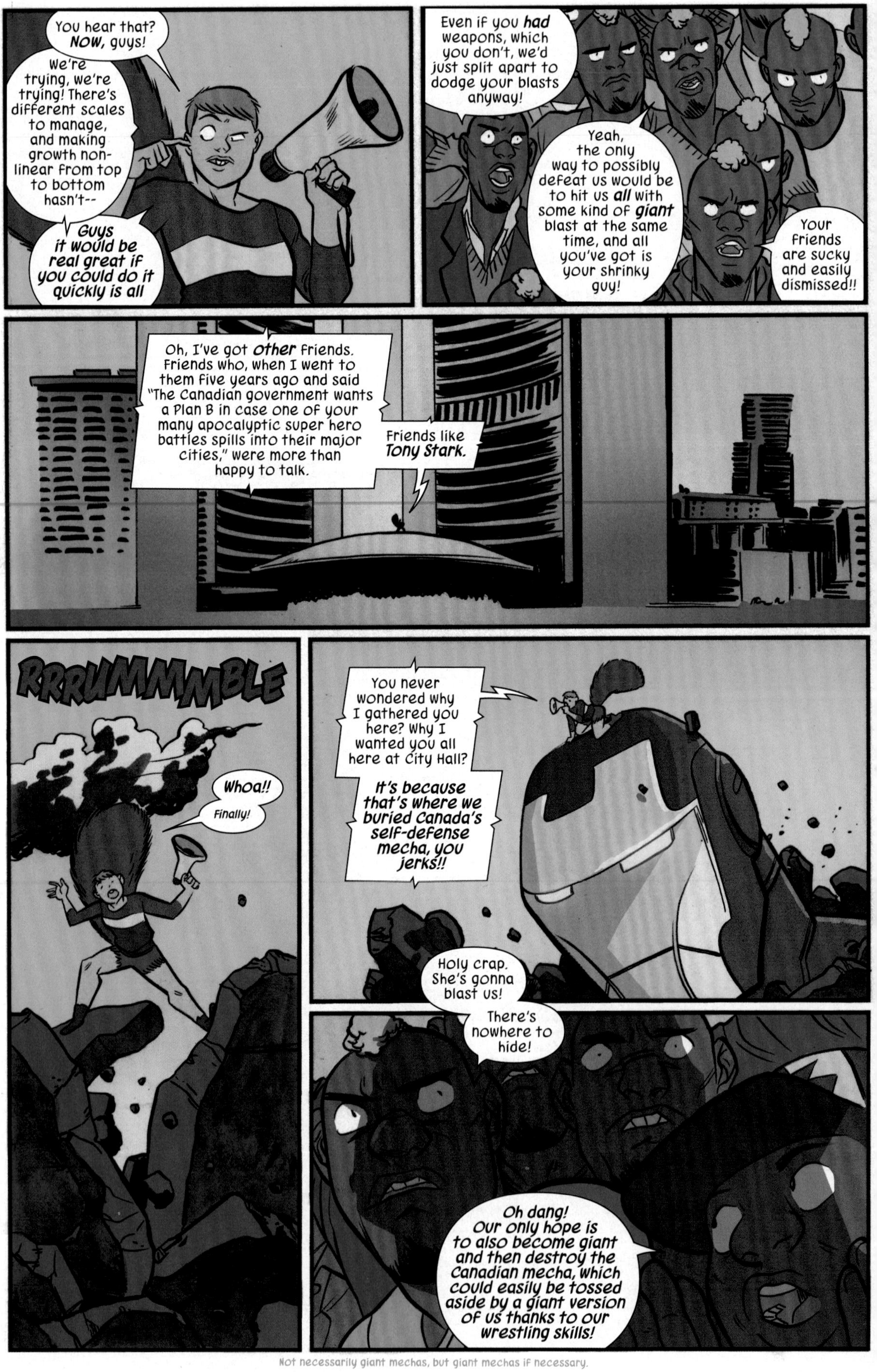
You hear that? NOW, guys!
We're trying, we're trying! There's different scales to manage, and making growth non-linear from top to bottom hasn't--
Guys it would be real great if you could do it quickly is all
Even if you had weapons, which you don't, we'd just split apart to dodge your blasts anyway!
Yeah, the only way to possibly defeat us would be to hit us all with some kind of giant blast at the same time, and all you've got is your shrinky guy!
Your friends are sucky and easily dismissed!!
Oh, I've got other friends. Friends who, when I went to them five years ago and said "The Canadian government wants a Plan B in case one of your many apocalyptic super hero battles spills into their major cities," were more than happy to talk.
Friends like Tony Stark.
RRRUMMMMBLE
Whoa!!
Finally!
You never wondered why I gathered you here? Why I wanted you all here at City Hall?
It's because that's where we buried Canada's self-defense mecha, you jerks!!
Holy crap. She's gonna blast us!
There's nowhere to hide!
Oh dang! Our only hope is to also become giant and then destroy the Canadian mecha, which could easily be tossed aside by a giant version of us thanks to our wrestling skills!

Not necessarily giant mechas, but giant mechas if necessary.

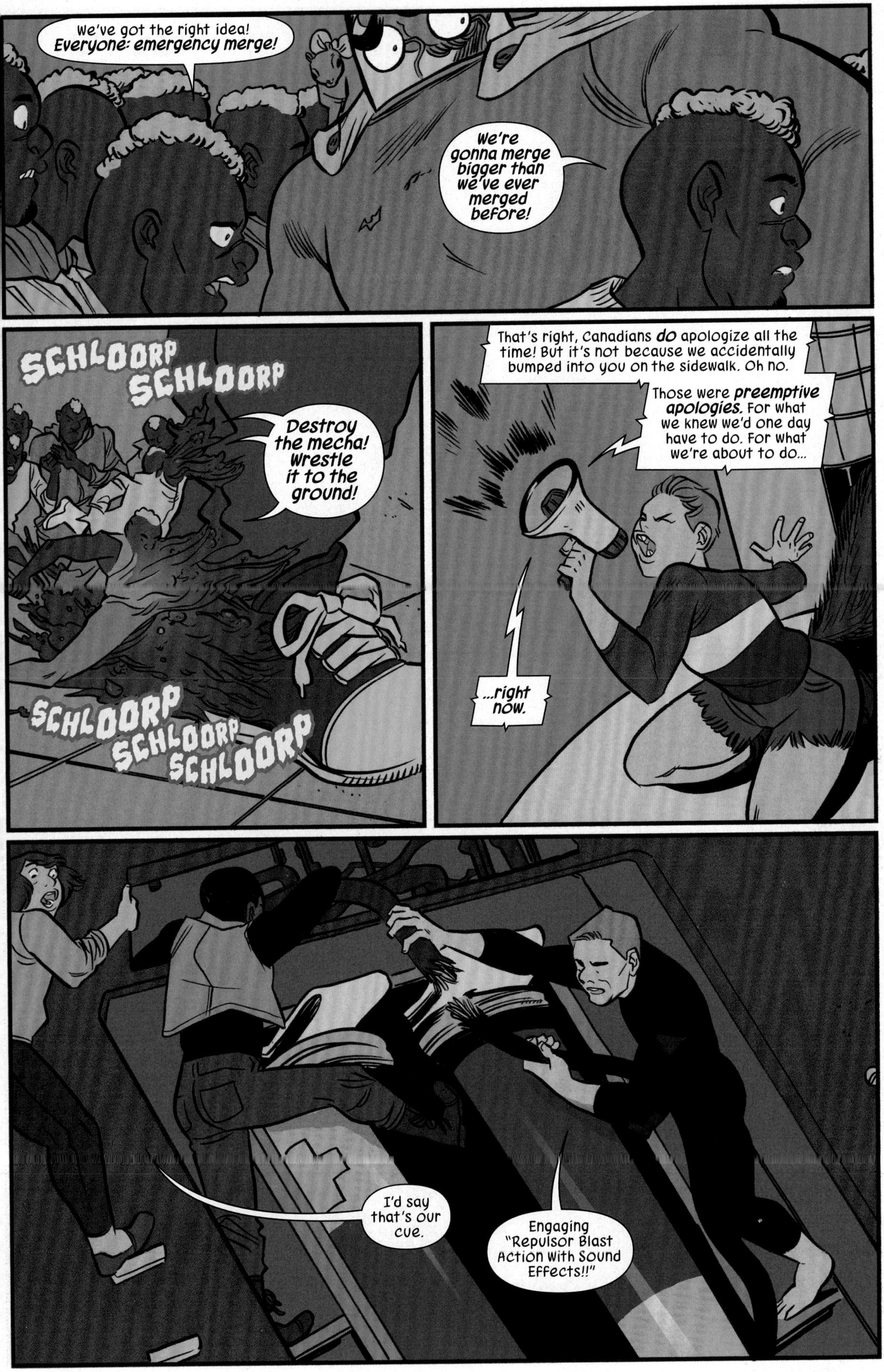
We've got the right idea! Everyone: emergency merge!
We're gonna merge bigger than we've ever merged before!
SCHLOORP SCHLOORP
Destroy the mecha! Wrestle it to the ground!
SCHLOORP SCHLOORP SCHLOORP
That's right, Canadians do apologize all the time! But it's not because we accidentally bumped into you on the sidewalk. Oh no.
Those were preemptive apologies. For what we knew we'd one day have to do. For what we're about to do...
...right now.
I'd say that's our cue.
Engaging "Repulsor Blast Action With Sound Effects!!"

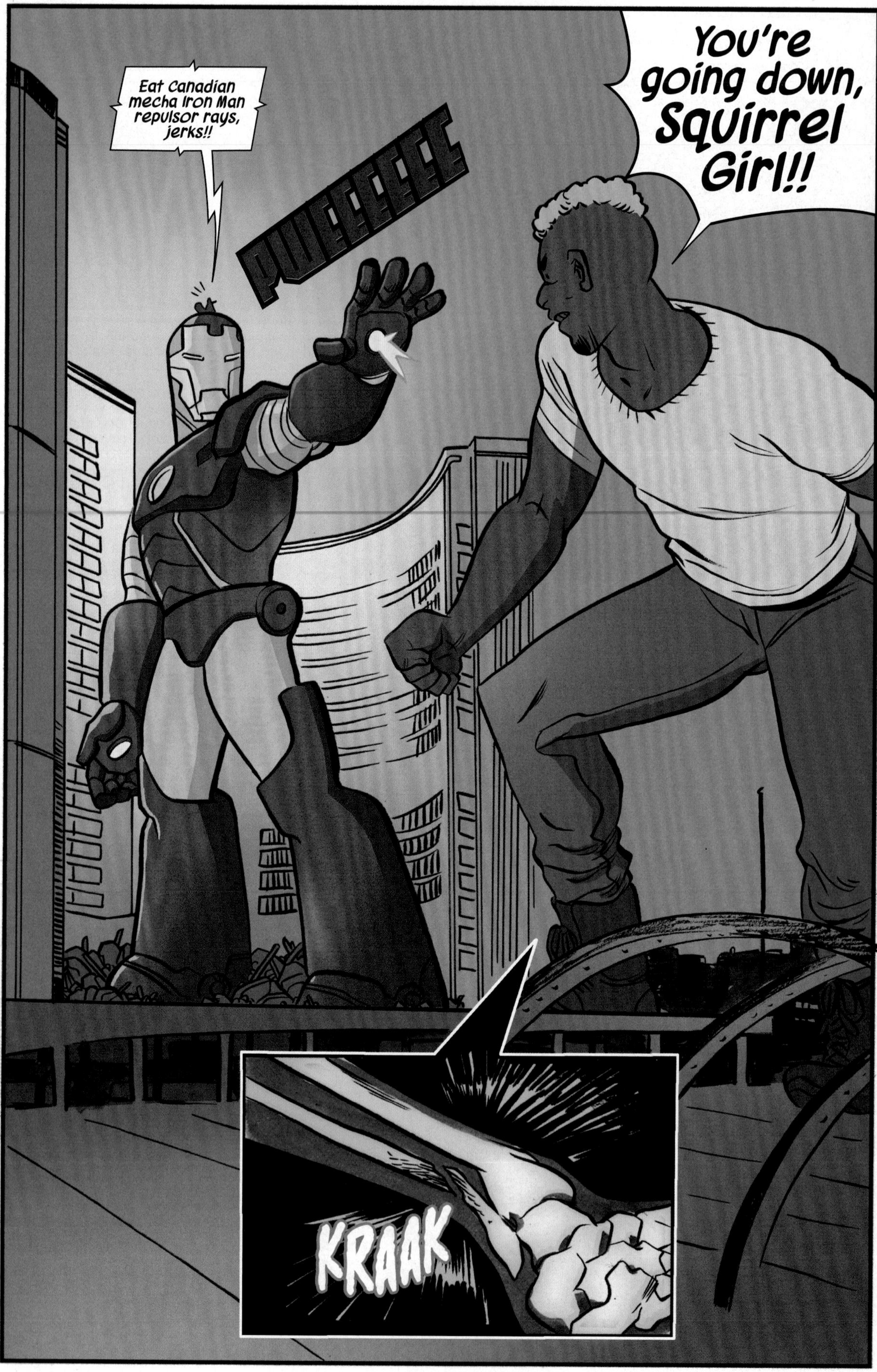
Eat Canadian mecha Iron Man repulsor rays, jerks!!
PWEEEEEE
You're going down, Squirrel Girl!!
KRAAK

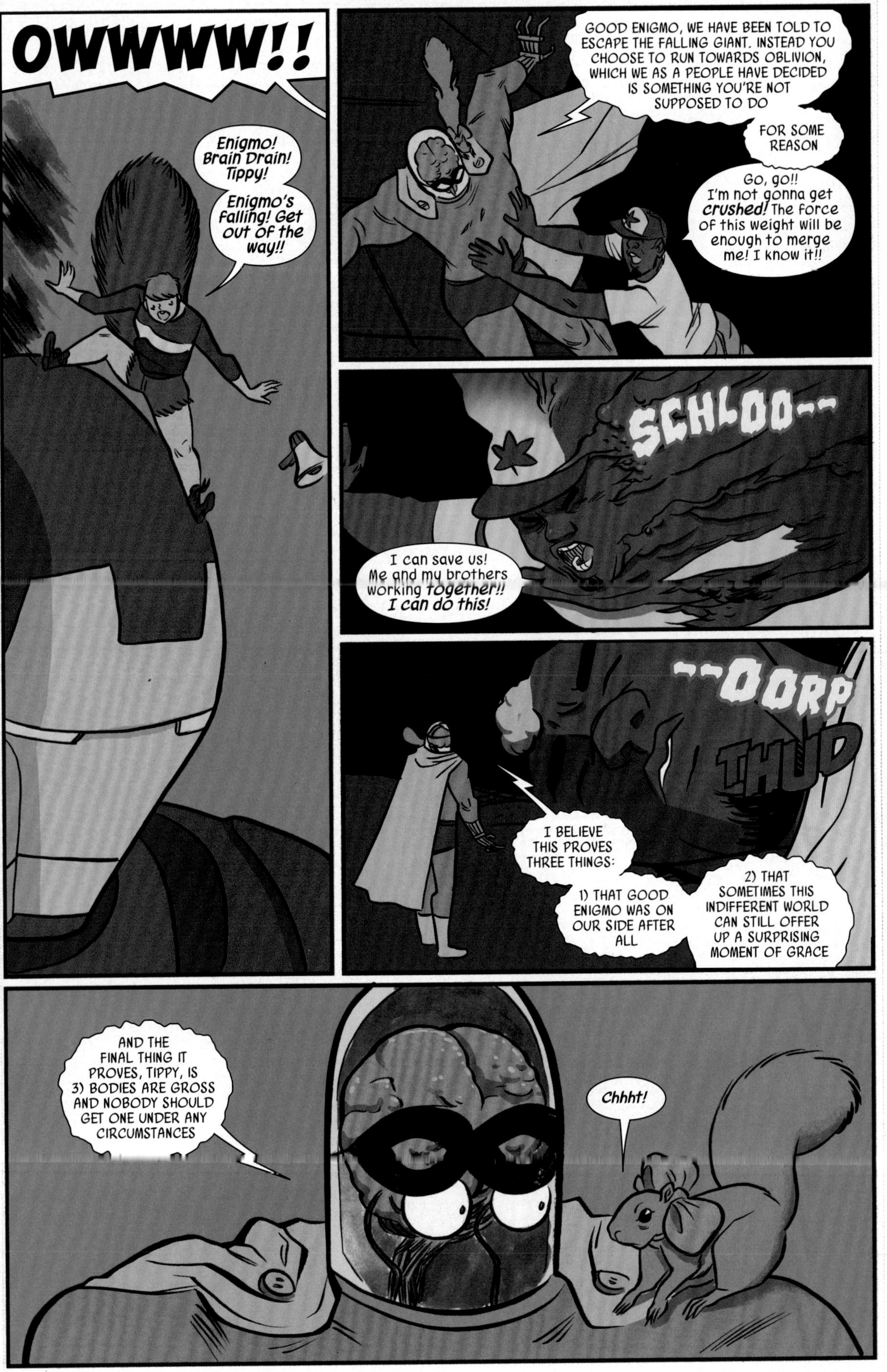
OWWWW!!
Enigmo! Brain Drain! Tippy!
Enigmo's falling! Get out of the way!!
GOOD ENIGMO, WE HAVE BEEN TOLD TO ESCAPE THE FALLING GIANT. INSTEAD YOU CHOOSE TO RUN TOWARDS OBLIVION, WHICH WE AS A PEOPLE HAVE DECIDED IS SOMETHING YOU'RE NOT SUPPOSED TO DO
FOR SOME REASON
Go, go!! I'm not gonna get crushed! The force of this weight will be enough to merge me! I know it!!
SCHLOO--
I can save us! Me and my brothers working together!! I can do this!
--OORP
THUD
I BELIEVE THIS PROVES THREE THINGS:
1) THAT GOOD ENIGMO WAS ON OUR SIDE AFTER ALL
2) THAT SOMETIMES THIS INDIFFERENT WORLD CAN STILL OFFER UP A SURPRISING MOMENT OF GRACE
AND THE FINAL THING IT PROVES, TIPPY, IS 3) BODIES ARE GROSS AND NOBODY SHOULD GET ONE UNDER ANY CIRCUMSTANCES
Chhht!

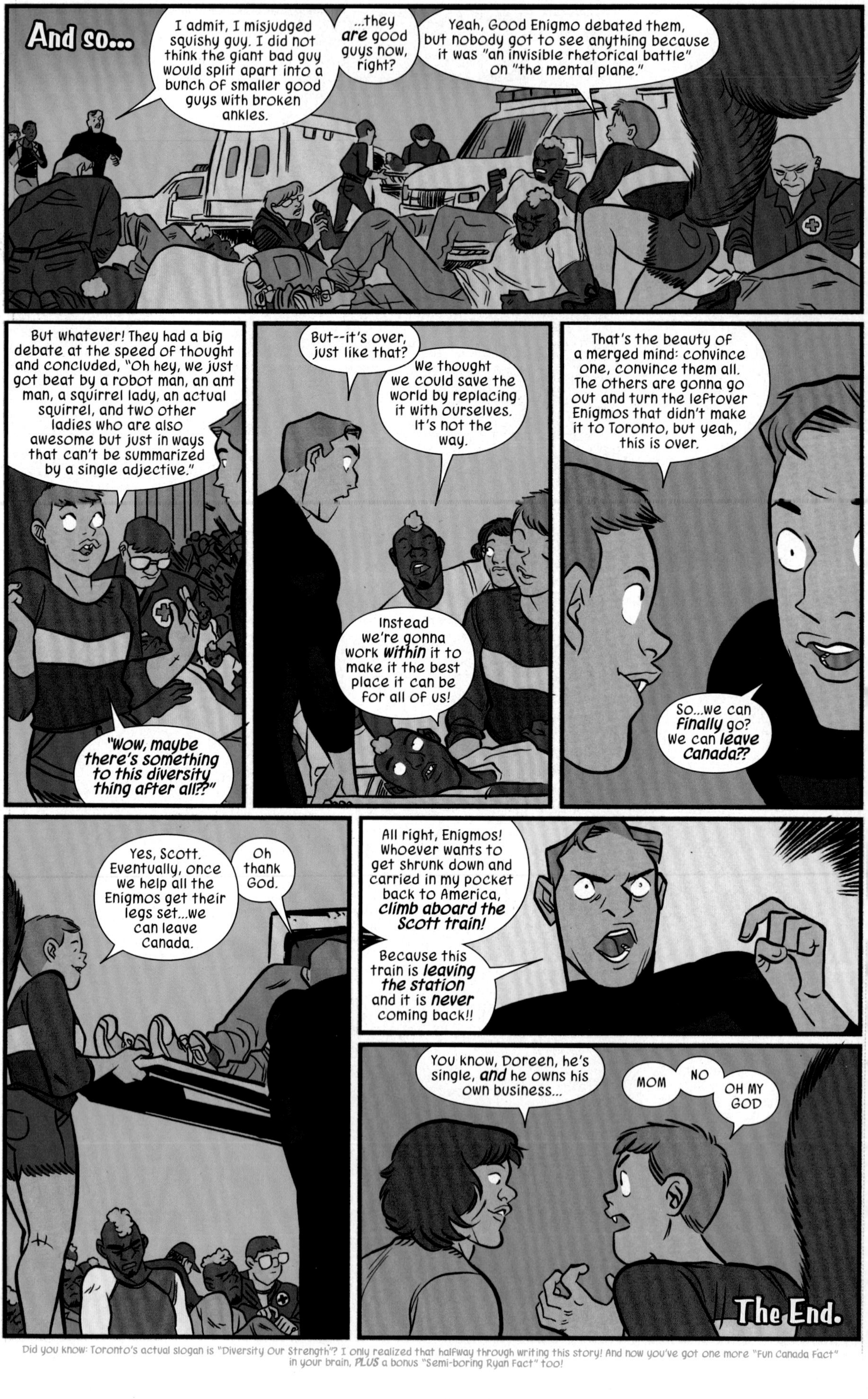
And so...
I admit, I misjudged squishy guy. I did not think the giant bad guy would split apart into a bunch of smaller good guys with broken ankles.
...they *are* good guys now, right?
Yeah, Good Enigmo debated them, but nobody got to see anything because it was "an invisible rhetorical battle" on "the mental plane."
But whatever! They had a big debate at the speed of thought and concluded, "Oh hey, we just got beat by a robot man, an ant man, a squirrel lady, an actual squirrel, and two other ladies who are also awesome but just in ways that can't be summarized by a single adjective."
"Wow, maybe there's something to this diversity thing after all??"
But--it's over, just like that?
We thought we could save the world by replacing it with ourselves. It's not the way.
Instead we're gonna work *within* it to make it the best place it can be for all of us!
That's the beauty of a merged mind: convince one, convince them all. The others are gonna go out and turn the leftover Enigmos that didn't make it to Toronto, but yeah, this is over.
So...we can *finally* go? We can *leave Canada??*
Yes, Scott. Eventually, once we help all the Enigmos get their legs set...we can leave Canada.
Oh thank God.
All right, Enigmos! Whoever wants to get shrunk down and carried in my pocket back to America, *climb aboard the Scott train!*
Because this train is *leaving the station* and it is *never* coming back!!
You know, Doreen, he's single, *and* he owns his own business...
MOM
NO
OH MY GOD
The End.

Did you know: Toronto's actual slogan is "Diversity Our Strength"? I only realized that halfway through writing this story! And now you've got one more "Fun Canada Fact" in your brain, *PLUS* a bonus "Semi-boring Ryan Fact" too!

SQUIRREL GIRL, NANCY, TIPPY, AND MAUREEN FINISHED THEIR VACATION IN NOVA SCOTIA, FAMOUS FOR ITS FIDDLE MUSIC, STRIKING NATURAL BEAUTY, ACADIAN CULTURE...AND REMARKABLY FEW SUPER VILLAINS.

THE CANADIAN GOVERNMENT GAVE ANT-MAN A BONUS FOR NOT SMASHING UP THE ENTIRE CITY HALL WHILE SAVING IT, WHICH HAPPENED TO BE FOR THE PRECISE AMOUNT ANT-MAN OWED FOR HIS LOST PLANE, SO THAT WAS NICE.

CANADA

TO ANT-MAN

PAY IN ORDER OF

TWO BILLION ONE MILLION

SCOTT'S ROLE IN SAVING THE WORLD GOT HIS BUSINESS A LOT OF ATTENTION...

...ENOUGH TO EASILY AFFORD A REPLACEMENT ANT-VAN.

BRAIN DRAIN CONTINUED TO FIGHT CRIME AND HIS OWN ENNUI IN NYC...

...BUT NOW IN A NEW COSTUME MADE FOR HIM BY MAUREEN.

ENIGMO DENOUNCED TRYING TO REPLACE HUMANITY WITH HIMSELF, AND INSTEAD, 14% OF HIS TOTAL BIOMASS PURSUED A MASTERS DEGREE IN THEORETICAL PHYSICS.

SCIENCE EVENTUALLY RECOVERED FROM BEING ABUSED BY BOTH PYM PARTICLES AND COSMIC RAYS, AND CONTINUES TO BE THE BEST WAY TO EXPLORE THE WORKINGS OF OUR UNIVERSE.

THE (REAL, FINAL) END.

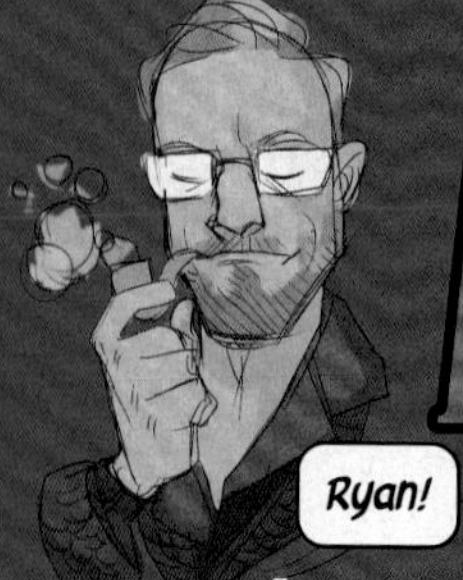
Ryan!

Letters From Nuts

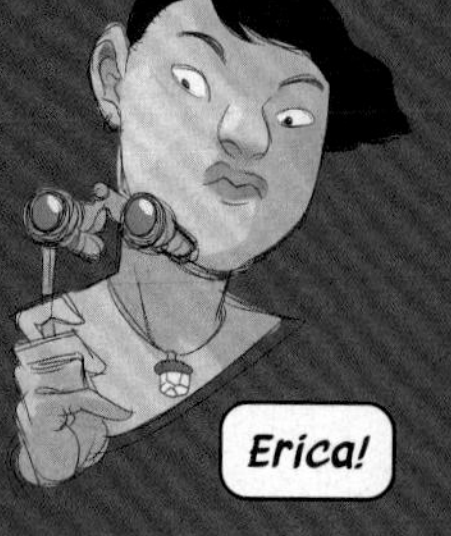
Erica!

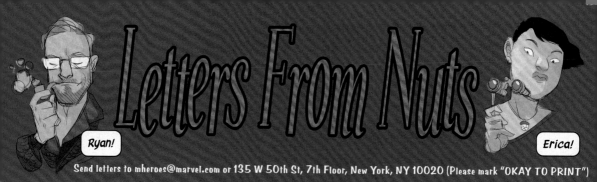

Send letters to mheroes@marvel.com or 135 W 50th St, 7th Floor, New York, NY 10020 (Please mark "OKAY TO PRINT")

You folks get many letters from young girls in whose lives you have been important, which is great. I am not a small girl. I am a guy who is approaching 50. Squirrel Girl is very important to my life.

For the last few years, I have been dealing with chronic pain, unemployment, and (unsurprisingly) depression. The Unbeatable Squirrel Girl has made me *literally* laugh out loud a bare minimum of once every single issue, often more. (Most recently with "So I cannot give it my full recommendation.") Laughs can be hard to come by. You deliver.

No pressure,
Alexx

RYAN: Alexx, thank you so much. That's what we're here for! I've got a friend with chronic pain and it is such a daily struggle, so to have unemployment and depression on top of that -- it's rough, dude. I know what we do is small in the grand scheme of things, but I'm really happy that we can help you out, even a little!

ERICA: I think one of the things that has surprised me the most is the range of people who have told me they enjoy the book. I'm really glad that we could make something that has positively affected your life.

Ryan and Erica:

Your mention of Koi Boi heading off to visit the ruins of the underwater kingdom of New Atlantis brought a couple of questions to mind:

1) Will you be presenting that as a Squirrel Girl special episode? There are usually technology raiders searching out hidden Atlantean technology in their ruins (not to mention trying to find Atlantean skeletons to sell on the alternative medicine black market). Surely Koi Boi is likely to run into one of them. If not, a guided Visitors' Board tour of the ruins might be quite beautiful. Unfortunately, I can't remember which destruction of Atlantis this ruin is from. Was it bombed, nuked, or biologically destroyed? Hmm, why was Koi Boi going there again?

2) Koi are fresh water fish. New Atlantis is in salt water. I seem to remember Koi Boi swimming in the harbor area so I assume that he can breathe heavily polluted salt water but can he also breathe fresh water? Does his amphibious nature allow him to breathe both? Does he have to use special breathing equipment in one water or the other? Did Tony Stark make the salt filter / infuser unit for him? Man, this would make a really interesting Biology 201 class at his college!

Thanks for an entertaining comic,
Geoffrey Tolle
Lord of Squirrels (as soon as I start my 40 generation domestication project).

RYAN: 1) I don't think we'll show it! Normally I'd say "use your imagination," but you have clearly already done this, so I guess all I can say is "thanks for using your imagination!" If you could fill out that plot to 20 pages and send over a script, I'd be happy to take the credit for it!!

2) I think Erica and I discussed this and we agreed Koi Boi could breathe both salt and fresh water, but I admit we did not work out the specifics! Although MAYBE the fact that the original Atlantis is in fresh water is the reason everyone's had such a hard time finding it! MAYBE??

ERICA: I'm pretty sure he's good in all types of water. He can talk to all the fish and really just had to pick one to go with for the name. "Fish Boy" just doesn't cut it, you know?

Guys, Atlantis was built on the ruins of the original Atlantis 8,000 years ago. Anything that was there from the Great Cataclysm is surely in an underwater museum or merged into the new construction (like Rome) by now.

Ryan and Erica,

Wow guys, this comic is just swell. Squirrel Girl is truly unbeatable, and Nancy is such a rad character, and Koi Boy and Chipmunk Hunk are undeniably the most perfectly named super heroes ever. And geez, Brain Drain is just trying so hard to be a good superhero and I just...I just want him to be happy. I love you, Brain Drain, and I will always be proud of you. No matter what.

Squirrelfully Yours,

Elisha Smith
Knoxville, TN

RYAN: Aw, thank you! I -- I really love Brain Drain too. I am surprised at how cute he is, and I love how Erica has turned a literal brain with a pair of eyes attached into somehow the most facially expressive character. SHE IS MAGIC.

ERICA: I love our crazy nihilist brain trapped in a robot body trying to be a super hero.

Dear Letters From Nuts,

I wanted to draw attention to an apparent discrepancy on the cover of issue #11. There, the binary numbering is displayed in six digits, 001011, whereas five digits, 01011, would seem more applicable, since Doreen teaches Count Nefaria (and us readers) how to count in binary on a single hand, and five fingers equal five digits. Sidenote: the English word "digit" comes from the Latin word for "finger" -- how appropriate!

At first, I thought the cover numbering might have something to do with squirrels having six fingers, but a hasty Google image search revealed that four front fingers and five hind fingers are the usual sciurine characteristics. I flipped through the issue again and found no evidence of polydactyly.

Then it dawned on me: the six-digit binary numbering must have come from Doctor Octopus, who is right there on the cover. Raising one arm and the two opposite tentacles while keeping his other three not-being-used-for-standing appendages lowered is naturally how Doc Ock would flash his digits!

Does this explanation entitle me to a No-Prize? I do hope so! I've long aspired to the rank of Titanic True Believer (T.T.B.), which would in turn bump me up to Permanent Marvelite Maximus (P.M.M.).

Best,
Morris Tichenor, R.F.O., Q.N.S., K.O.F.
Toronto, ON

P.S. More etymology fun: the Latin word "digitus" probably derives from "dico" (meaning "to speak" + the suffix "-itus"). I like to image Romans gesticulated wildly whenever they spoke.

P.P.S. I want to second Erica's assertion that Nomad's Lorenzo Lamas phase is "the BEST Nomad." Thanks for giving a shout-out to one of my favorite '90s titles.

RYAN: Man I love a letter that starts out with "HERE IS A PROBLEM" and ends with "NEVERMIND, I HAVE COME UP WITH A SOLUTION TO THE PROBLEM THAT ONLY

REQUIRES YOU PRETEND THAT YOU WERE SMARTER THAN YOU ACTUALLY ARE," which is something I am more than willing to do and may actually already be doing. It is my understanding that No-Prizes are for THIS VERY THING, which makes me extremely excited about No-Prizes. My understanding that they're just pictures of empty envelopes makes me LESS excited, but, well, here we are. (Also the padded zeroes worked nicely from a design perspective, so really, TWO good reasons to do it that way.) ENJOY THE PRIZE:

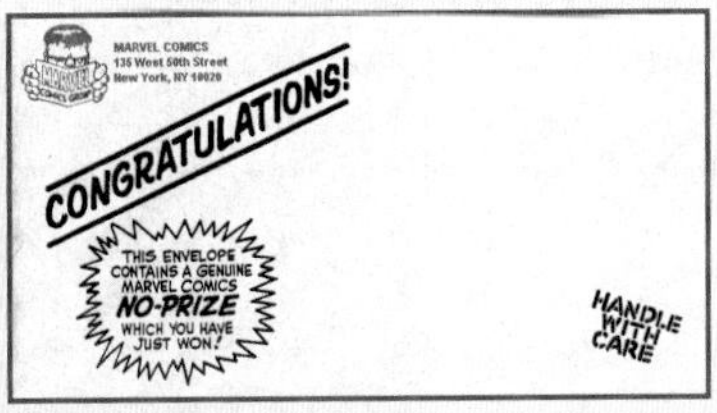
MARVEL COMICS
135 West 50th Street
New York, NY 10020
CONGRATULATIONS!
THIS ENVELOPE CONTAINS A GENUINE MARVEL COMICS NO-PRIZE WHICH YOU HAVE JUST WON!
HANDLE WITH CARE

ERICA: I... still haven't read #11, but what's important is that the issue you're currently reading got to the printers by the deadline.

I'm really hoping that now that Steve is on the run in the Marvel Cinematic U, we're going to get at least a moment of him with his hair grown out riding a motorcycle around. I know that he wasn't Nomad during that time, but we have to work with what we're given. Also, we know he can ride a motorcycle.

Dear Squirrel Girl Crew:

I enjoyed Squirrel Girl's run-in with the Mole Man. It looks like next month, we can expect Dr. Octopus and Venom. While Squirrel Girl certainly has taken on some of Marvel's big name villains, I recently became interested in one of the lesser lights. Might I suggest that Squirrel Girl versus the legend-in-her-own-mind White Rabbit would have some great possibilities?

Sincerely
Robert Fisher

RYAN: The time delay on these letters means you have already (hopefully!) read the comic and seen what happens! Doc Ock and Venom are two of my favorite bad guys, so it was a treat to put them both in the same issue (KINDA, AGAIN, I CAN ONLY ASSUME YOU READ IT BUT DON'T WANT TO SPOIL ANYTHING). In any case, to answer your question, I just looked up the White Rabbit and she has a giant robot rabbit that fires missiles, so I'm already totally down with her whole thing.

ERICA: If you've read this issue, it probably means you just finished a three-issue arc starring a character who has only been in TWO OTHER ISSUES IN ALL OF MARVEL'S 70+ YEAR HISTORY. We're into the deep cuts too, is all I'm sayin'. I feel like one of the hardest parts of doing this is picking who the villain will be each time. We're literally going through that right now planning for issue #17. I feel like this is the one thing we have trouble agreeing on sometimes.

Another cracker from Ryan and Erica - kicking off with Spider-Man getting in on the Twitter conversation - and who is he kidding when he says that his webshooters make that "thwip" sound? We know that just like Wolverine, he makes that noise himself.

Count Nefaria was wonderful and the footnotes were right, we were all doing the counting on our fingers too. Very elegant solution to the nightmare about exams, which we've all had.

There are lots of good comics about at the moment, but Squirrel Girl, each and every issue is just a JOY. Easily the nicest lead character around - and isn't it lovely to show that you don't have to be dark or angsty or driven to be a compelling lead - you can actually be kind and perky too.

(Jacob - the facial expression on Count Nefaria's face in the "no way, you've got to teach me" panel was just perfect)

Many thanks

Andrew Pack
Brighton, England

RYAN: Yeah, Jacob did a terrific job on that issue, and I loved that we got to show that Doreen's dreams are a little brighter than the real world. That seems to fit, you know? Thank you for all these kind words, and I can only hope that future authors continue to characterize Count Nefaria as "a Dracula who likes numbers." IT WORKS, YO.

ERICA: I was so glad we got Jacob. I went to Wil with two names for who I'd like to use and Jacob wasn't even sure he could do it at the time, but we diiiiid iiiiit.

Dear Ryan, Erica, & Rico,

I first started reading Unbeatable Squirrel Girl after seeing a copy of the 1st volume at my library and thinking, "well, this looks ridiculous but potentially fun." Turns out it wasn't ridiculous (ok, maybe a little bit, but absolutely in a good way), and was more than just fun. I've been hooked on the adventures of Doreen, Tippy-Toe, & co. ever since. So much so that I cosplayed as Squirrel Girl for NYCC this year, and actually got to meet all of you (which was awesome)!

One of my favorite things about Squirrel Girl is that she doesn't just use the powers of squirrel, but those of girl as well. I love a good superhero fight scene, and Doreen can definitely kick butt (it's right there in her catchphrase) but my favorite moments are the ones where she uses reason, friendship, and sometimes even computer science to save the day. It's so refreshing to see a clever, optimistic, and ultimately inspiring superhero like Squirrel Girl who knows that it's often better to talk things out and solve problems with brains rather than fists.

Keep on eating nuts & kicking butts (and writing amazing new stories for Squirrel Girl)!

Rachel

P.S. I wish I could've gotten a photo with Rico too, but my friend had wandered off with the camera. Thank you so much for the button though, Rico! No one has asked me about my squirrel powers yet, but I remain hopeful.

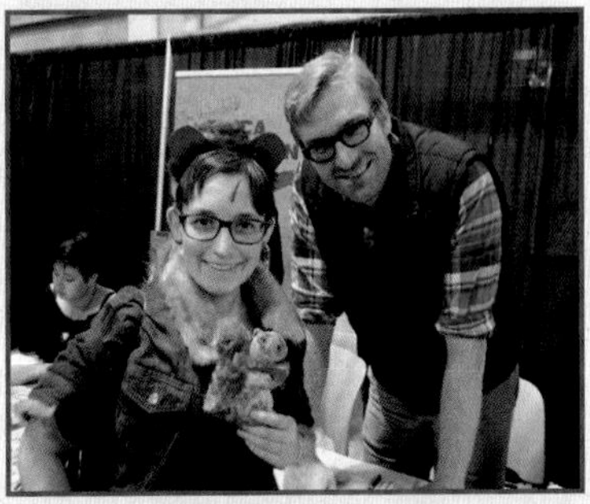

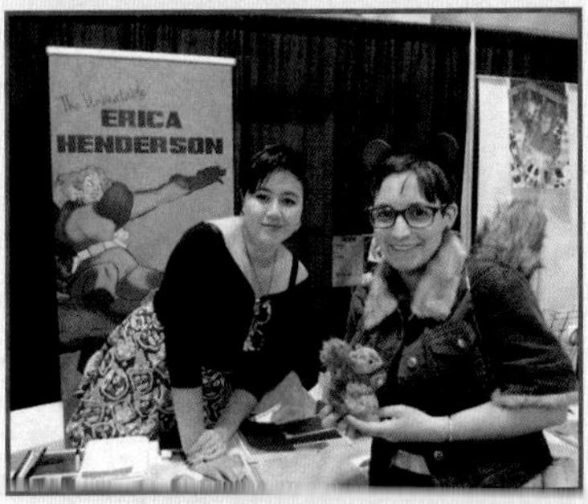
ERICA
HENDERSON

RYAN: Rachel, it was SO GREAT to meet you at NYCC! At that show I was given my very own stuffed Tippy-Toe by a fan, so now I can pass as -- well, not Squirrel Girl, but Squirrel Earl at least. Your costume is amazing, and this letter is the best. I like the photo with Erica the best because it shows off your tail -- IT WAS A REALLY WELL-MADE TAIL, EVERYONE! Fun fact: NYCC was the first time Rico and I met in real life, and then later on we all went out to dinner and ate delicious guacamole. WE LIVED OUR BEST LIVES THAT DAY.

Next Issue:

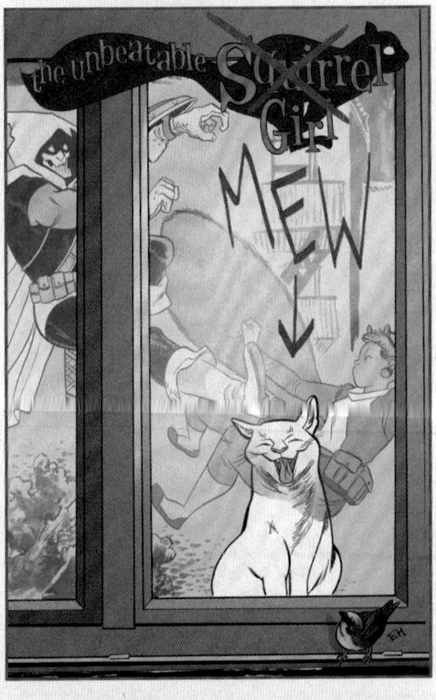
the unbeatable Squirrel Girl
MEW
EH

Attention, Squirrel Scouts! Make sure to check out our production blog, **unbeatablesquirrelgirl.tumblr.com**, where we post behind-the-scenes stuff on how the book gets made, along with all sorts of cool things *you* make: fanart, cosplay, whatever!

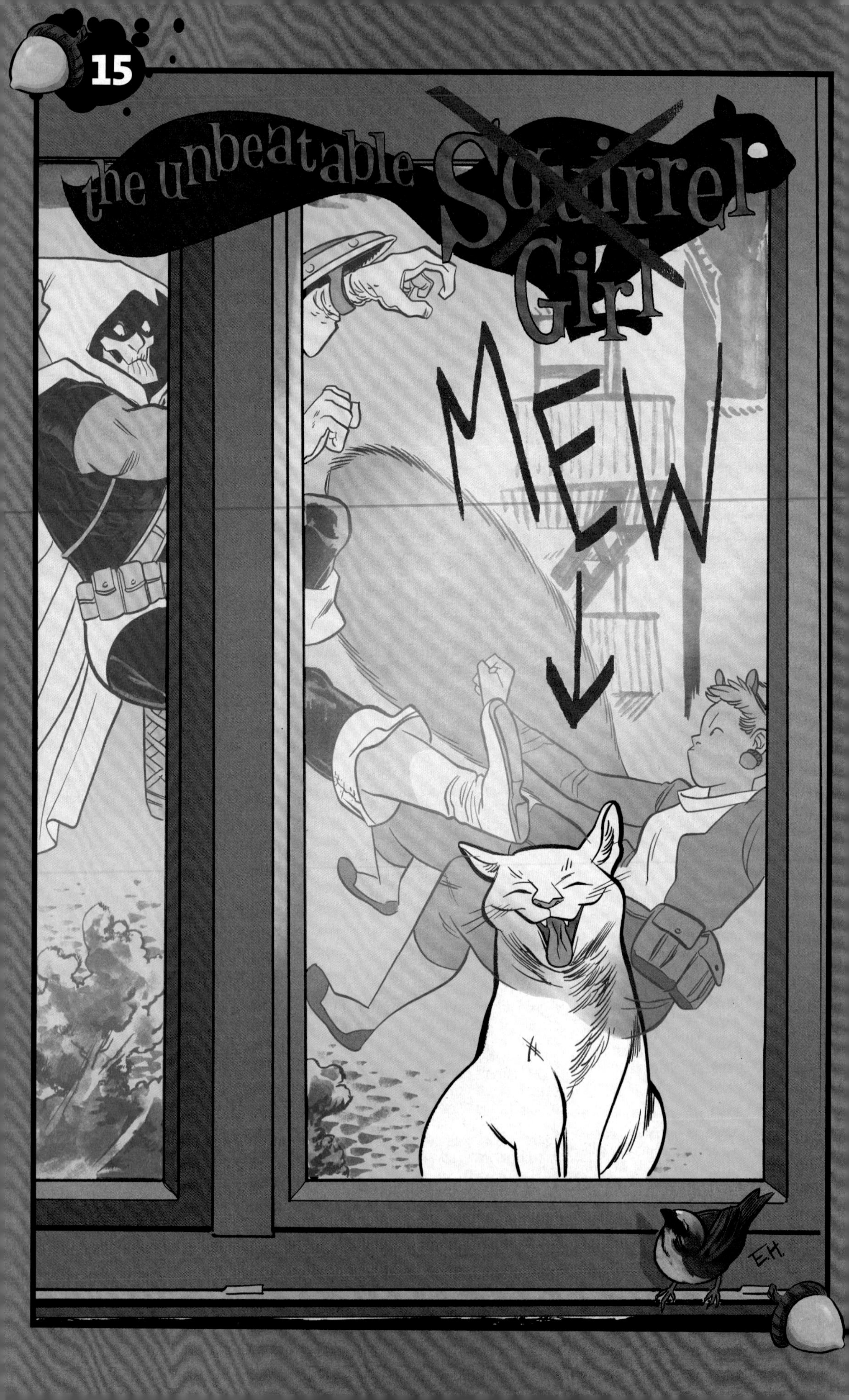
15
the unbeatable Squirrel Girl
MEW
E.H.

*Doreen Green isn't just a second-year computer science student: she secretly also has all the powers of both squirrel and girl! She uses her amazing abilities to fight crime **and** be as awesome as possible. You know her as...**The Unbeatable Squirrel Girl!** Find out what she's been up to, with...*

Squirrel Girl *in a nutshell*

Nancy Whitehead @sewwiththeflo
zcadfewg5ttyniu,o;

Nancy Whitehead @sewwiththeflo
Hey everyone, sorry, my cat got on my keyboard and somehow posted that. Pretty cute though, right? Anyway, test post please ignore.

Nancy Whitehead @sewwiththeflo
';,l;joih87t67r5d4dsaqzdx

Nancy Whitehead @sewwiththeflo
Once more, sorry, Mew walked on my laptop again. Less cute the second time. I'll keep it closed from now on.

Nancy Whitehead @sewwiththeflo
hrzayus5f3iu6t54h76p8k70[k98;'--]\

Nancy Whitehead @sewwiththeflo
Okay okay she got on my phone this time but I PROMISE Mew will stop posting on my account.

Nancy Whitehead @sewwiththeflo
Thank you all for following me on social media today and I hoped you enjoyed this unscheduled #content.

Nancy Whitehead @sewwiththeflo
fmgnsjkbehrftyqu27334dfd5yn7c5jmikn,ob,lm;n9',

Nancy Whitehead @sewwiththeflo
Mew, how is this happening

Nancy Whitehead @sewwiththeflo
How is this happening, Mew

Nancy Whitehead @sewwiththeflo
XSCDV32CDN43KJ54HK6LUUMIK9OP97LKI

Nancy Whitehead @sewwiththeflo
Sorry, I'm sorry, I don't know how this keeps being a thing. I put my laptop under the bed WHILE LOGGED OUT, and yet here we are??

Nancy Whitehead @sewwiththeflo
VDSABCwvce32j43t56hy86jk98..l;jk

Nancy Whitehead @sewwiththeflo
Look all I can say is: if you followed me on this site then you knew the risks.

Squirrel Girl @unbeatablesg
@sewwiththeflo Maybe you should ask Mew to put her social media posts on... PAWS

Nancy Whitehead @sewwiththeflo
@unbeatablesg xacf435hy6gngj7ti7tj

Nancy Whitehead @sewwiththeflo
@unbeatablesg OKAY SHE'S REPLYING TO YOU NOW, HOLY COW, THIS IS CRAZY, WHAT IS GOING ON

Squirrel Girl @unbeatablesg
@sewwiththeflo I agree it's...CLAWS for concern

Nancy Whitehead @sewwiththeflo
@unbeatablesg I THINK I FIGURED IT OUT, YOU HAVE TO HIT CTRL+ENTER TO POST AND HER NATURAL GAIT REACHES THOSE TWO KEYS

Squirrel Girl @unbeatablesg
@sewwiththeflo but how is she getting the laptop open though??

Nancy Whitehead @sewwiththeflo
@unbeatablesg Listen, Mew is the best cat and therefore I'm sure she [illegible] but I'm CERTAIN now I've figured it out.

Nancy Whitehead @sewwiththeflo
@unbeatablesg It won't happen again. EVER.

Nancy Whitehead @sewwiththeflo
zwdreh4u7oi98p-['9=-=;p0lomnybtcdexweaq

Nancy Whitehead @sewwiththeflo
MEW

Nancy Whitehead @sewwiththeflo
WHY

Nancy Whitehead @sewwiththeflo
WHY, MEW

search!

#zcrg5ju7,i;

#lknmjguifte4w3q

#zcdvtnmukil;;;;;;;;;;

#8dfuetryt3#4

#cyuu6ui7jjmmm

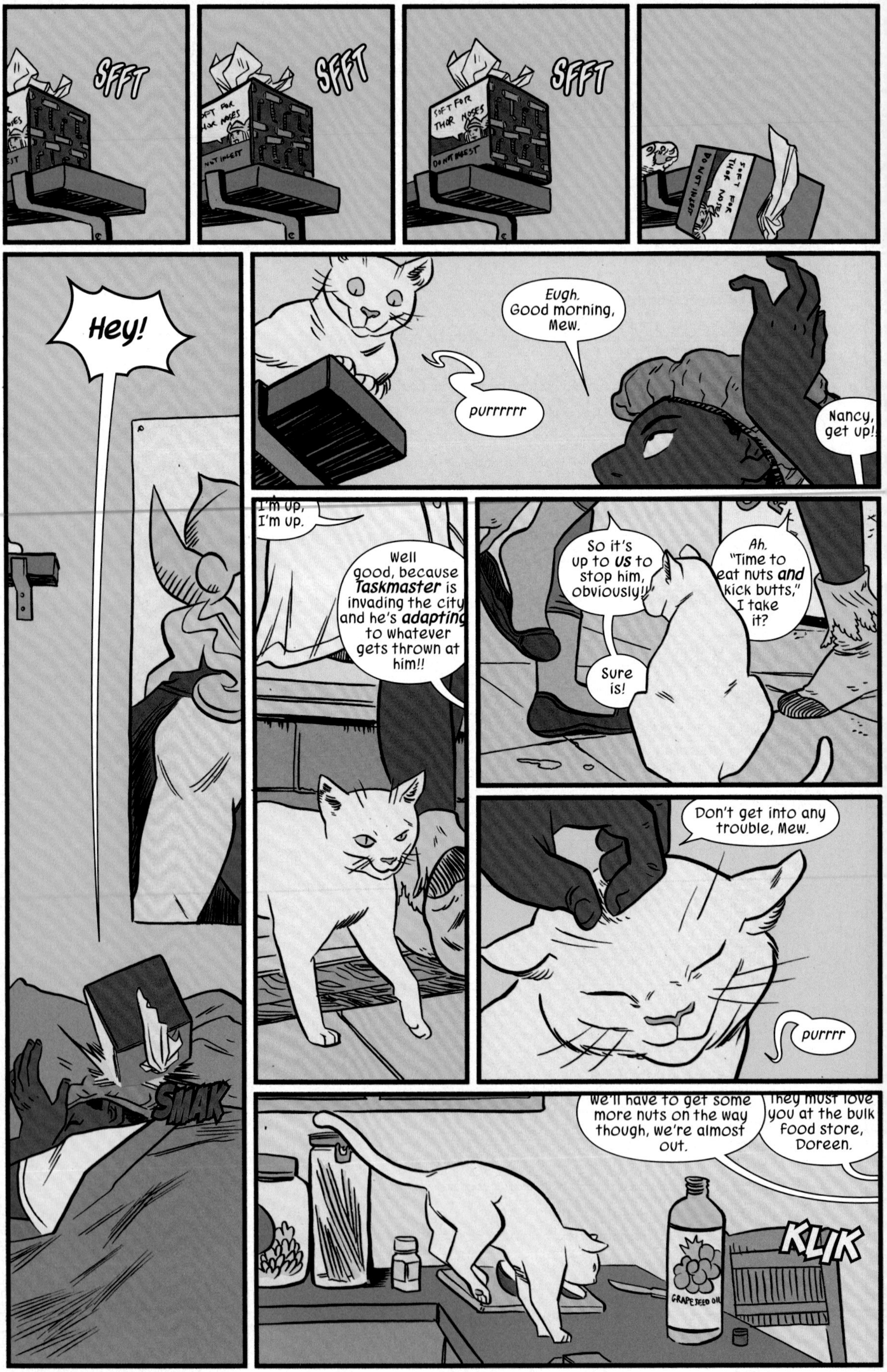
SFFT
SOFT FOR THOR NOSES
DO NOT INGEST
SFFT
SFFT
SOFT FOR THOR NOSES
DO NOT INGEST
Hey!
SMAK
Eugh. Good morning, Mew.
purrrrrr
Nancy, get up!!
I'm up, I'm up.
Well good, because Taskmaster is invading the city and he's adapting to whatever gets thrown at him!!
So it's up to us to stop him, obviously!!
Sure is!
Ah. "Time to eat nuts and kick butts," I take it?
Don't get into any trouble, Mew.
purrrr
We'll have to get some more nuts on the way though, we're almost out.
They must love you at the bulk food store, Doreen.
GRAPESEED OIL
KLIK

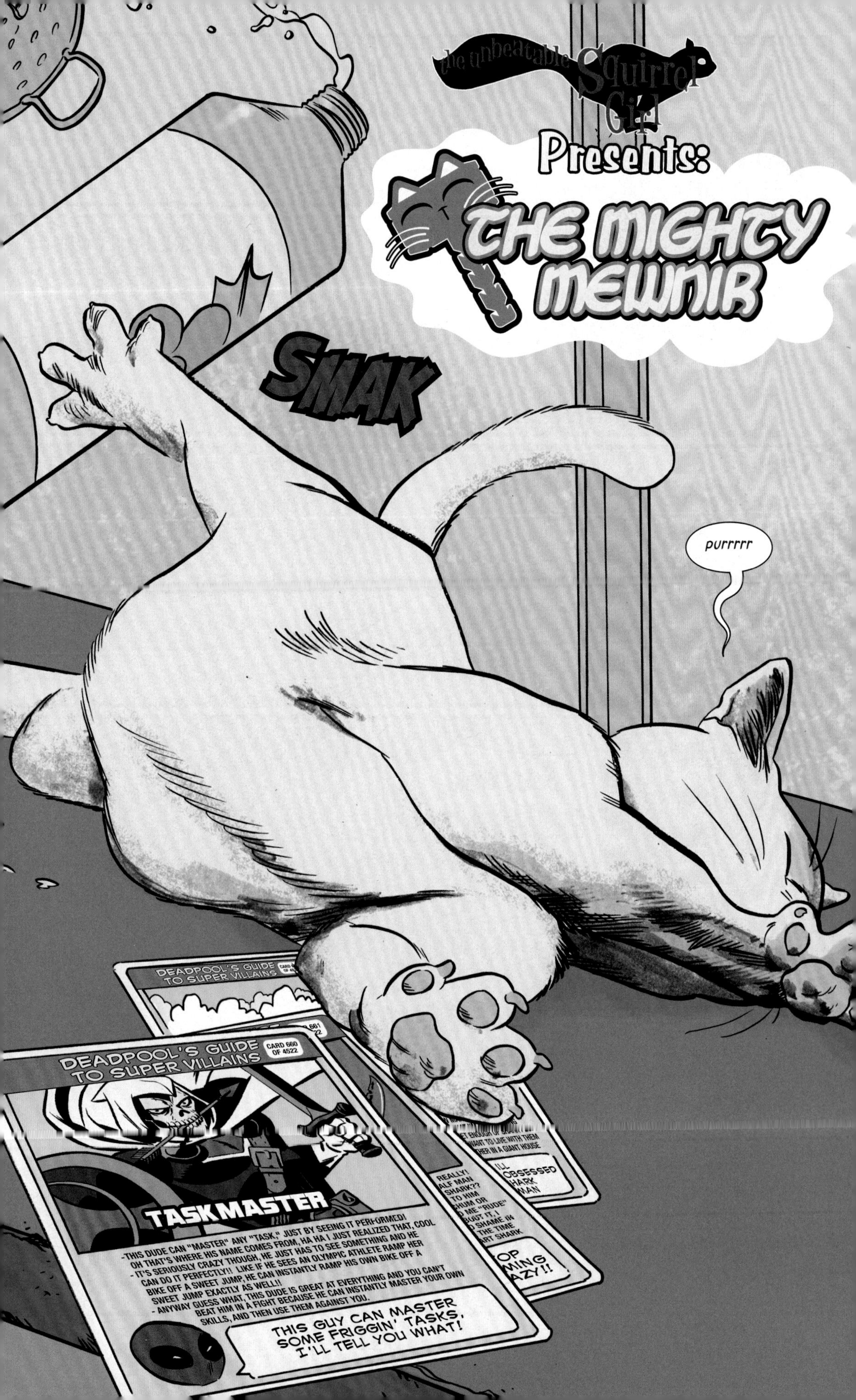

the unbeatable Squirrel Girl
Presents:
THE MIGHTY MEWNIR
SMAK
purrrrr
DEADPOOL'S GUIDE TO SUPER VILLAINS
DEADPOOL'S GUIDE TO SUPER VILLAINS
CARD 660 OF 4522
TASKMASTER
-THIS DUDE CAN "MASTER" ANY "TASK," JUST BY SEEING IT PERFORMED! OH THAT'S WHERE HIS NAME COMES FROM, HA HA I JUST REALIZED THAT, COOL
- IT'S SERIOUSLY CRAZY THOUGH, HE JUST HAS TO SEE SOMETHING AND HE CAN DO IT PERFECTLY!! LIKE IF HE SEES AN OLYMPIC ATHLETE RAMP HER BIKE OFF A SWEET JUMP, HE CAN INSTANTLY RAMP HIS OWN BIKE OFF A SWEET JUMP EXACTLY AS WELL!!
- ANYWAY GUESS WHAT, THIS DUDE IS GREAT AT EVERYTHING AND YOU CAN'T BEAT HIM IN A FIGHT BECAUSE HE CAN INSTANTLY MASTER YOUR OWN SKILLS, AND THEN USE THEM AGAINST YOU.
THIS GUY CAN MASTER SOME FRIGGIN' TASKS, I'LL TELL YOU WHAT!

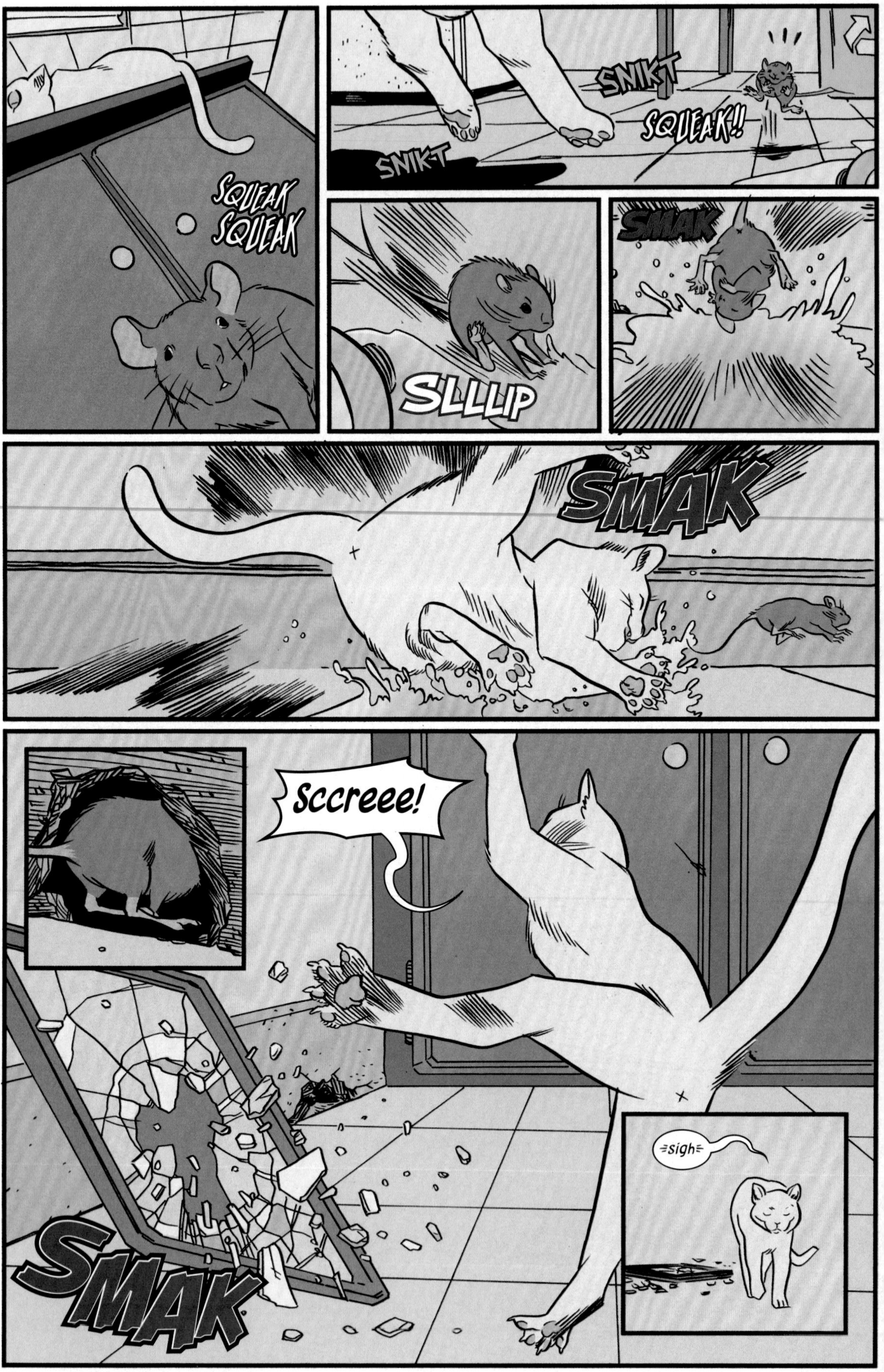
SQUEAK
SQUEAK
SNIKT
SNIKT
SQUEAK!!
SLLLIP
SMAK
SMAK
Sccreee!
SMAK
sigh

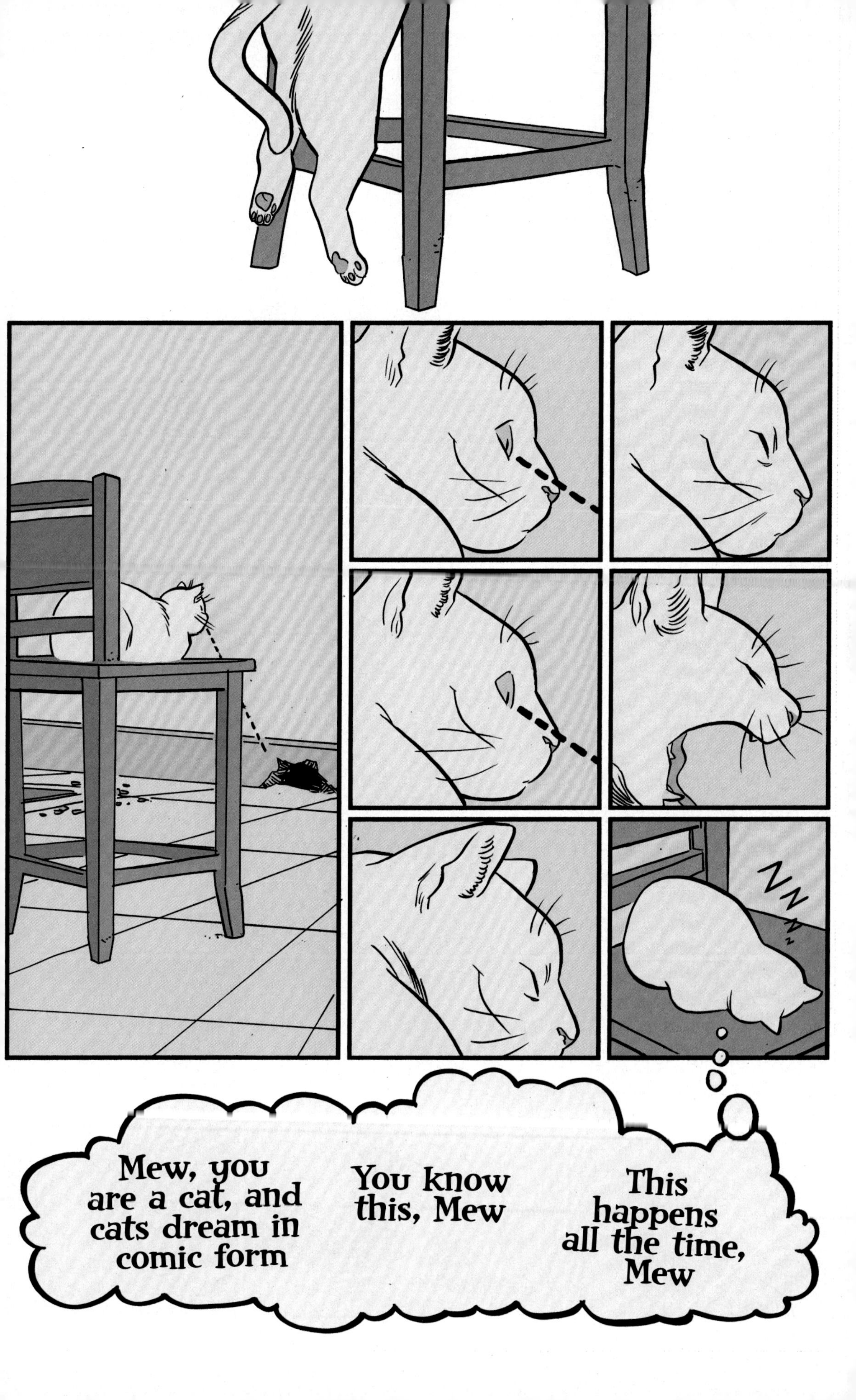
Mew, you are a cat, and cats dream in comic form
You know this, Mew
This happens all the time, Mew

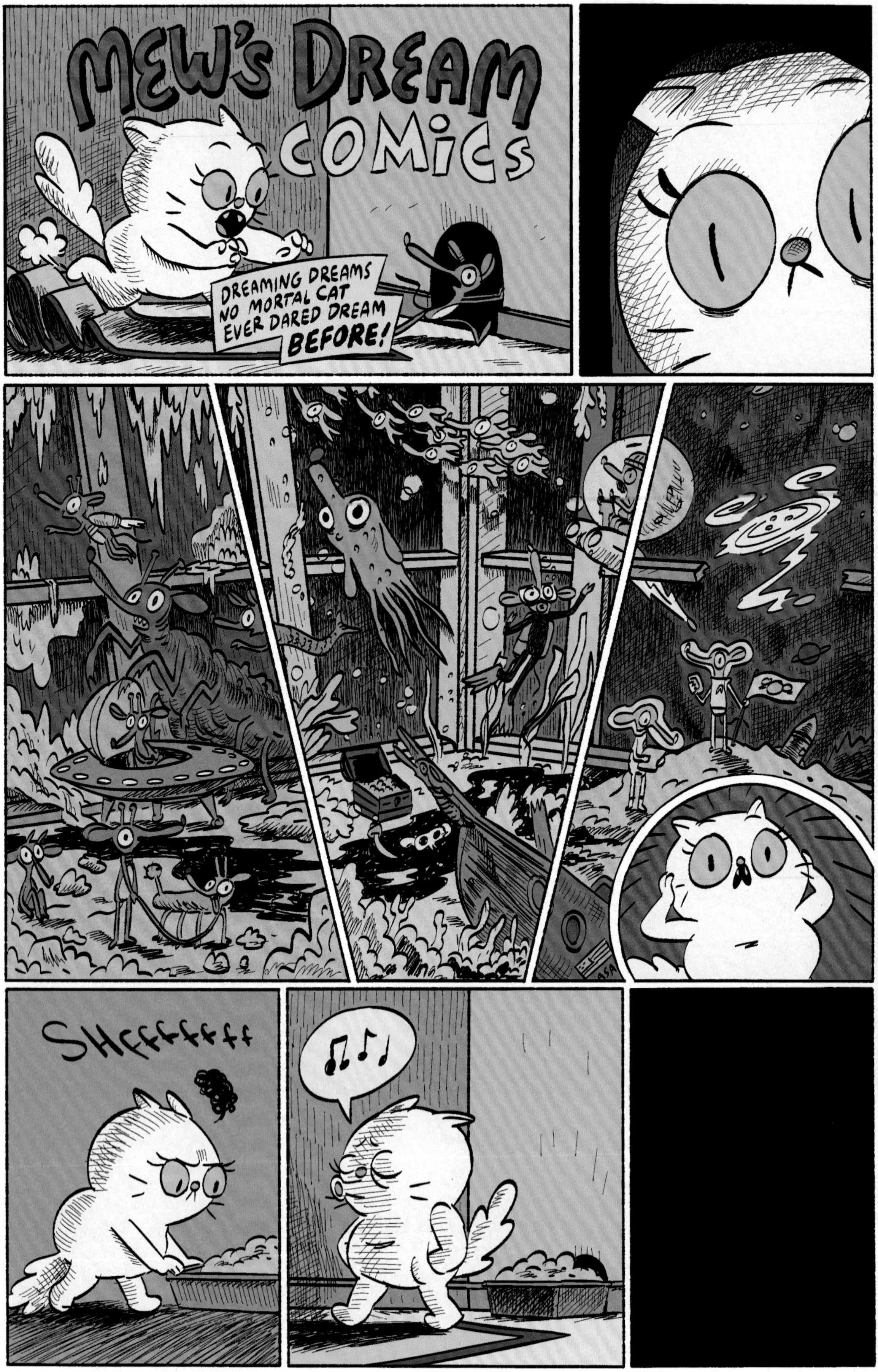
MEW'S DREAM
COMICS
DREAMING DREAMS NO MORTAL CAT EVER DARED DREAM BEFORE!
SHffffff

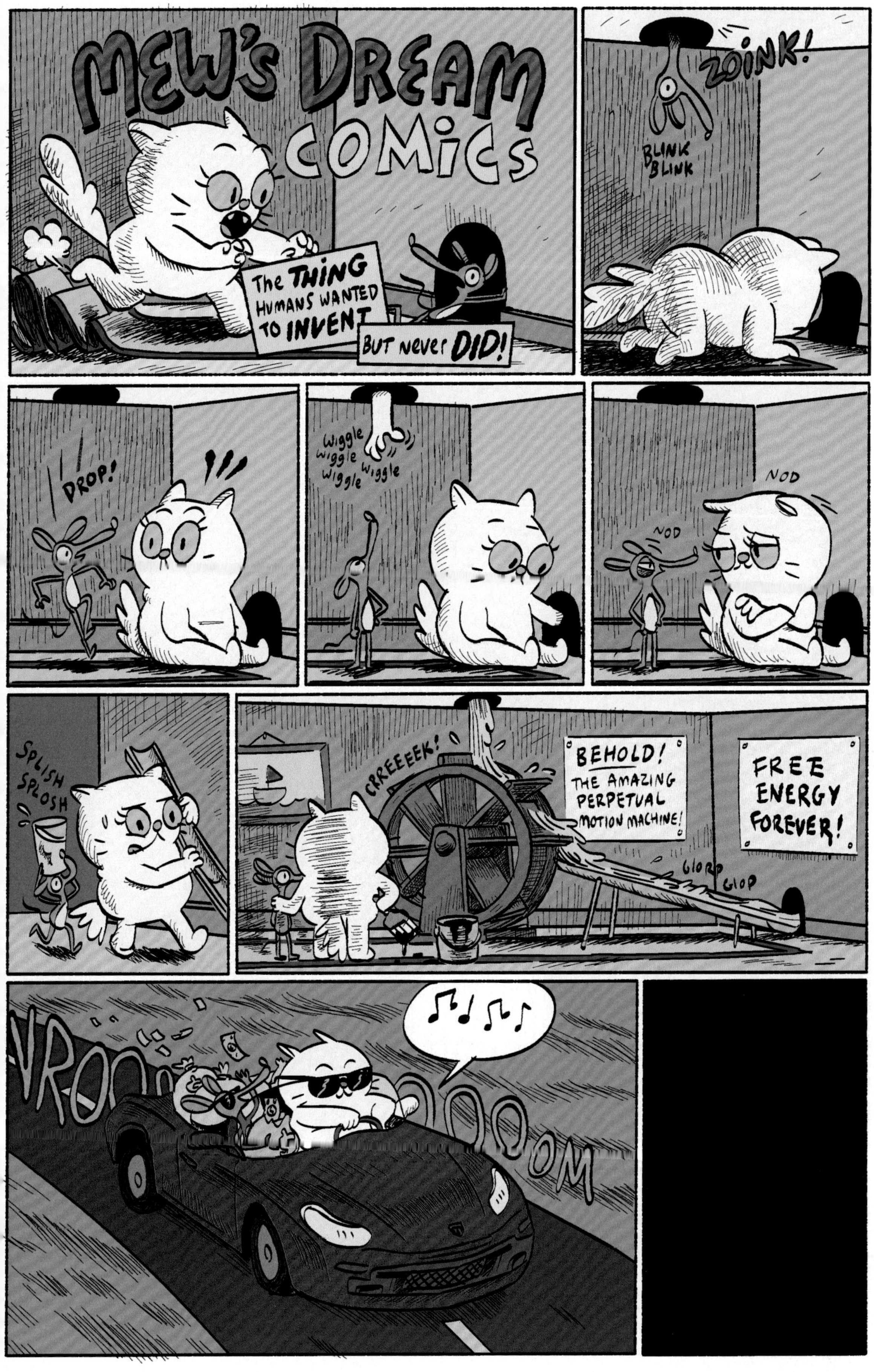
MEW'S DREAM COMICS
The THING HUMANS WANTED TO INVENT
BUT never DID!
ZOINK!
BLINK BLINK
DROP!
Wiggle wiggle wiggle wiggle
NOD
NOD
SPLISH SPLOSH
CREEEEK!
BEHOLD! THE AMAZING PERPETUAL MOTION MACHINE!
FREE ENERGY FOREVER!
GLORP GLOP
VROOOOOOOOM

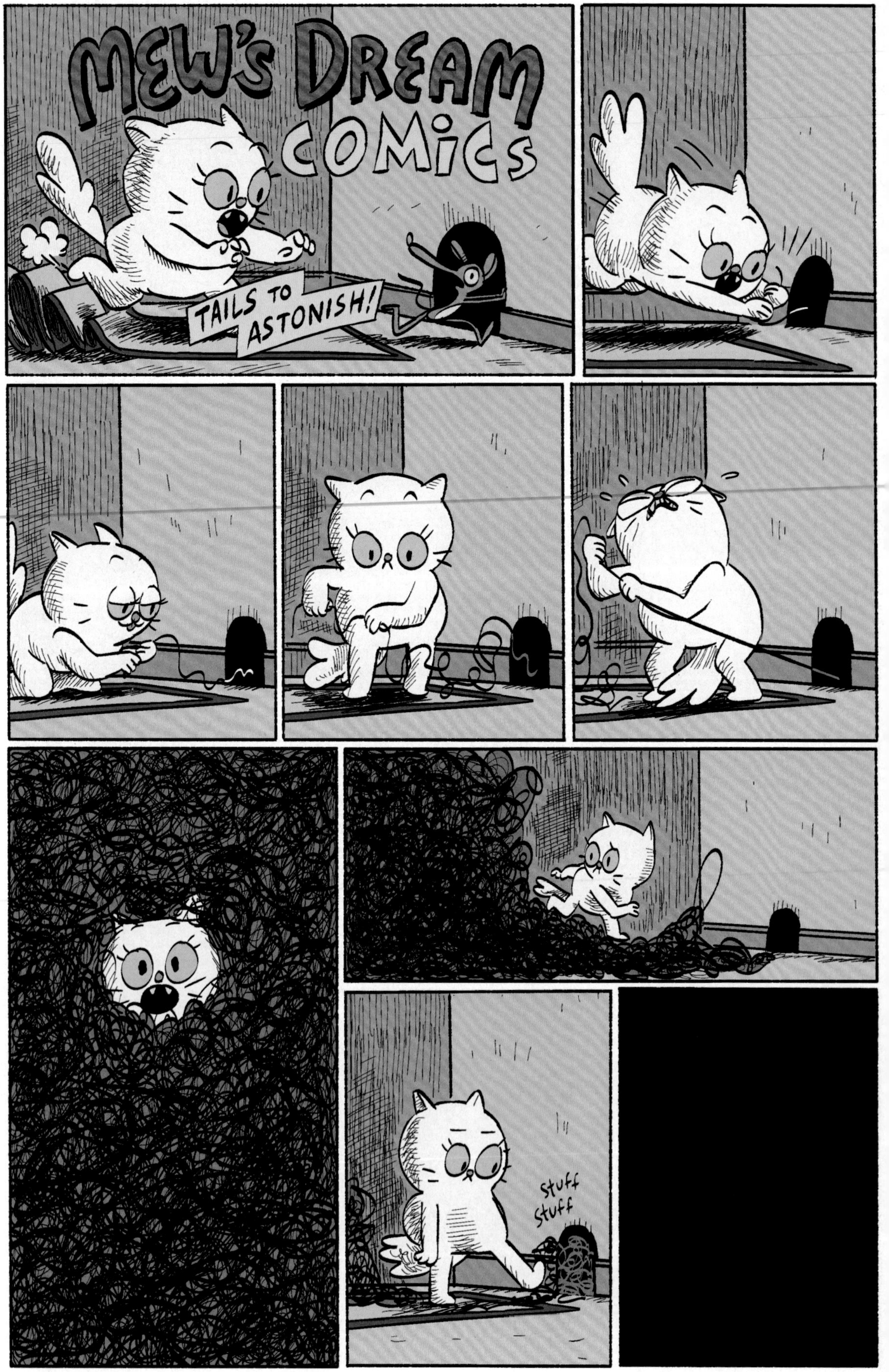
MEW'S DREAM COMICS
TAILS TO ASTONISH!
STUFF STUFF

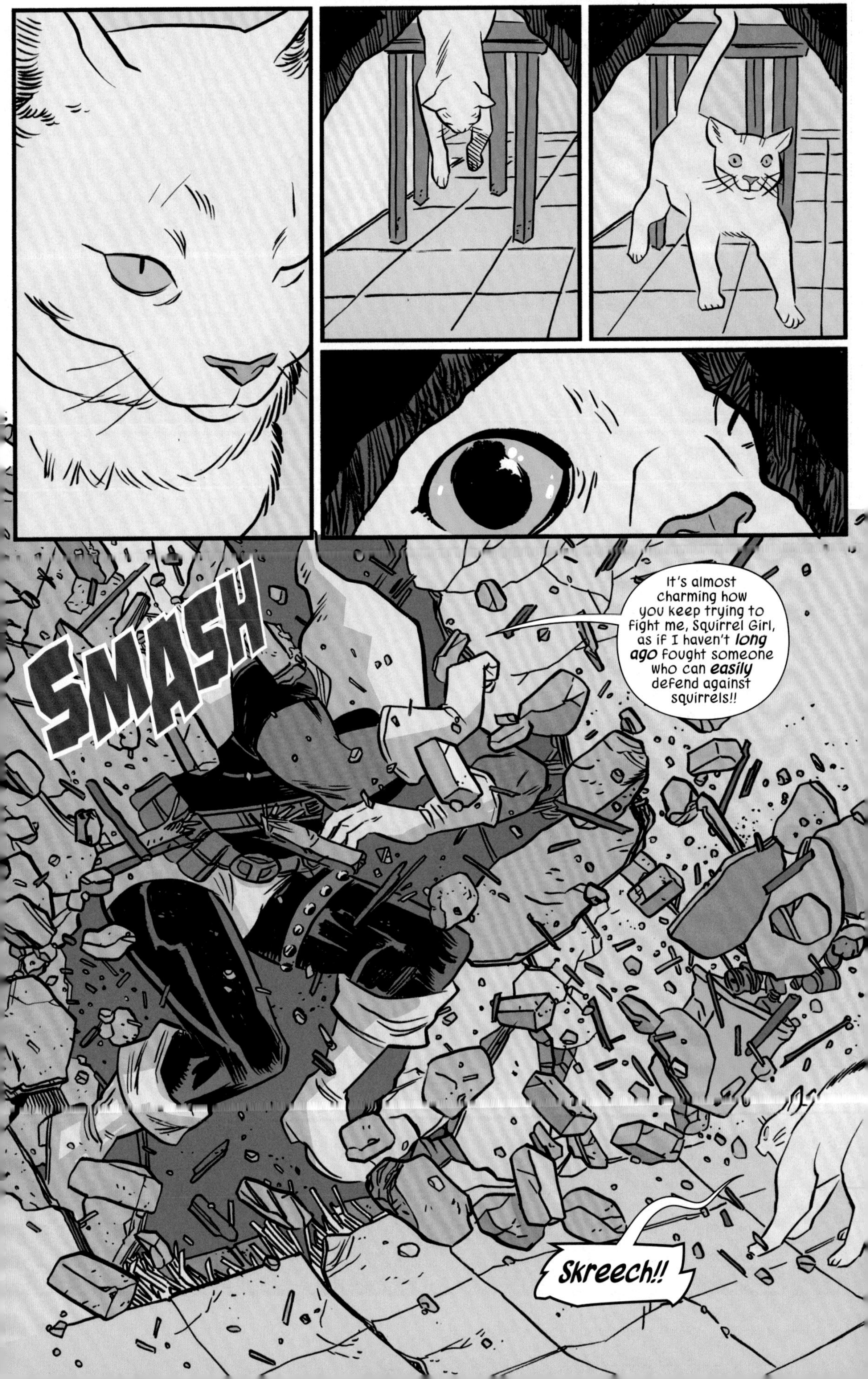
SMASH
It's almost charming how you keep trying to fight me, Squirrel Girl, as if I haven't long ago fought someone who can easily defend against squirrels!!
Skreech!!

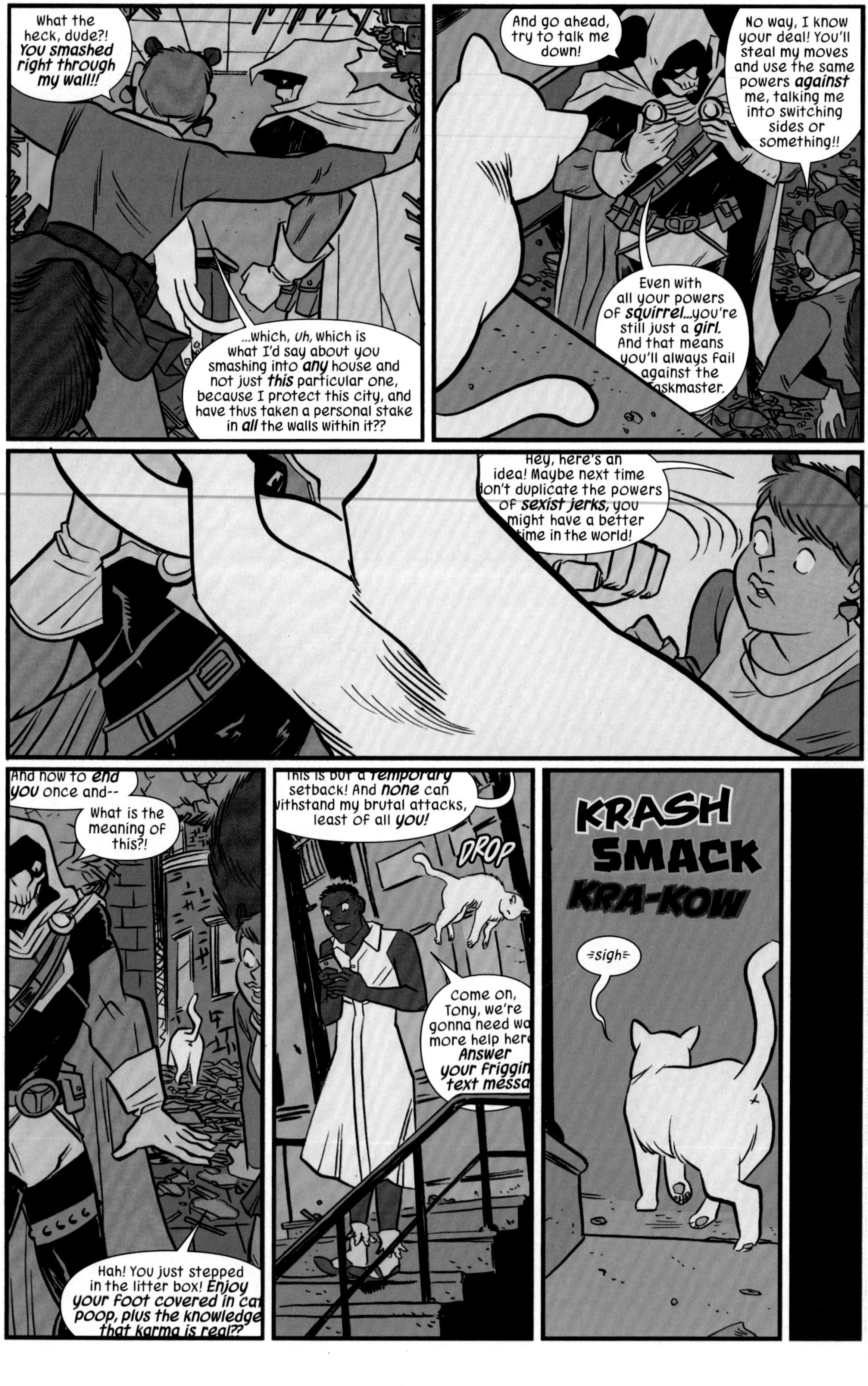

What the heck, dude?! You smashed right through my wall!!
...Which, uh, which is what I'd say about you smashing into any house and not just this particular one, because I protect this city, and have thus taken a personal stake in all the walls within it??
And go ahead, try to talk me down!
No way, I know your deal! You'll steal my moves and use the same powers against me, talking me into switching sides or something!!
Even with all your powers of squirrel...you're still just a girl. And that means you'll always fail against the
Hey, here's an idea! Maybe next time
don't duplicate the powers of sexist jerks, you might have a better
time in the world!
And how to end you once and--
What is the meaning of this?!
Hah! You just stepped in the litter box! Enjoy your foot covered in ca
poop, plus the knowledge that karma is real??
This is but a temporary setback! And none can
withstand my brutal attacks, least of all you!
DROP
Come on, Tony, we're gonna need wa
more help here
Answer your friggin
text messa
KRASH
SMACK
KRA-KOW
sigh

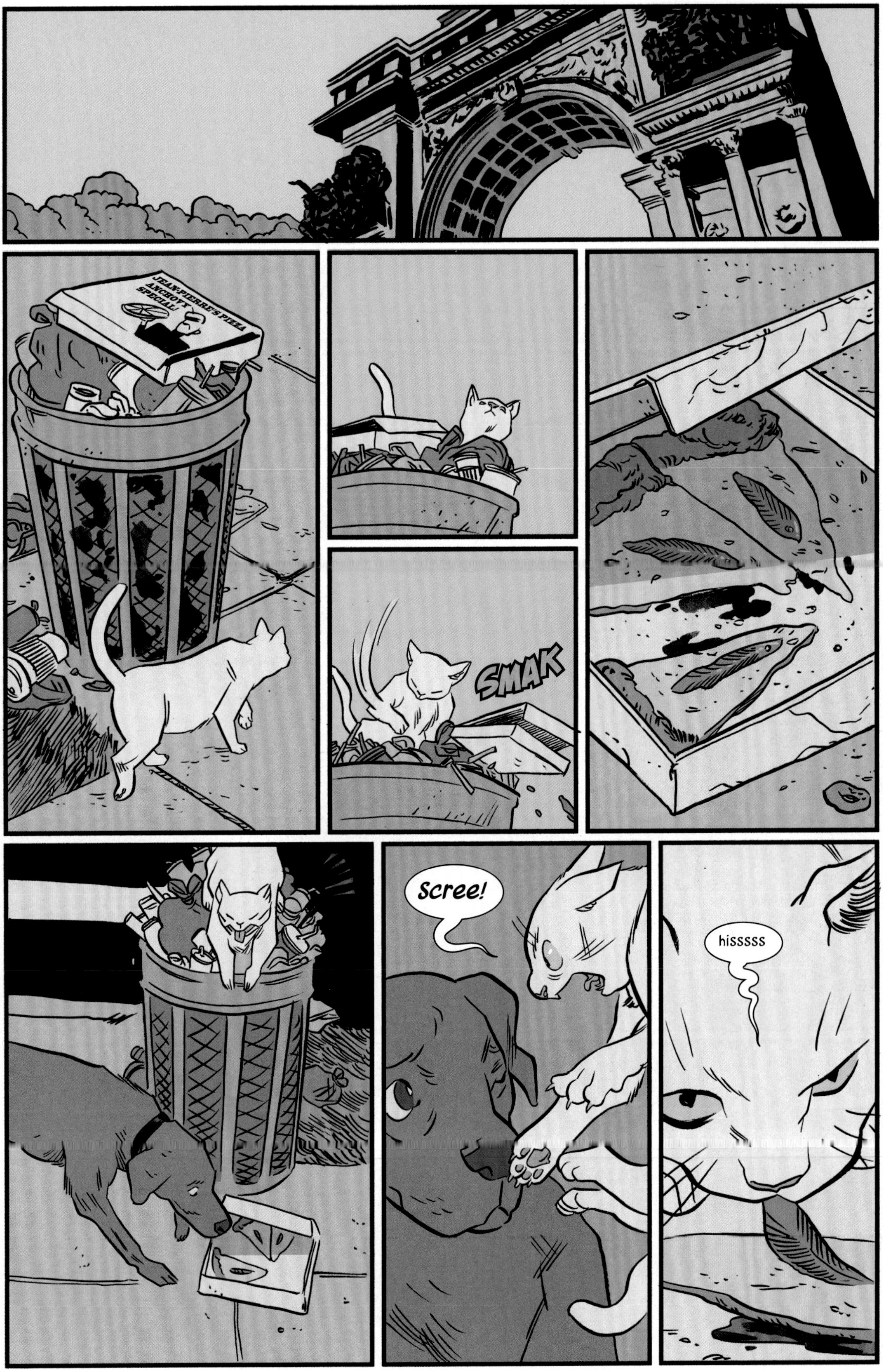
JEAN-PIERRE'S PIZZA
ANCHOVY SPECIAL!
SMAK
Scree!
hissssss

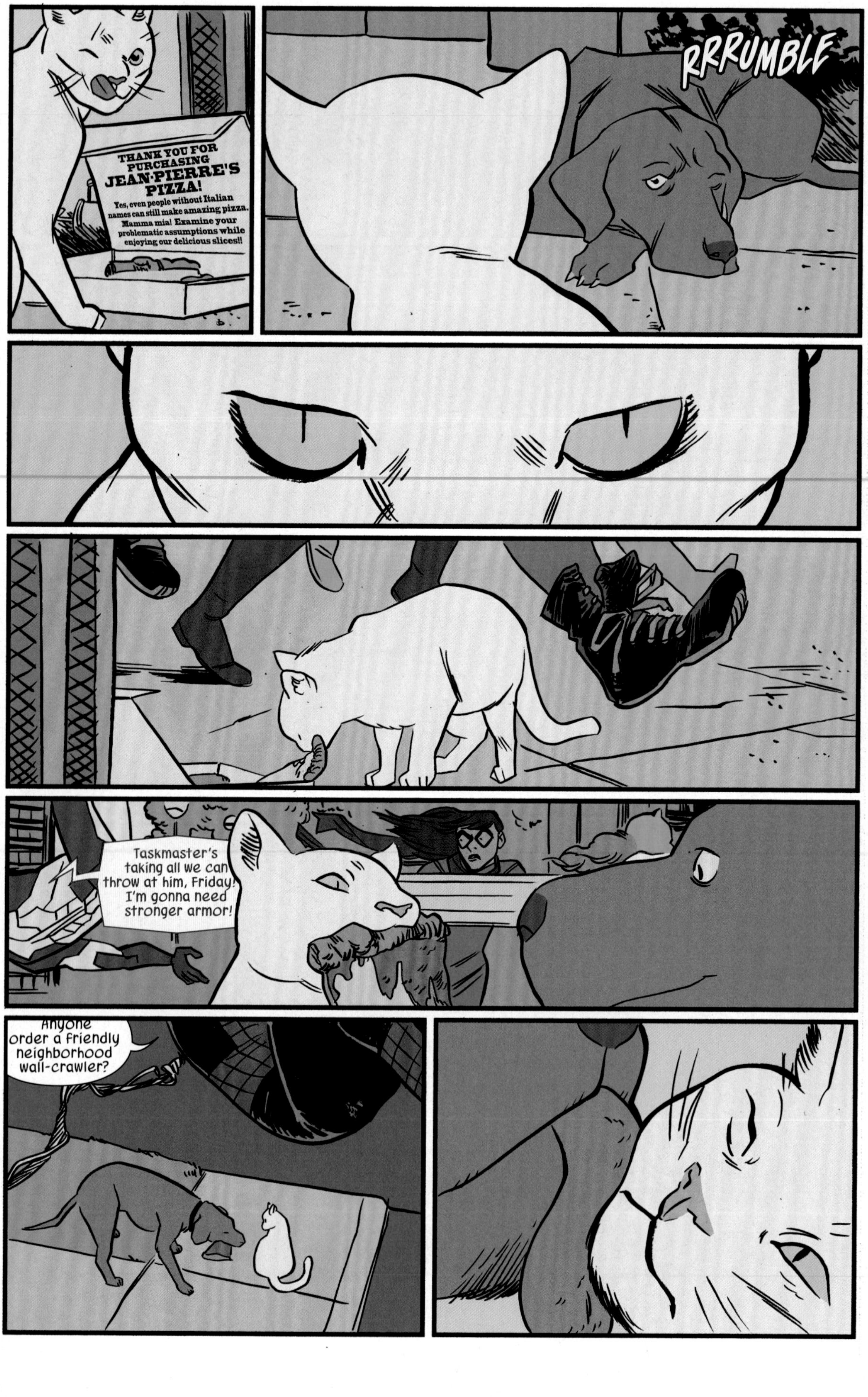
THANK YOU FOR PURCHASING JEAN-PIERRE'S PIZZA!
Yes, even people without Italian names can still make amazing pizza. Mamma mia! Examine your problematic assumptions while enjoying our delicious slices!!
RRRUMBLE
Taskmaster's taking all we can throw at him, Friday! I'm gonna need stronger armor!
Anyone order a friendly neighborhood wall-crawler?

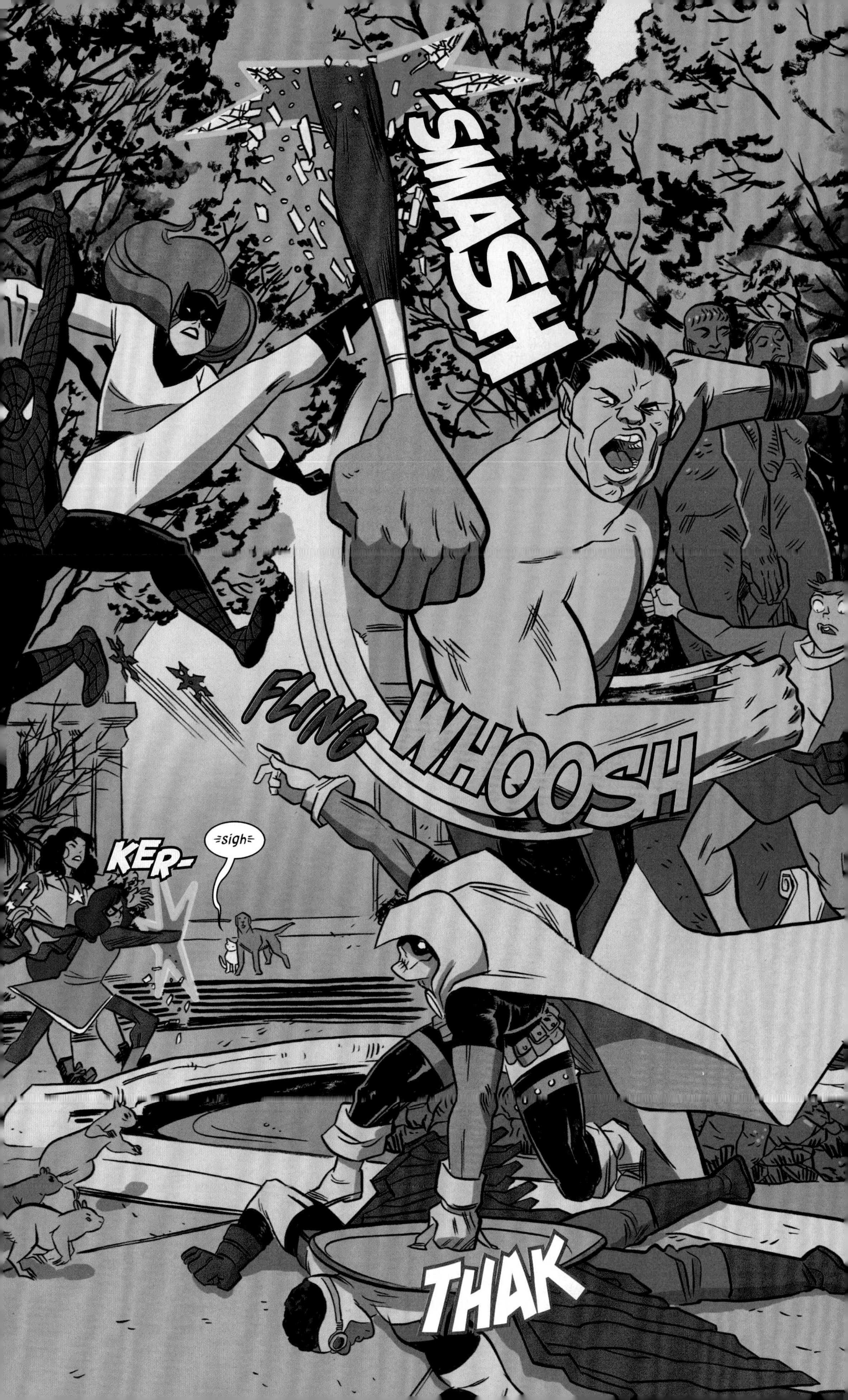
SMASH
FLING
WHOOSH
KER-
sigh
THAK

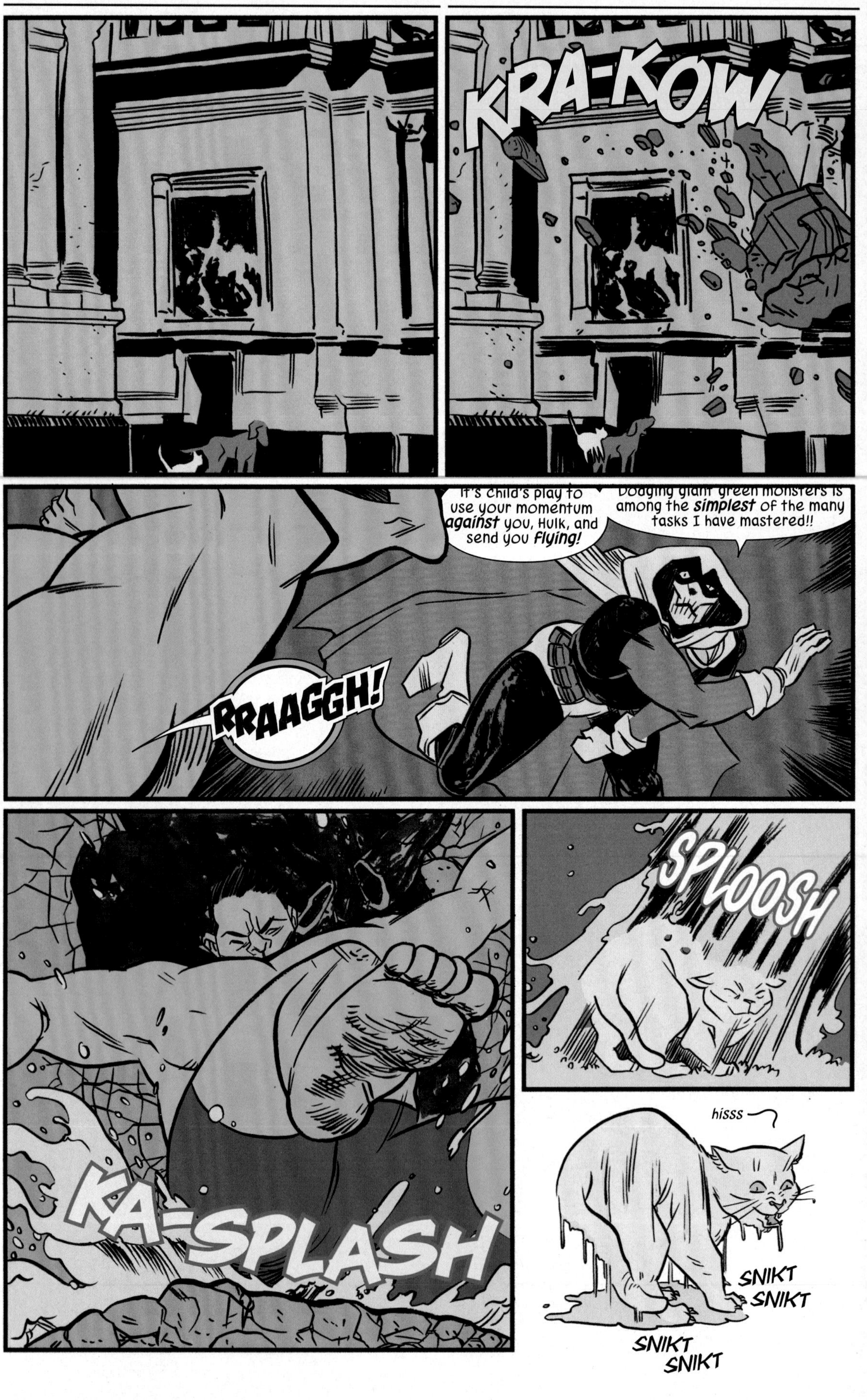
KRA-KOW
It's child's play to use your momentum against you, Hulk, and send you flying!
Dodging giant green monsters is among the simplest of the many tasks I have mastered!!
RRAAGGH!
KA-SPLASH
SPLOOSH
hisss
SNIKT
SNIKT
SNIKT
SNIKT

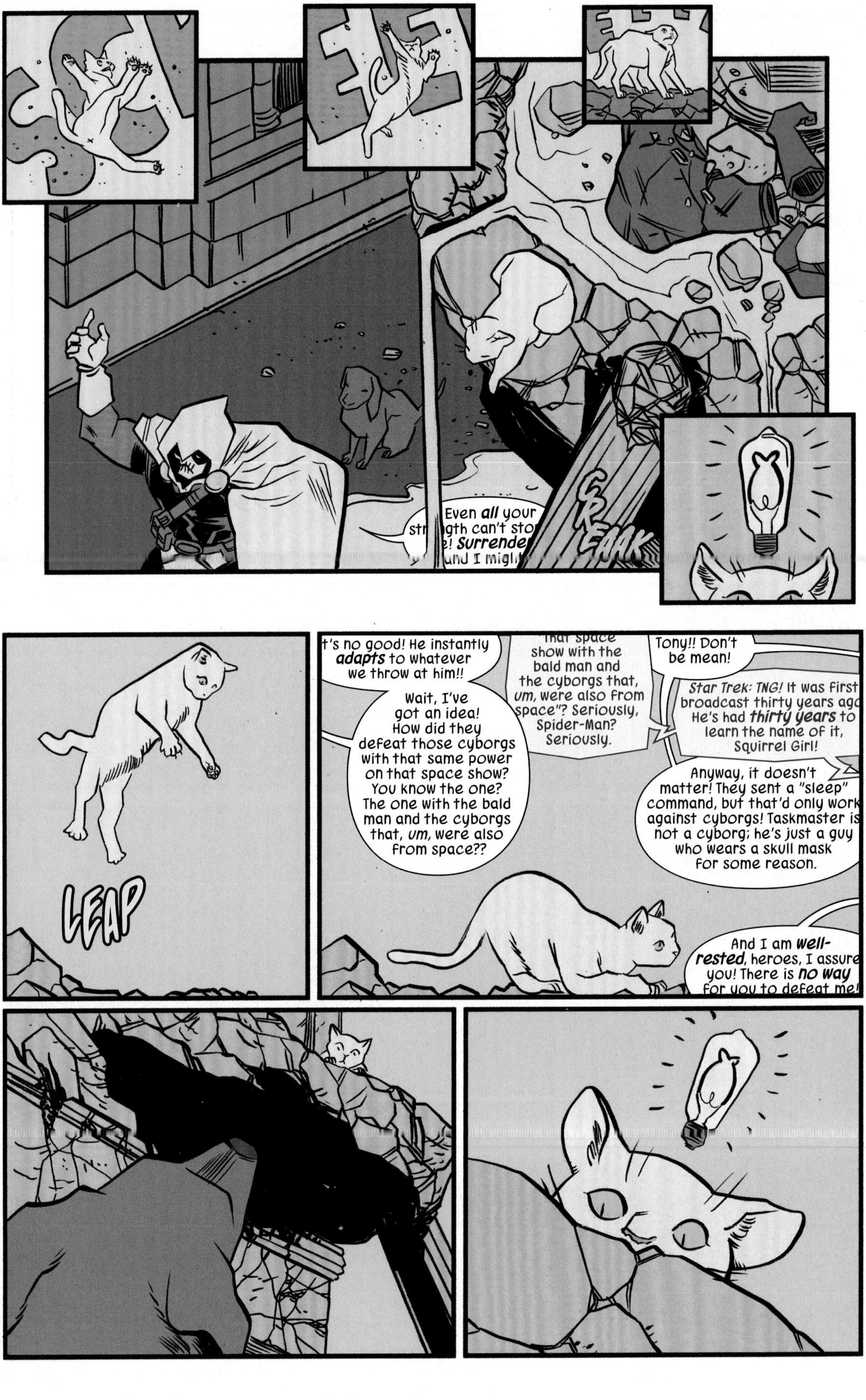
Even all your strength can't stop me! Surrender and I might
CREAAK
LEAP
It's no good! He instantly adapts to whatever we throw at him!!
Wait, I've got an idea! How did they defeat those cyborgs with that same power on that space show? You know the one? The one with the bald man and the cyborgs that, um, were also from space??
"That space show with the bald man and the cyborgs that, um, were also from space"? Seriously, Spider-Man? Seriously.
Tony!! Don't be mean!
Star Trek: TNG! It was first broadcast thirty years ago. He's had thirty years to learn the name of it, Squirrel Girl!
Anyway, it doesn't matter! They sent a "sleep" command, but that'd only work against cyborgs! Taskmaster is not a cyborg; he's just a guy who wears a skull mask for some reason.
And I am well-rested, heroes, I assure you! There is no way for you to defeat me!

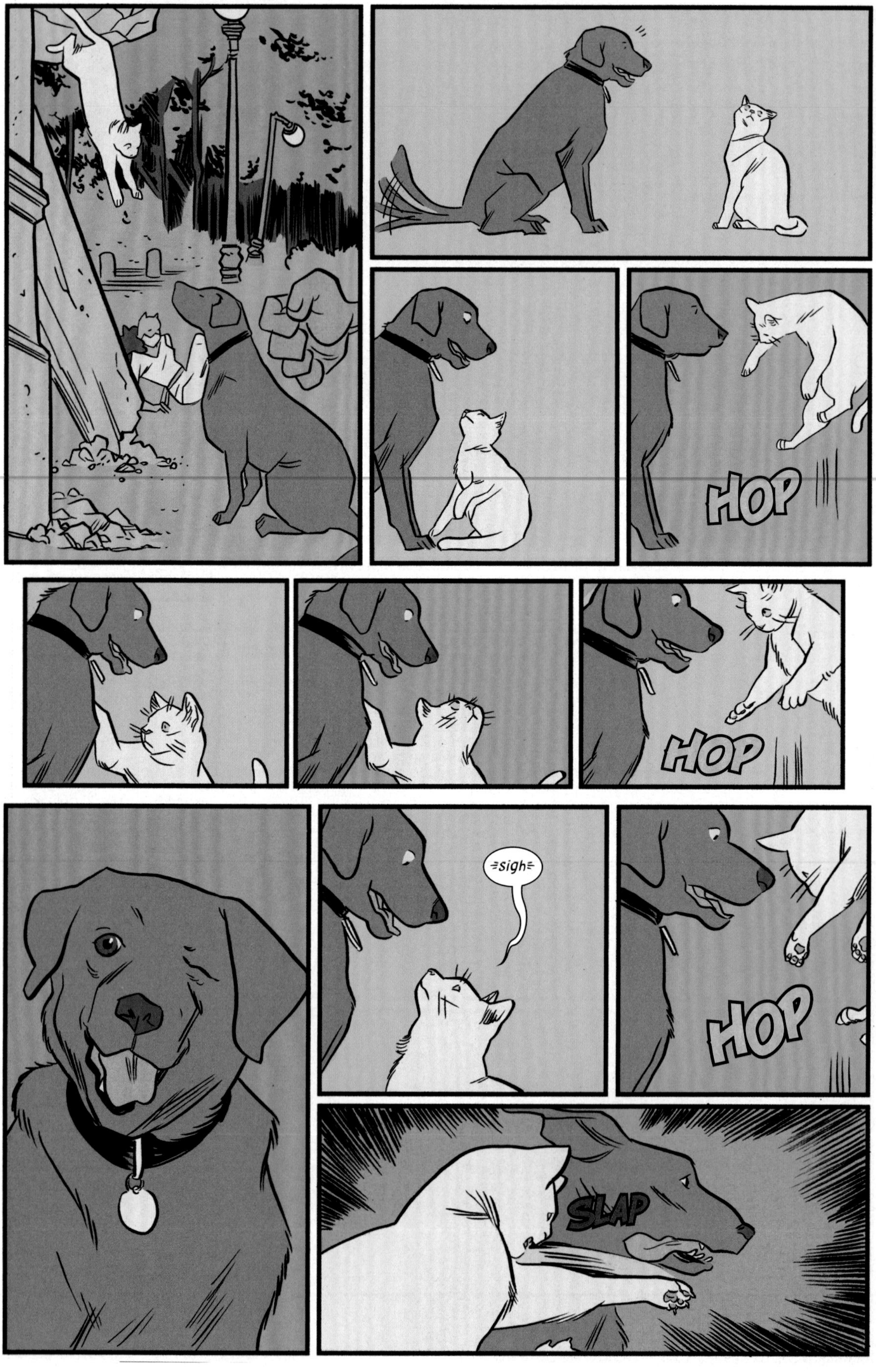
HOP
HOP
sigh
HOP
SLAP

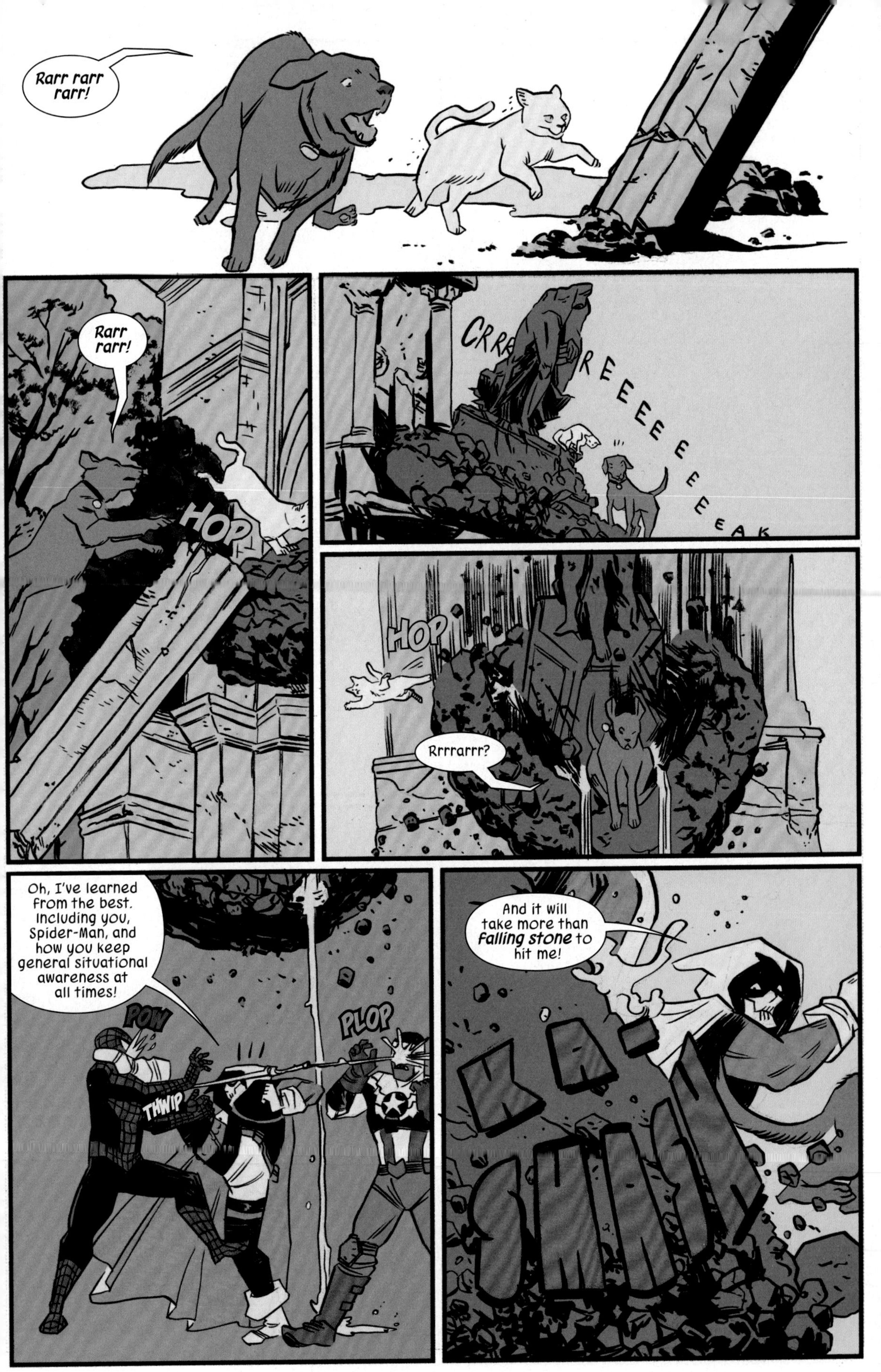
Rarr rarr rarr!
Rarr rarr!
HOP
CRRREEEEEEEEEEAK
HOP
Rrrrarrr?
Oh, I've learned from the best. Including you, Spider-Man, and how you keep general situational awareness at all times!
POW
PLOP
THWIP
And it will take more than *falling stone* to hit me!
KA-SHAK

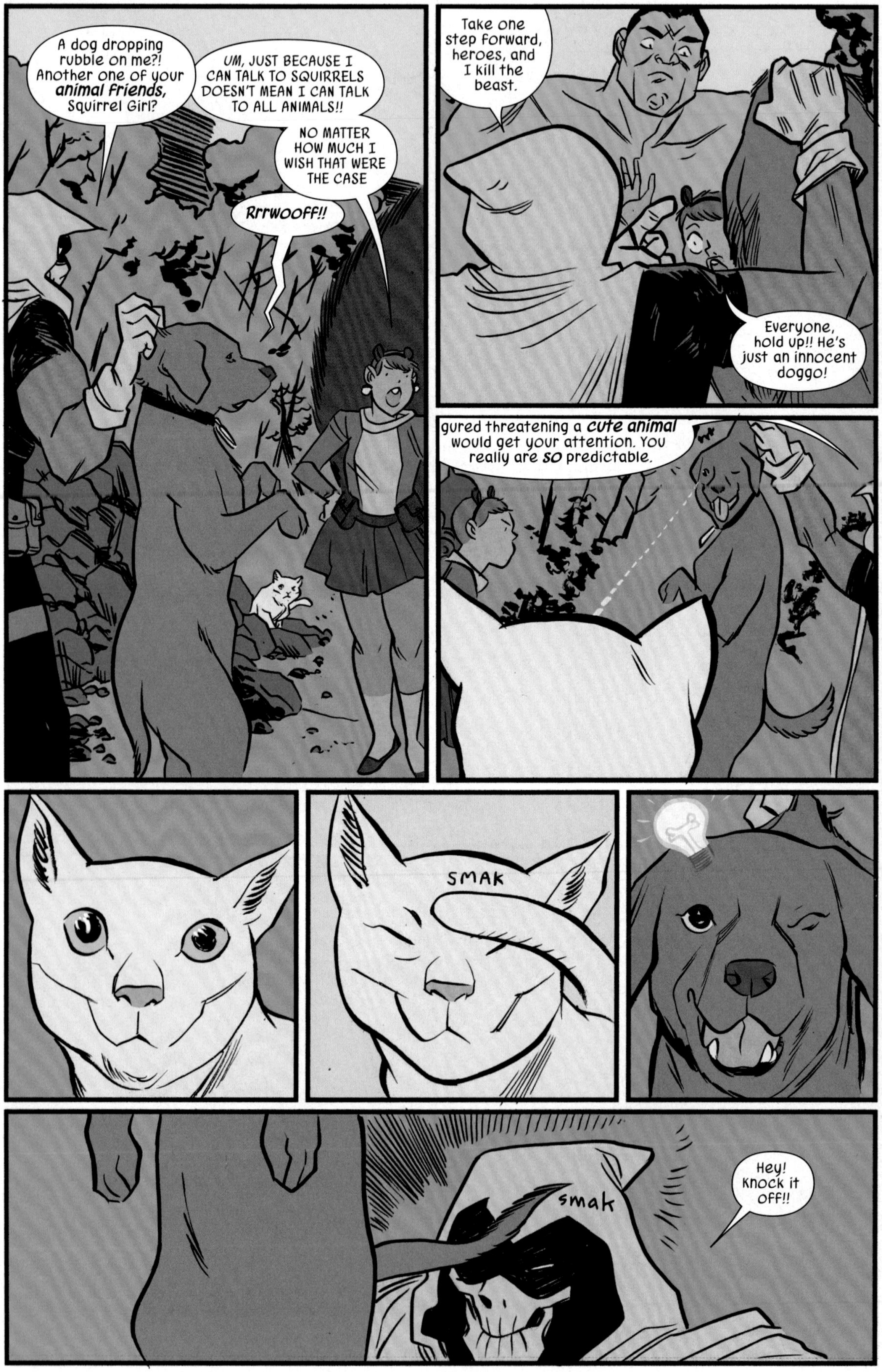
A dog dropping rubble on me?! Another one of your animal friends, Squirrel Girl?
UM, JUST BECAUSE I CAN TALK TO SQUIRRELS DOESN'T MEAN I CAN TALK TO ALL ANIMALS!!
NO MATTER HOW MUCH I WISH THAT WERE THE CASE
Rrrwooff!!
Take one step forward, heroes, and I kill the beast.
Everyone, hold up!! He's just an innocent doggo!
gured threatening a cute animal would get your attention. You really are SO predictable.
SMAK
smak
Hey! Knock it off!!

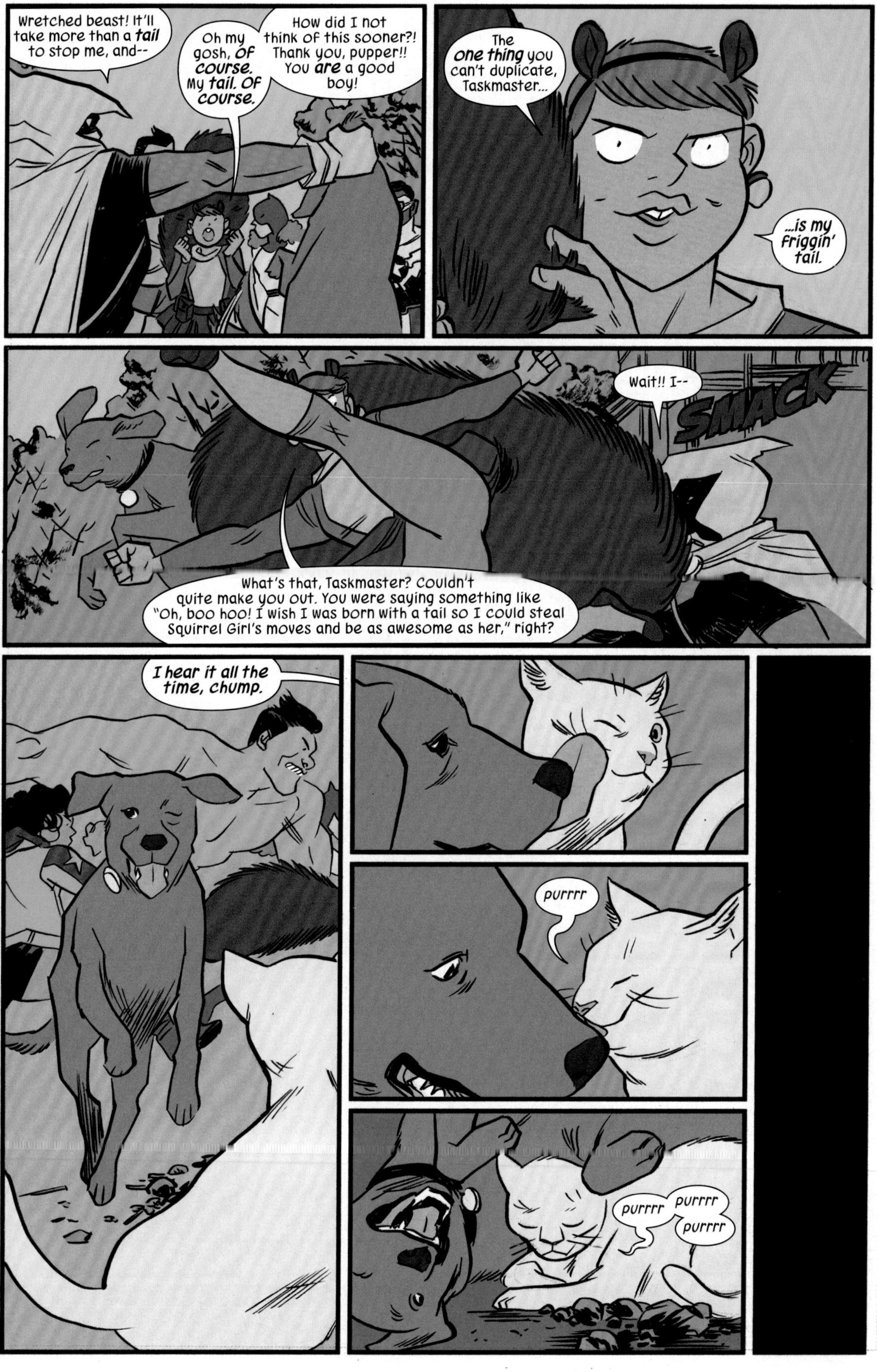
Wretched beast! It'll take more than a tail to stop me, and--
Oh my gosh, of course. My tail. Of course.
How did I not think of this sooner?! Thank you, pupper!! You are a good boy!
The one thing you can't duplicate, Taskmaster...
...is my friggin' tail.
Wait!! I--
SMACK
What's that, Taskmaster? Couldn't quite make you out. You were saying something like "Oh, boo hoo! I wish I was born with a tail so I could steal Squirrel Girl's moves and be as awesome as her," right?
I hear it all the time, chump.
purrrr
purrrr
purrrr
purrrr

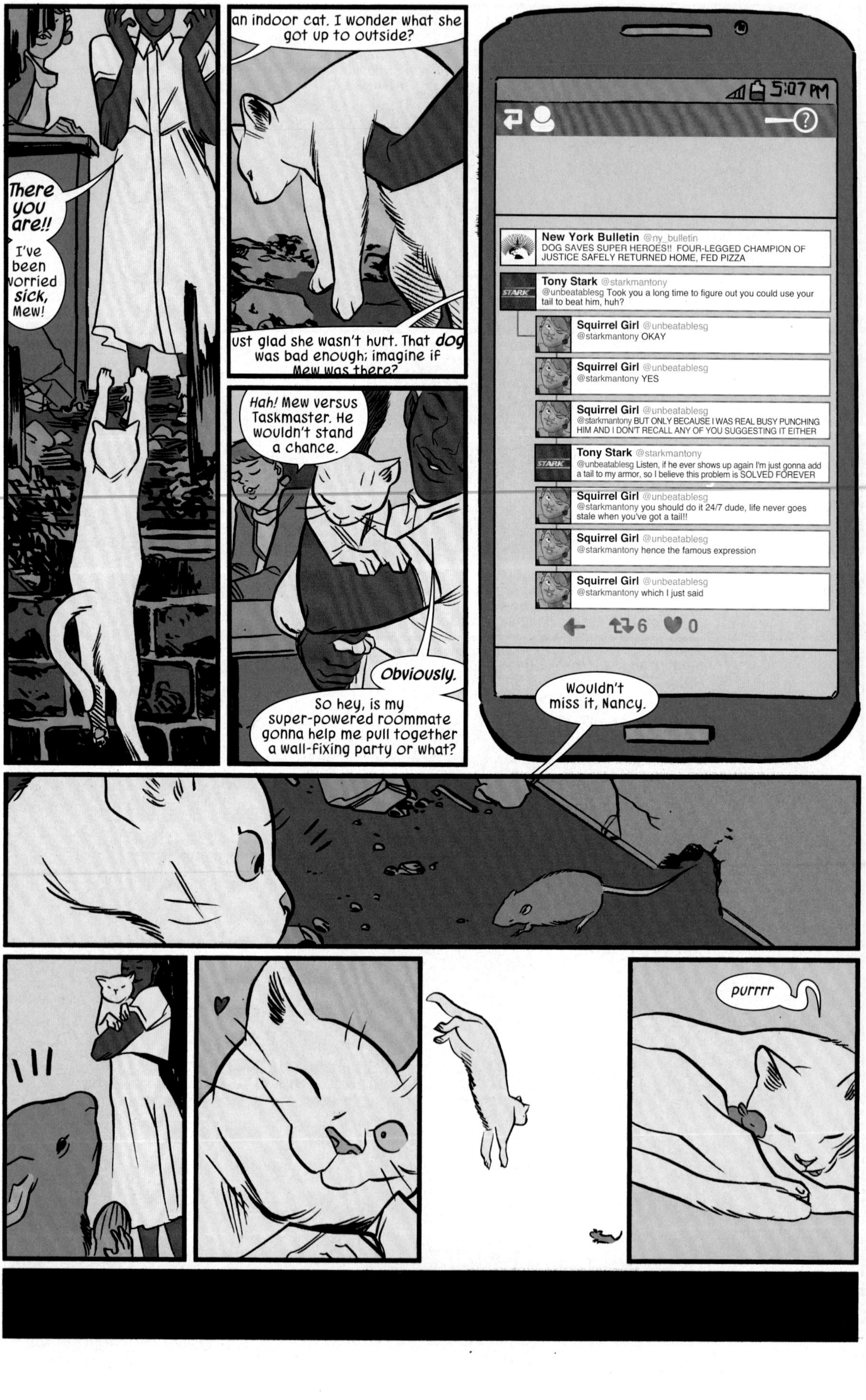

There you are!!
I've been worried sick, Mew!
an indoor cat. I wonder what she got up to outside?
ust glad she wasn't hurt. That dog was bad enough; imagine if Mew was there?
Hah! Mew versus Taskmaster. He wouldn't stand a chance.
Obviously.
So hey, is my super-powered roommate gonna help me pull together a wall-fixing party or what?
5:07 PM
New York Bulletin @ny_bulletin
DOG SAVES SUPER HEROES!! FOUR-LEGGED CHAMPION OF JUSTICE SAFELY RETURNED HOME, FED PIZZA
Tony Stark @starkmantony
@unbeatablesg Took you a long time to figure out you could use your tail to beat him, huh?
Squirrel Girl @unbeatablesg
@starkmantony OKAY
Squirrel Girl @unbeatablesg
@starkmantony YES
Squirrel Girl @unbeatablesg
@starkmantony BUT ONLY BECAUSE I WAS REAL BUSY PUNCHING HIM AND I DON'T RECALL ANY OF YOU SUGGESTING IT EITHER
Tony Stark @starkmantony
@unbeatablesg Listen, if he ever shows up again I'm just gonna add a tail to my armor, so I believe this problem is SOLVED FOREVER
Squirrel Girl @unbeatablesg
@starkmantony you should do it 24/7 dude, life never goes stale when you've got a tail!!
Squirrel Girl @unbeatablesg
@starkmantony hence the famous expression
Squirrel Girl @unbeatablesg
@starkmantony which I just said
6
0
Wouldn't miss it, Nancy.
purrrr

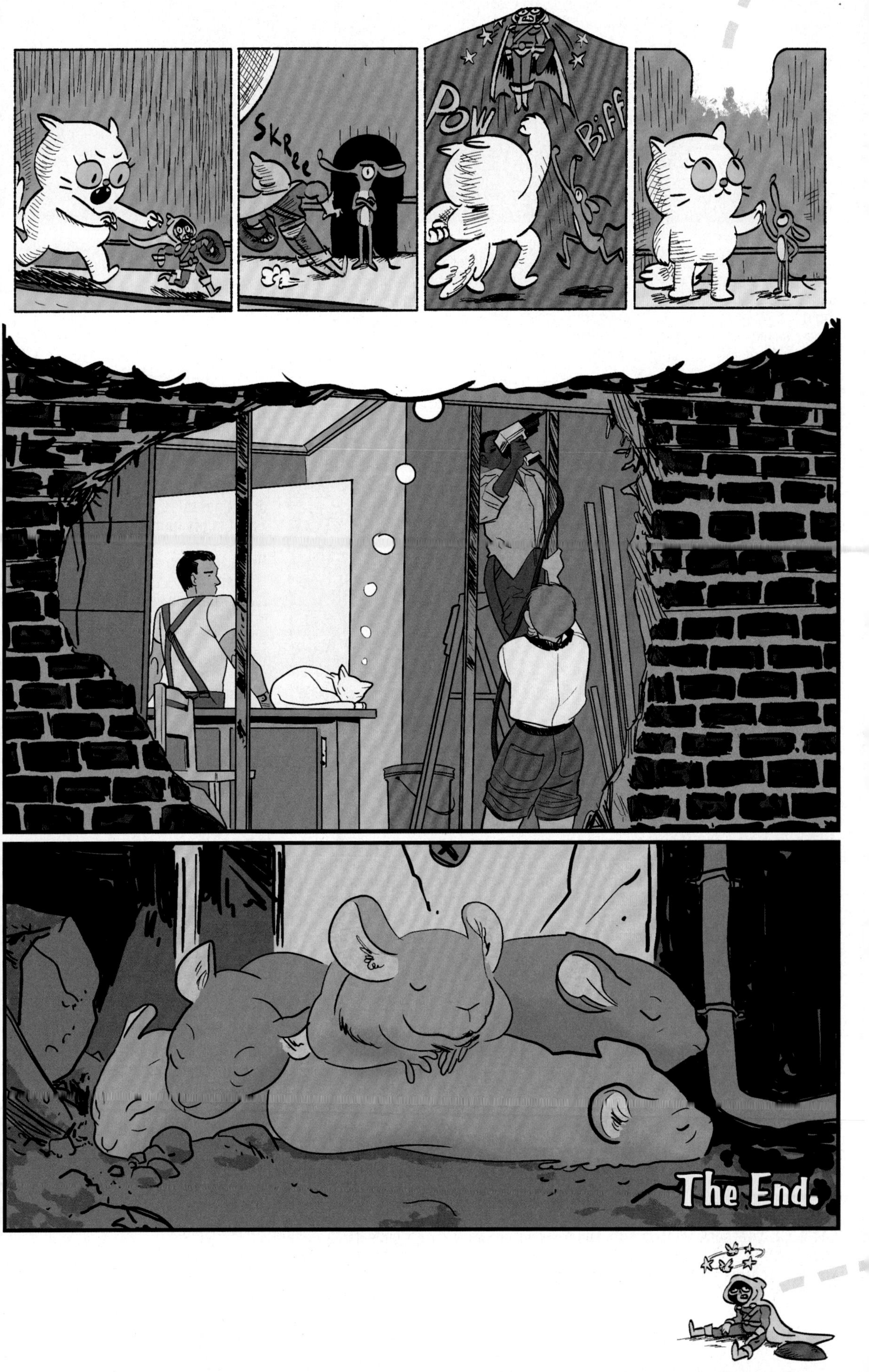
SKReee
POW
Biff
The End.

Letters From Nuts

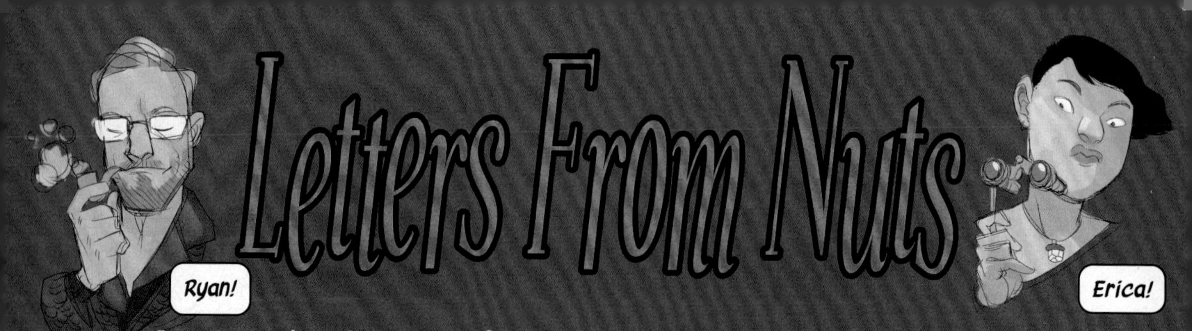
Ryan!
Erica!

Send letters to mheroes@marvel.com or 135 W 50th St, 7th Floor, New York, NY 10020 (Please mark "OKAY TO PRINT")

Ryan, Erica and Rico,

Thank you for all of the hard work, talent and dedication you all put into this wonderful, wonderful book each month. It had been nearly fifteen years since I've picked up a print comic every issue without fail, but your book has brought me back into the fold.

After your first issue #1 I made THE UNBEATABLE SQUIRREL GIRL a habit very specifically so that I'd have a box of comics to share with my daughter as soon as she's able to flip through them. I've become assured that I made the right choice for two reasons. First of all, you folks continue to produce an amazing, smart, insightful and funny all-ages comic and you show no signs of slowing down. Second, she's only eighteen months old and is absolutely obsessed with acorns. Every time she goes outside we wind up finding a few acorns around the living room later. Doreen must have some tough-soled shoes, because I swear those acorn caps are worse than Lego bricks to step on.

Nuts to you all,
Daniel and Carolyn Tauber

RYAN: Aw, that's great! I've got a nephew too who just turned three and while he's not quiiiite at the point yet where he's reading comics, I'm really excited for him to start. I am SO READY to be the cool uncle. I've got comics in my house, I've got lots of neat toys and a giant lime green stuffed T-Rex from *Dinosaur Comics* – I AM READY. Perhaps he'll be reading this letter column in a few years and be like, "A time when I was so young that I didn't read comics? IMPOSSIBLE." ALSO: I didn't know stepping on acorn caps was worse than stepping on Lego, but I am happy to take your word for it and would absolutely not like to find out with personal experience.

ERICA: Pro tip: glue down the caps. I learned this from cosplayers and jewelry makers. But yay! I'm glad we could get you back into comics and have provided you with something you can share with your daughter in the future.

Thank you for coming to Lethbridge Word on the Street and the signing at Kapow. My husband and I have been fans of your work for years and are so excited that you are involved in an incredible Marvel comic. I wish we had some better pictures of our Unbeatable Squirrel Boy but he was also very excited.

Miranda
Alberta, Canada

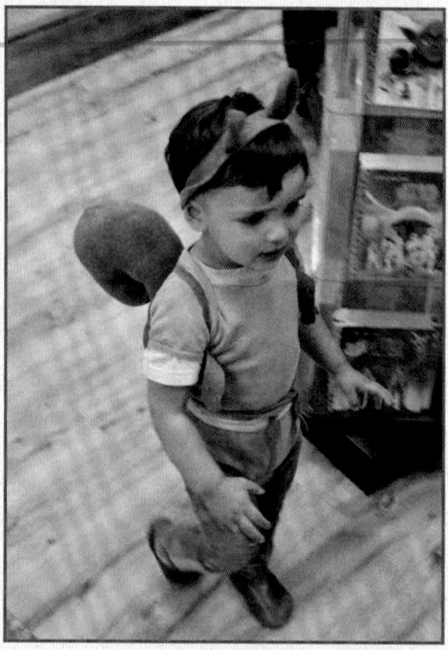

RYAN: Miranda, THIS WAS THE BEST. Your Squirrel Boy was truly unbeatable, and it was hilarious how the second he was dressed up he ran off (because he was shy? Because ADVENTURE BECKONED??). Everyone else: If you've never been to Lethbridge, Alberta, Canada, I recommend it! I went for a walk while I was there and came across HENDERSON LAKE, which I can only assume was named after Erica Henderson, so I instantly felt welcome and at home.

ERICA: That lake thing is probably correct.

Ryan and Erica,

Wow guys, this comic is just swell. Squirrel Girl is truly unbeatable, and Nancy is such a rad character, and Koi Boy and Chipmunk Hunk are undeniably the most perfectly named super heroes ever. And geez, Brain Drain is just trying so hard to be a good super hero and I just...I just want him to be happy. I love you, Brain Drain, and I will always be proud of you. No matter what.

Squirrelfully Yours,
Elisha Smith
Knoxville, TN

RYAN: Thank you, Elisha! Brain Drain believes in himself and tries his best, and that is all anyone can ask!

ERICA: My only regret is that we didn't get to do more scenes of Brain Drain in his human costume.

Ryan and Erica,

Thank you so much for making me realize how awesome Squirrel Girl is! Your comic makes me crack up every time I read it, especially the "In A Nutshell" segment from Issue 11. It's quite possibly one of the best comics I've read! Squirrel Girl is, thanks to this comic, my favorite Marvel hero. I mean, come on! She's beat up Thanos, Galactus, and even the entire Marvel universe! Anyways, once again, thank you guys!

Ethan

RYAN: Thanks, Ethan! I really enjoy writing the "In A Nutshell" recap pages, and I also like that all the accounts there are real. I would argue it makes total sense that Tony Stark, international CEO and billionaire, would hang out online with Doreen Green. Also, if you haven't picked up our THE UNBEATABLE SQUIRREL GIRL BEATS UP THE MARVEL UNIVERSE! original graphic novel (it's an all-new story!), then what are you waiting for? I don't want to spoil anything, but I'll say this: the Marvel Universe does absolutely get beat up.

ERICA: Aw! Thanks! We like her a lot too.

"In this world, even a brain in a jar in a robot body can only do so much." You took the words right out of my mouth. Nicely observed! Brain Drain, Brain Drain, Brain Drain. He's all of it. Were he a man, he'd be my main. He brings the pain! His reign can't be disdained! He brings a presence to this plane that others only feign! If you mess with him you best be prayin'! Yeah, like that.

Ryan North and Erica Henderson, you two are still rocking it like a magikist. Rico Renzi and Travis Lanham and Wil Moss are doing this as well. I'd like to reiterate - this time into lettercol canon - that Ryan "Ry No" North should have SG fight a duo composed of the Rhino and a new villaness named the Air-Hen. For no reason I can explain, the latter's given name should be Peppy Bosworth.

Keep it up!
John Velousis

RYAN: John, this Brain Drain theme song is a thing of beauty. And PERSONALLY, I think the Rhino (who is already a Marvel villain, so: CHECK) and the Air-Hen should team up and go on adventures. Erica, do you want to go on an adventure? We are currently in Leeds in the United Kingdom for the Thought Bubble convention, so I guess we're already on one??

ERICA: I love how much people love Brain Drain. It hadn't even been that long since we introduced him but I was already dying to bring him back. Ryan and I were having breakfast adventures in Leeds. Who can eat the most breakfast?? (Ryan. Ryan can.)

Hello, True Believers,

Thought you might appreciate the Squirrel Girl costume my wife helped create for my 10-year-old daughter Fiona. Happy Halloween!

(And yes, those are totally comics in the background.)

James VanOsdol
Chicago, IL

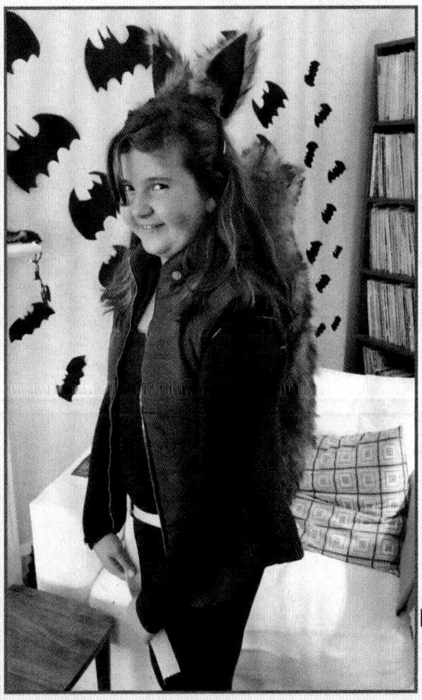

costume is unbeatable and I certainly hope at Halloween when people opened their doors and saw her they just emptied their entire bowls of candy into her pillowcase. I WILL ACCEPT NOTHING LESS.

ERICA: I hope those bats are year-round décor. Fun times goth house. ANYWAY – Fiona looks great! This makes me happy because I don't think I've seen trick-or-treaters since I left for college. Halloween is not just for rowdy adults, people!

Okay, that's all the room we have this month. DO NOT MISS THE NEXT ISSUE! Why? Because it's a special celebration of the 25th anniversary of Squirrel Girl's first appearance! With a short story by none other than SG's co-creator Will Murray! And you'll maybe (MAYBE!) even learn Squirrel Girl's origin!!!!!!!!!!!!!!!!!!!!!!!!! (And yes, that was twenty-five exclamation points.)

Next Issue:

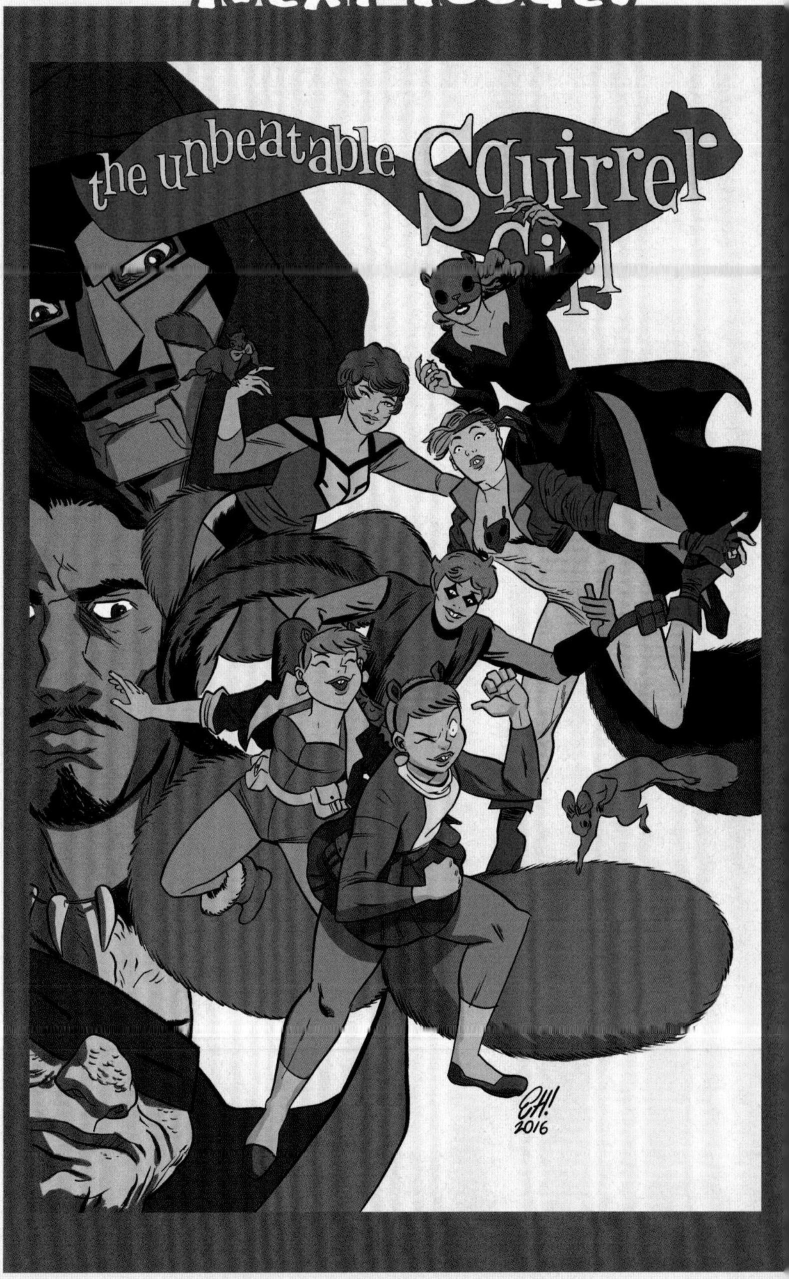
the unbeatable Squirrel Girl
EH! 2016

Attention, Squirrel Scouts! Make sure to check out our production blog, **unbeatablesquirrelgirl.tumblr.com**, where we post behind-the-scenes stuff on how the book gets made, along with all sorts of cool things *you* make: fanart, cosplay, whatever!

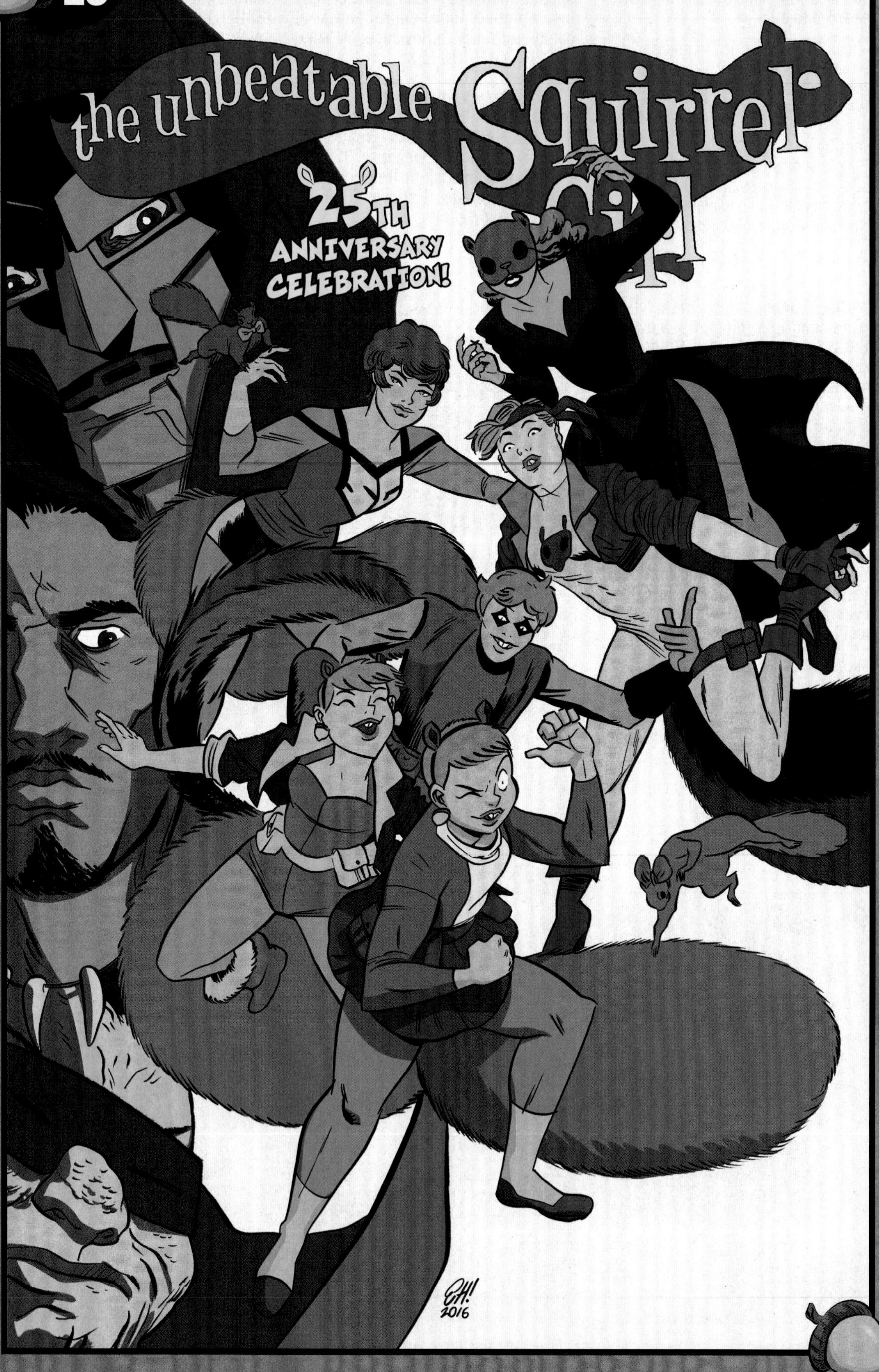
the unbeatable Squirrel Girl
25TH ANNIVERSARY CELEBRATION!
EH! 2016

*Doreen Green isn't just a second-year computer science student: she secretly also has all the powers of both squirrel and girl! She uses her amazing abilities to fight crime and be as awesome as possible. You know her as...**The Unbeatable Squirrel Girl!** Find out what she's been up to, with...*

Squirrel Girl in a nutshell

Squirrel Girl @unbeatablesg
IT'S MY BIRTHDAY!! I'M 20 YEARS OLD!! EVERYONE GET REAL EXCITED BECAUSE I WAS BORN...TWENTY YEARS AGO...THIS VERY NIGHT!

Squirrel Girl @unbeatablesg
Fav to wish me happy birthday, RT to wish me an EXTRA happy birthday

Nancy W. @sewwiththeflo
@unbeatablesg Have we worked out the etiquitte of wishing YOURSELF a happy birthday on social media?

Squirrel Girl @unbeatablesg
@sewwiththeflo what if YOU wished me happy birthday, then I could RT that? what if that was a thing we made happen

Nancy W. @sewwiththeflo
Happy birthday to Squirrel Girl, who is both one of my favorite super heroes AND one of my favorite people.

Squirrel Girl @unbeatablesg
@sewwiththeflo aww Nancy!! <3 <3 <3

Tony Stark @starkmantony
@unbeatablesg Are you having a party? Assuming you are having a party, can I come?

Squirrel Girl @unbeatablesg
@starkmantony YES BUT YOU HAVE TO WEAR THE ARMOR

Tony Stark @starkmantony
@unbeatablesg Is this a setup to get me so hepped up on cake that you can convince me to let YOU wear the armor?

Squirrel Girl @unbeatablesg
@starkmantony haha no

Squirrel Girl @unbeatablesg
@starkmantony it's my birthday

Squirrel Girl @unbeatablesg
@starkmantony i'm definitely ending up in that armor tony

Squirrel Girl @unbeatablesg
@starkmantony none can deny me my one true birthday wish

Odinson @num1odinson
@unbeatablesg I pray thee, might Asgardians come to thy party??

Nancy W. @sewwiththeflo
@num1odinson YES BRING LOKI

Odinson @num1odinson
@sewwiththeflo Though I may no longer wield Mjolnir, that does not mean I have been demoted to my brother's secretary service.

Nancy W. @sewwiththeflo
@num1odinson Hmm wow that's a super weird way to spell "yes I will absolutely bring Loki to this party and also Thor, excellent idea Nancy"

Nancy W. @sewwiththeflo
@unbeatablesg I'd be interested in knowing how that little baby born 20 years ago became Squirrel Girl.

Squirrel Girl @unbeatablesg
@sewwiththeflo YES! YES. It is an amazing story.

Nancy W. @sewwiththeflo
@unbeatablesg ...And?

Squirrel Girl @unbeatablesg
@sewwiththeflo And it goes...a little something...A'LIKE THIS.

Nancy W. @sewwiththeflo
@unbeatablesg ...

Nancy W. @sewwiththeflo
@unbeatablesg ...so were you going to post something after that, or

search!

#meetcute
#followtheleaper
#monkeyjoe
#properconcussiontreatment
#fishyhulk
#avengersassemble

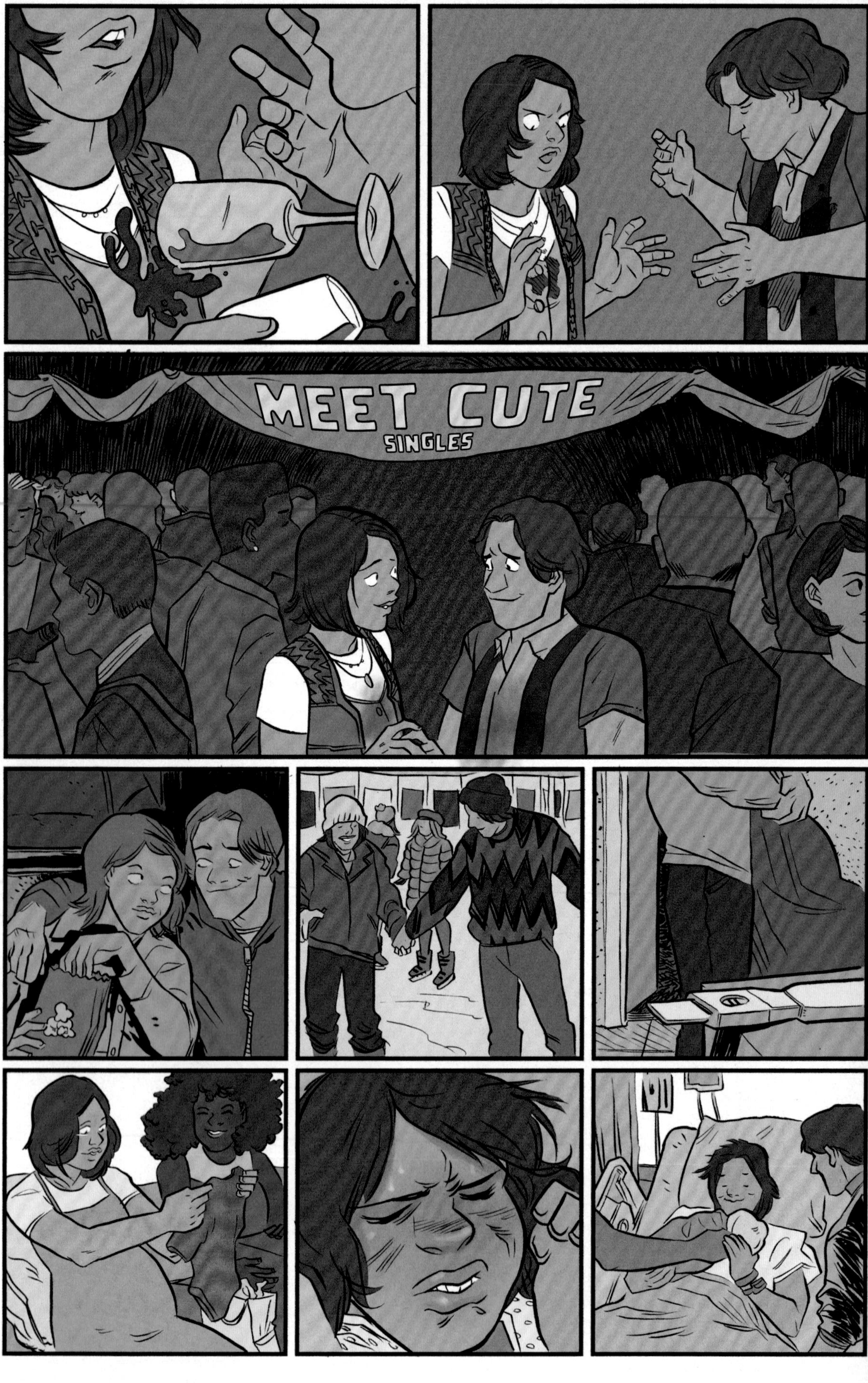
MEET CUTE
SINGLES

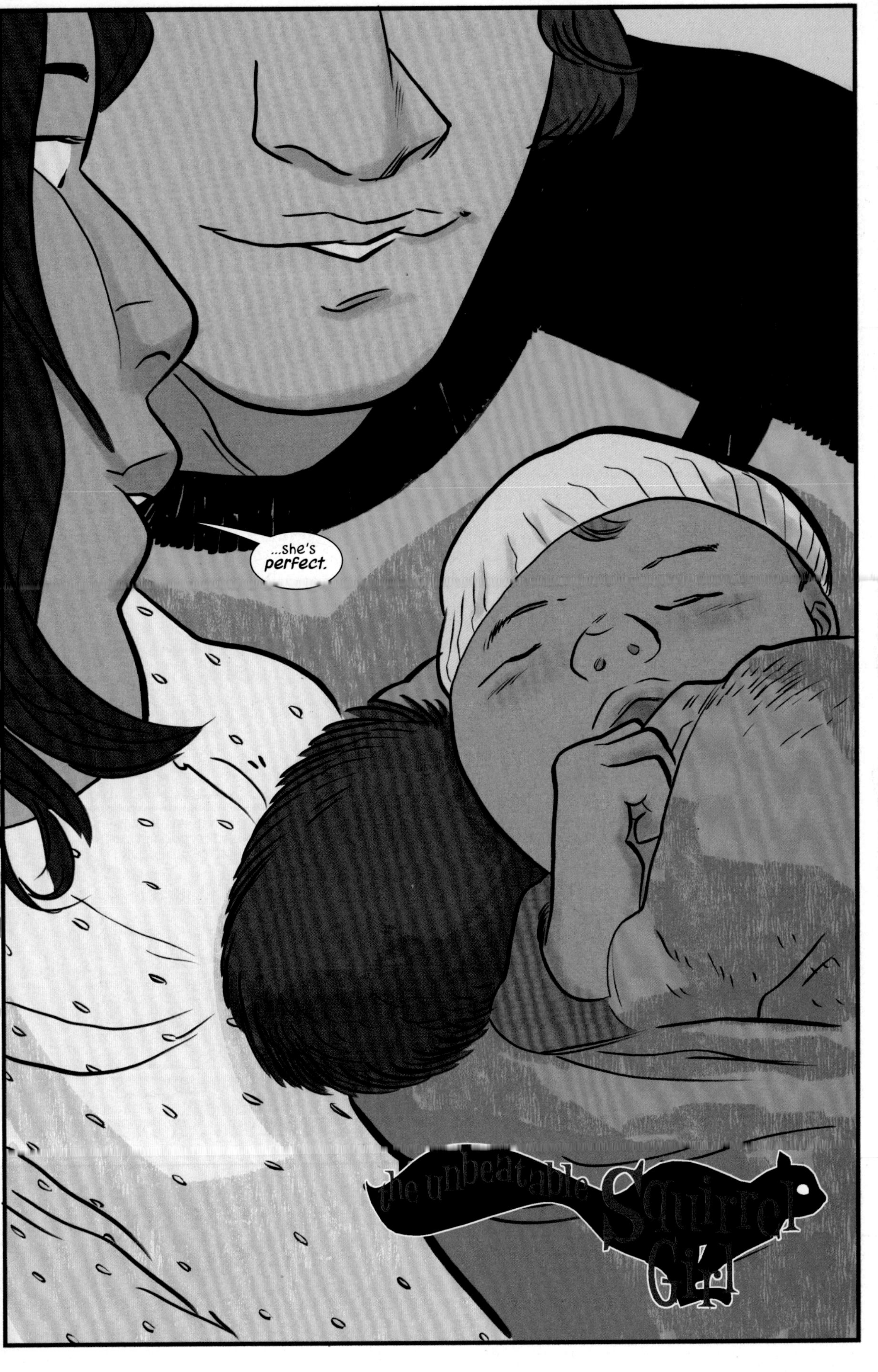
...she's perfect.
the unbeatable Squirrel Girl

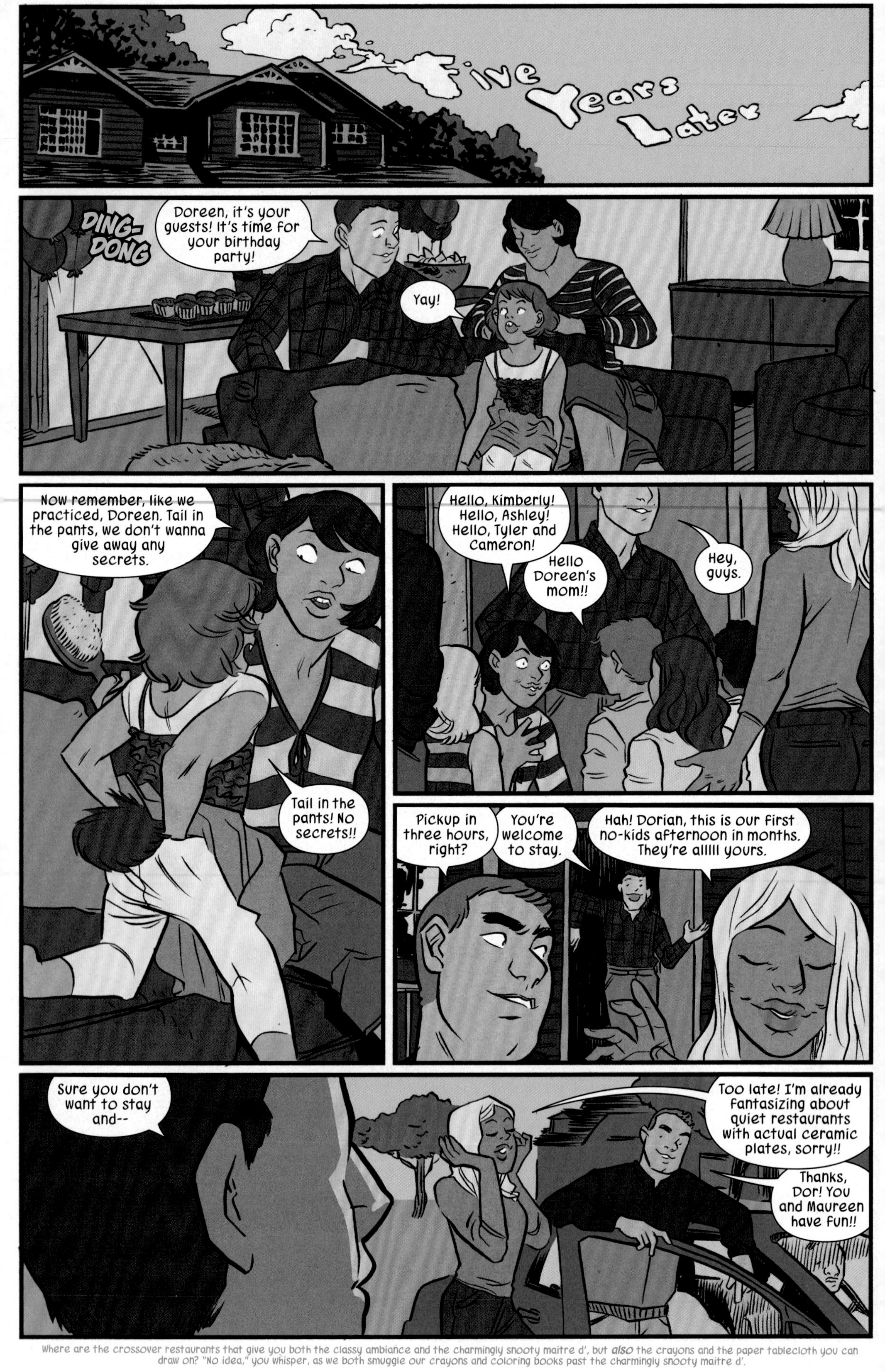
Five Years Later
DING-DONG
Doreen, it's your guests! It's time for your birthday party!
Yay!
Now remember, like we practiced, Doreen. Tail in the pants, we don't wanna give away any secrets.
Tail in the pants! No secrets!!
Hello, Kimberly! Hello, Ashley! Hello, Tyler and Cameron!
Hello Doreen's mom!!
Hey, guys.
Pickup in three hours, right?
You're welcome to stay.
Hah! Dorian, this is our first no-kids afternoon in months. They're alllll yours.
Sure you don't want to stay and--
Too late! I'm already fantasizing about quiet restaurants with actual ceramic plates, sorry!!
Thanks, Dor! You and Maureen have fun!!

Where are the crossover restaurants that give you both the classy ambiance and the charmingly snooty maitre d', but *also* the crayons and the paper tablecloth you can draw on? "No idea," you whisper, as we both smuggle our crayons and coloring books past the charmingly snooty maitre d'.

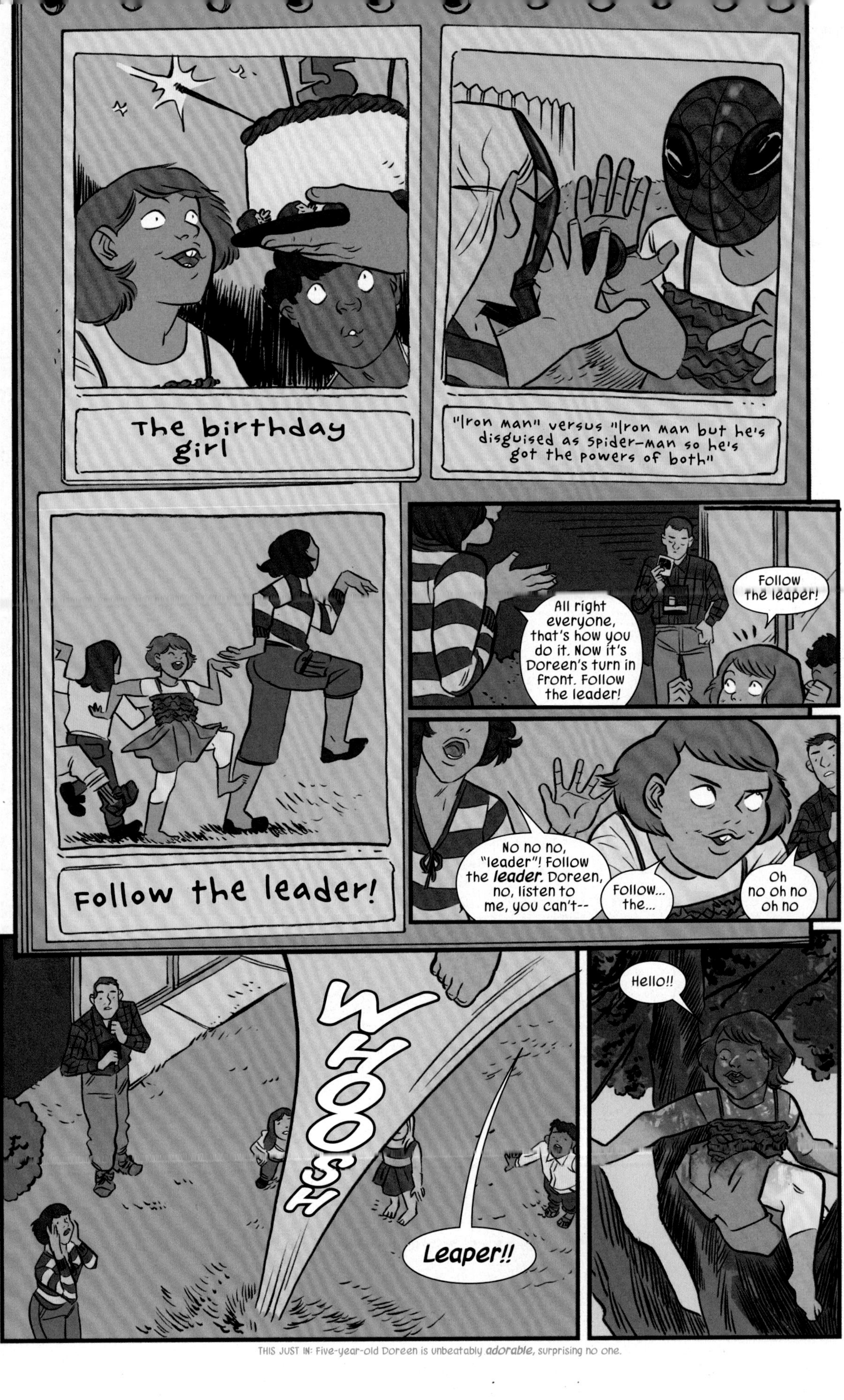
The birthday girl
"Iron Man" versus "Iron Man but he's disguised as Spider-Man so he's got the powers of both"
Follow the leader!
All right everyone, that's how you do it. Now it's Doreen's turn in front. Follow the leader!
Follow the leaper!
No no no, "leader"! Follow the *leader.* Doreen, no, listen to me, you can't--
Follow... the...
Oh no oh no oh no
WHOOSH
Leaper!!
Hello!!

THIS JUST IN: Five-year-old Doreen is unbeatably *adorable,* surprising no one.

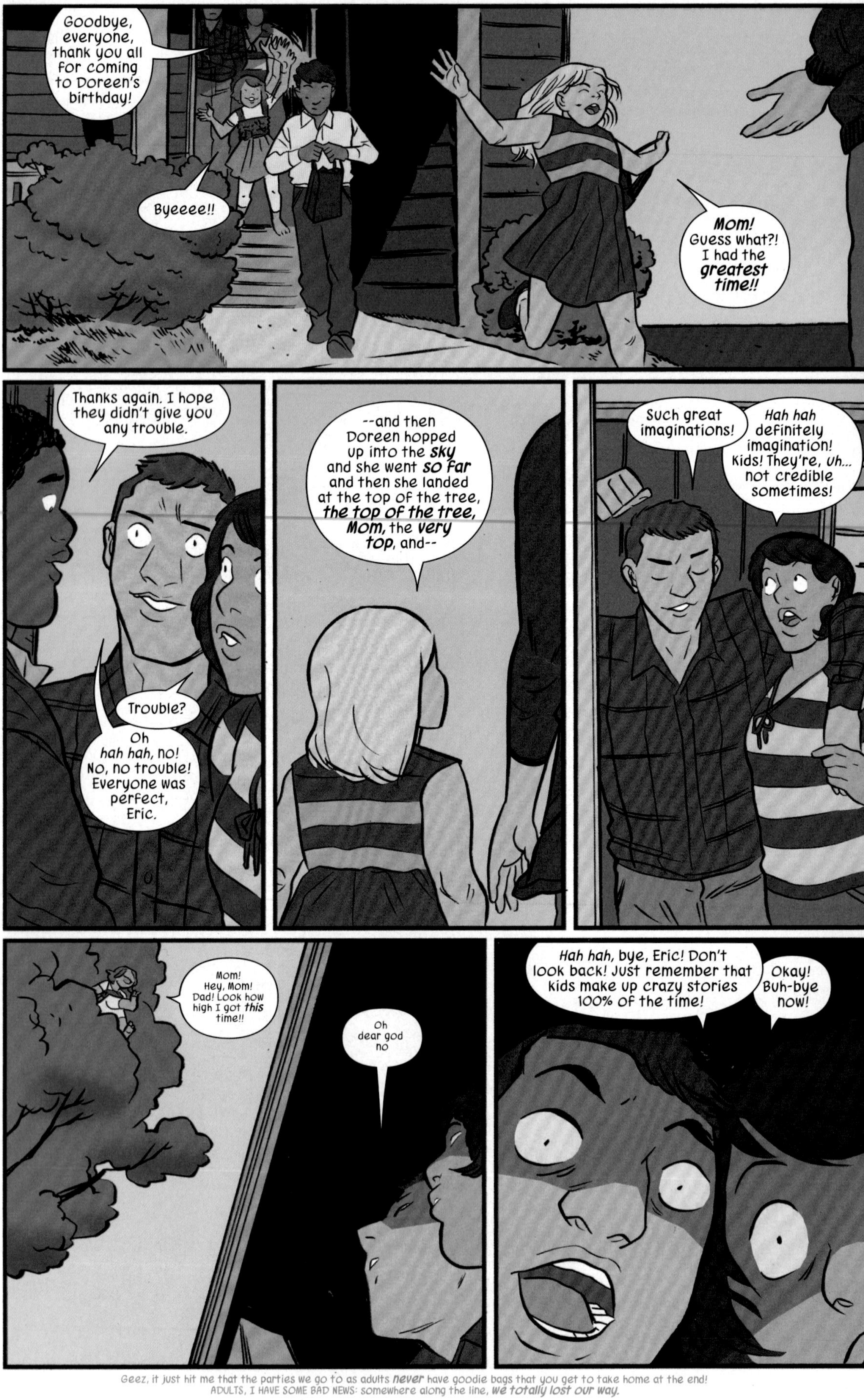
Goodbye, everyone, thank you all for coming to Doreen's birthday!
Byeeee!!
Mom! Guess what?! I had the greatest time!!
Thanks again. I hope they didn't give you any trouble.
Trouble?
Oh hah hah, no! No, no trouble! Everyone was perfect, Eric.
--and then Doreen hopped up into the sky and she went so far and then she landed at the top of the tree, the top of the tree, Mom, the very top, and--
Such great imaginations!
Hah hah definitely imagination! Kids! They're, uh... not credible sometimes!
Mom! Hey, Mom! Dad! Look how high I got this time!!
Oh dear god no
Hah hah, bye, Eric! Don't look back! Just remember that kids make up crazy stories 100% of the time!
Okay! Buh-bye now!

Geez, it just hit me that the parties we go to as adults *never* have goodie bags that you get to take home at the end! ADULTS, I HAVE SOME BAD NEWS: somewhere along the line, *we totally lost our way.*

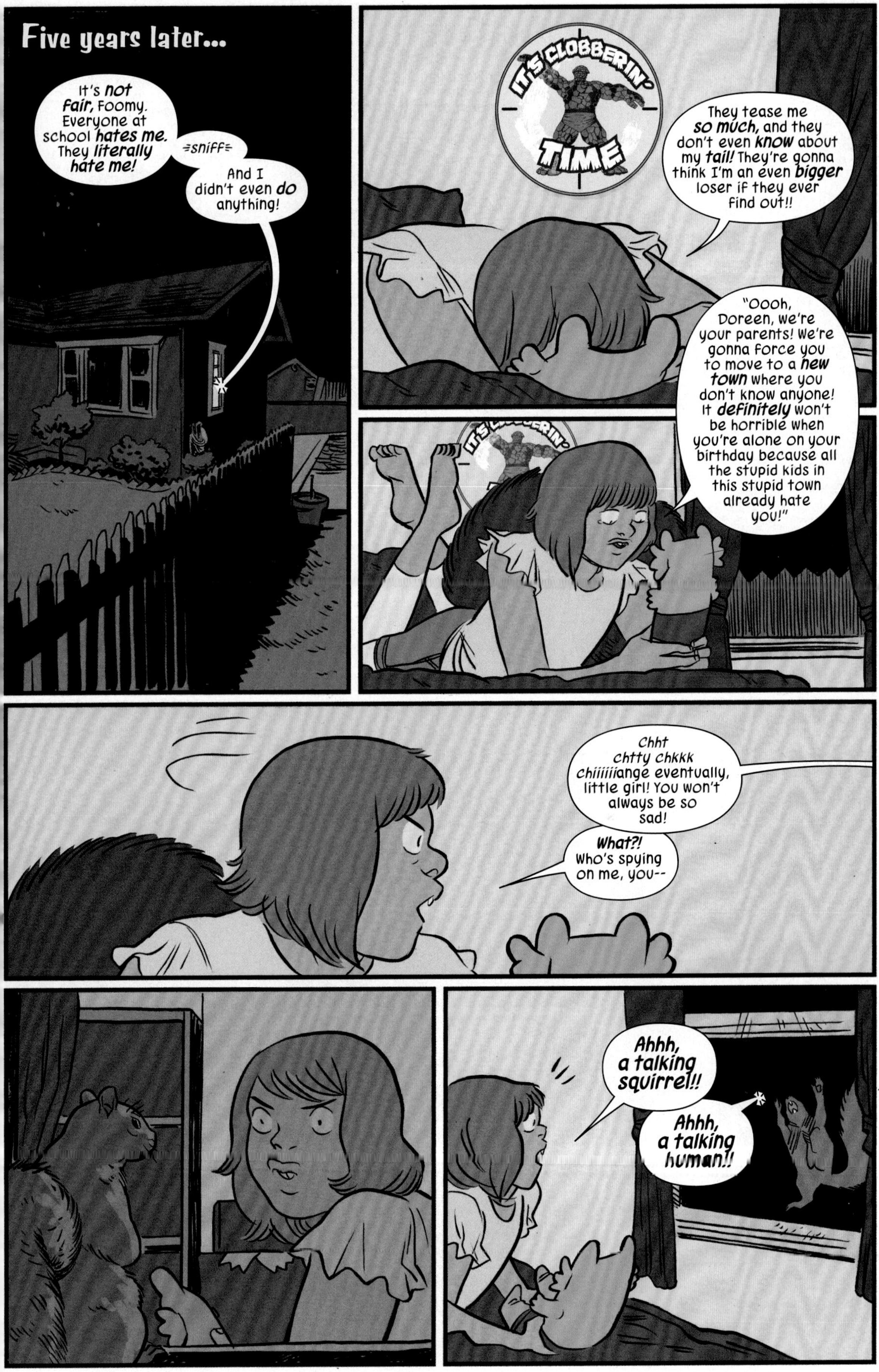
Five years later...
It's not fair, Foomy. Everyone at school hates me. They literally hate me!
=sniff=
And I didn't even do anything!
IT'S CLOBBERIN' TIME
They tease me so much, and they don't even know about my tail! They're gonna think I'm an even bigger loser if they ever find out!!
"Oooh, Doreen, we're your parents! We're gonna force you to move to a new town where you don't know anyone! It definitely won't be horrible when you're alone on your birthday because all the stupid kids in this stupid town already hate you!"
Chht chtty chkkk chiiiiiiange eventually, little girl! You won't always be so sad!
What?! Who's spying on me, you--
Ahhh, a talking squirrel!!
Ahhh, a talking human!!

I am happy to report that close reading of Doreen's Thing clock suggests that it's *always* clobbering time. Please, govern yourselves accordingly.

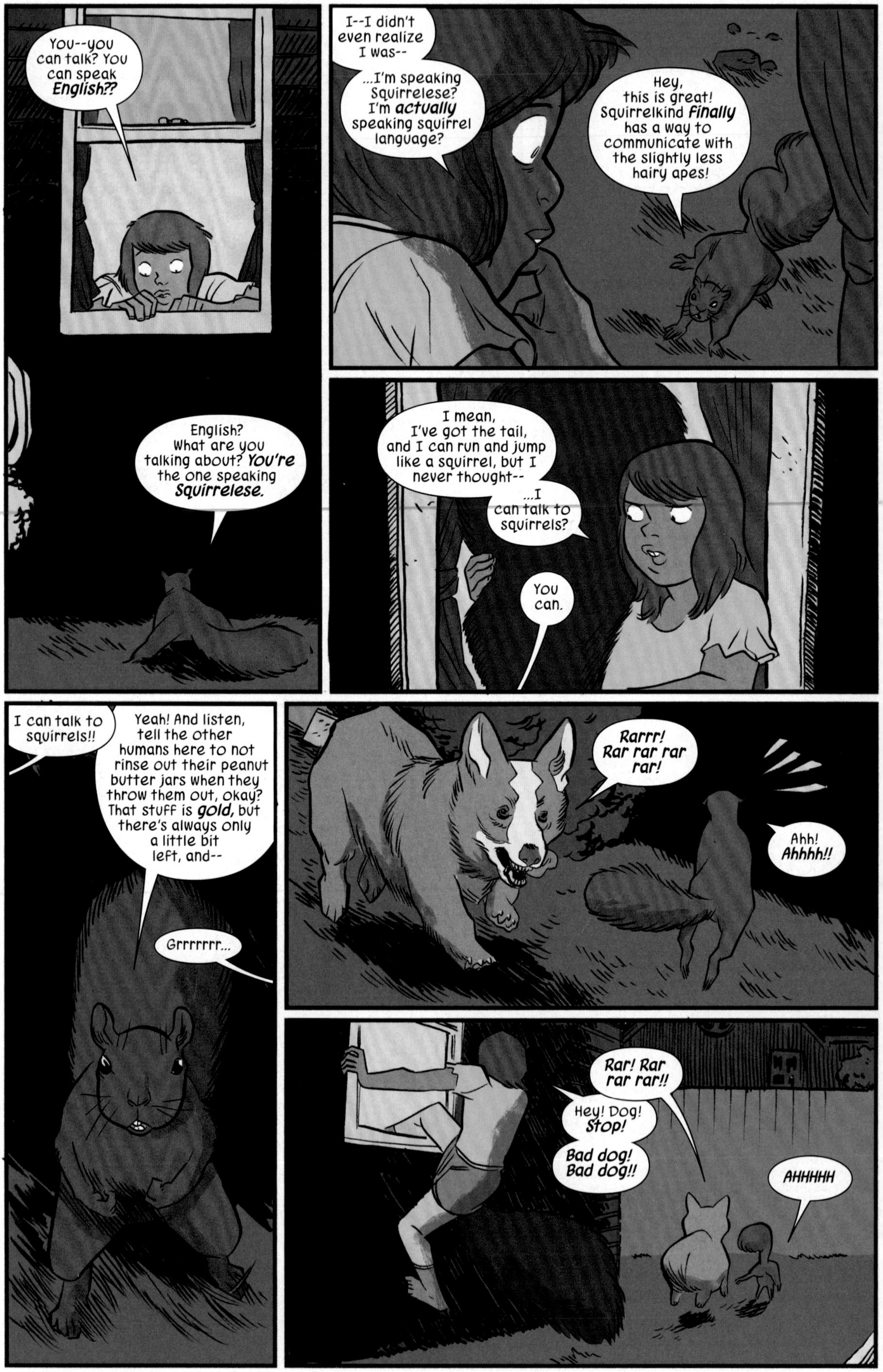
You--you can talk? You can speak English??
I--I didn't even realize I was--
...I'm speaking Squirrelese? I'm actually speaking squirrel language?
Hey, this is great! Squirrelkind finally has a way to communicate with the slightly less hairy apes!
English? What are you talking about? You're the one speaking Squirrelese.
I mean, I've got the tail, and I can run and jump like a squirrel, but I never thought--
...I can talk to squirrels?
You can.
I can talk to squirrels!!
Yeah! And listen, tell the other humans here to not rinse out their peanut butter jars when they throw them out, okay? That stuff is gold, but there's always only a little bit left, and--
Grrrrrrr...
Rarrr! Rar rar rar rar!
Ahh! Ahhhh!!
Rar! Rar rar rar!!
Hey! Dog! Stop!
Bad dog! Bad dog!!
AHHHHH

This squirrel learns he can communicate with a new species for the very first time, and the very first message he transmits is "send more peanut butter." This, sadly, once again confirms that it was actually a good idea to not put squirrels in charge of the messages sent into deep space on the *Voyager* spacecraft.

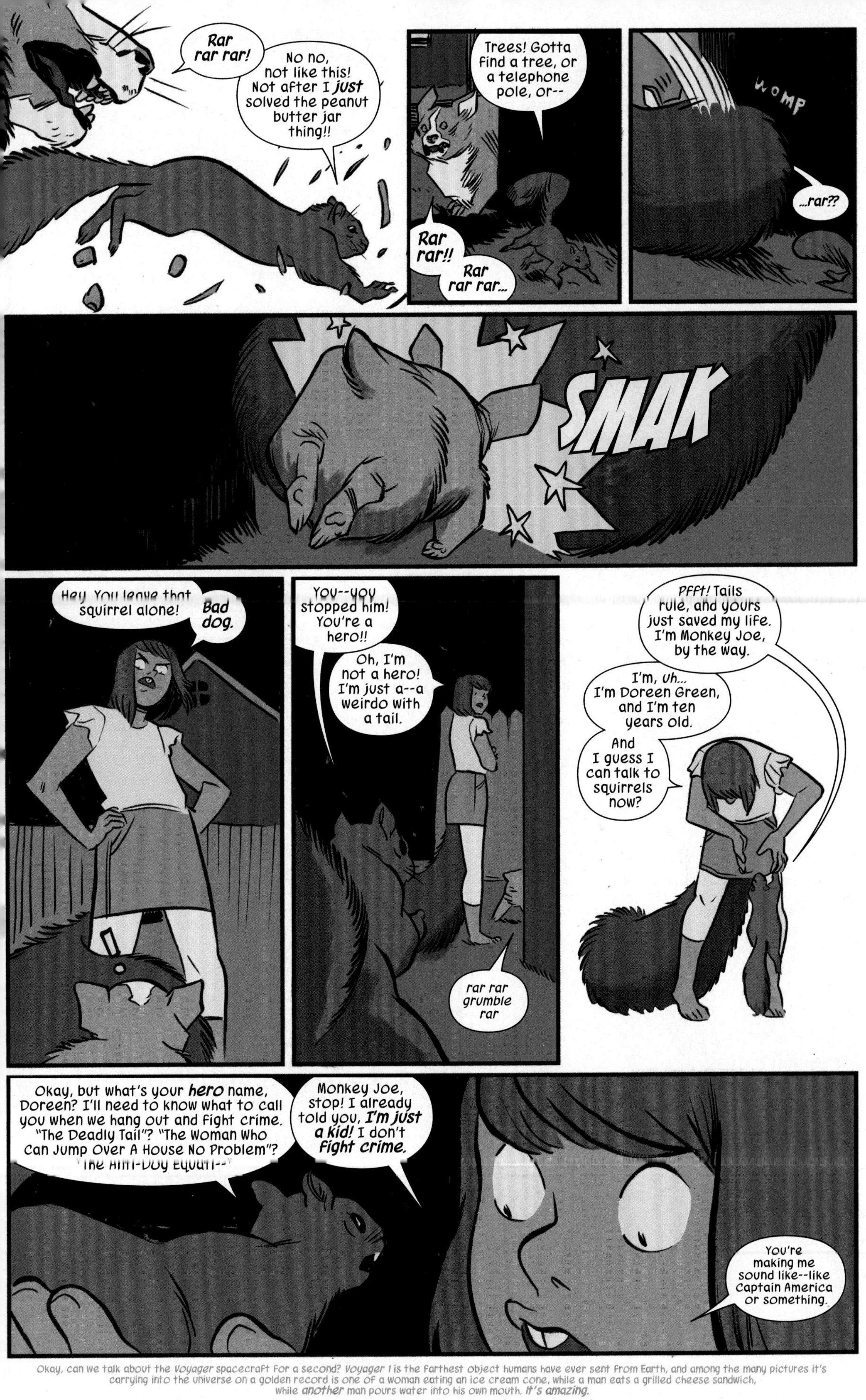

Rar rar rar!
No no, not like this! Not after I *just* solved the peanut butter jar thing!!
Trees! Gotta find a tree, or a telephone pole, or--
Rar rar!!
Rar rar rar...
WOMP
...rar??
SMAK
Hey! You leave that squirrel alone!
Bad dog.
You--you stopped him! You're a hero!!
Oh, I'm not a hero! I'm just a--a weirdo with a tail.
rar rar grumble rar
Pfft! Tails rule, and yours just saved my life. I'm Monkey Joe, by the way.
I'm, uh... I'm Doreen Green, and I'm ten years old.
And I guess I can talk to squirrels now?
Okay, but what's your **hero** name, Doreen? I'll need to know what to call you when we hang out and fight crime. "The Deadly Tail"? "The Woman Who Can Jump Over A House No Problem"? "The Anti-Dog Equati--"
Monkey Joe, stop! I already told you, ***I'm just a kid!*** I don't ***fight crime.***
You're making me sound like--like Captain America or something.

Okay, can we talk about the *Voyager* spacecraft for a second? *Voyager 1* is the farthest object humans have ever sent from Earth, and among the many pictures it's carrying into the universe on a golden record is one of a woman eating an ice cream cone, while a man eats a grilled cheese sandwich, while ***another*** man pours water into his own mouth. ***It's amazing.***

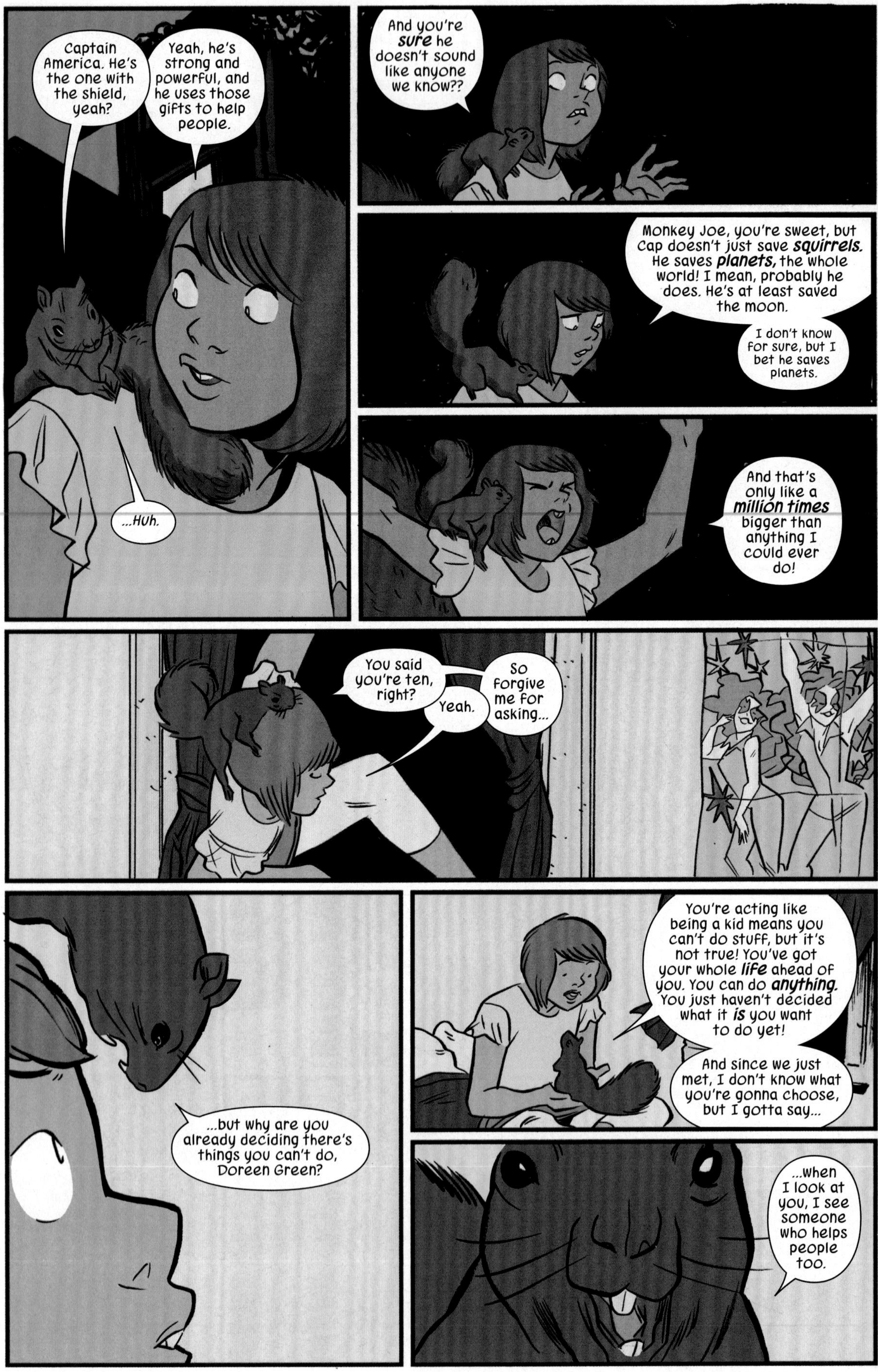
Captain America. He's the one with the shield, yeah?
Yeah, he's strong and powerful, and he uses those gifts to help people.
...Huh.
And you're *sure* he doesn't sound like anyone we know??
Monkey Joe, you're sweet, but Cap doesn't just save *squirrels.* He saves *planets,* the whole world! I mean, probably he does. He's at least saved the moon.
I don't know for sure, but I bet he saves planets.
And that's only like a *million times* bigger than anything I could ever do!
You said you're ten, right?
Yeah.
So forgive me for asking...
...but why are you already deciding there's things you can't do, Doreen Green?
You're acting like being a kid means you can't do stuff, but it's not true! You've got your whole *life* ahead of you. You can do *anything.* You just haven't decided what it *is* you want to do yet!
And since we just met, I don't know what you're gonna choose, but I gotta say...
...When I look at you, I see someone who helps people too.

I can't point you to the precise comic where Captain America saves the moon, but I'm certain there is one. And if there isn't, guess what: *I am so ready to write it.*

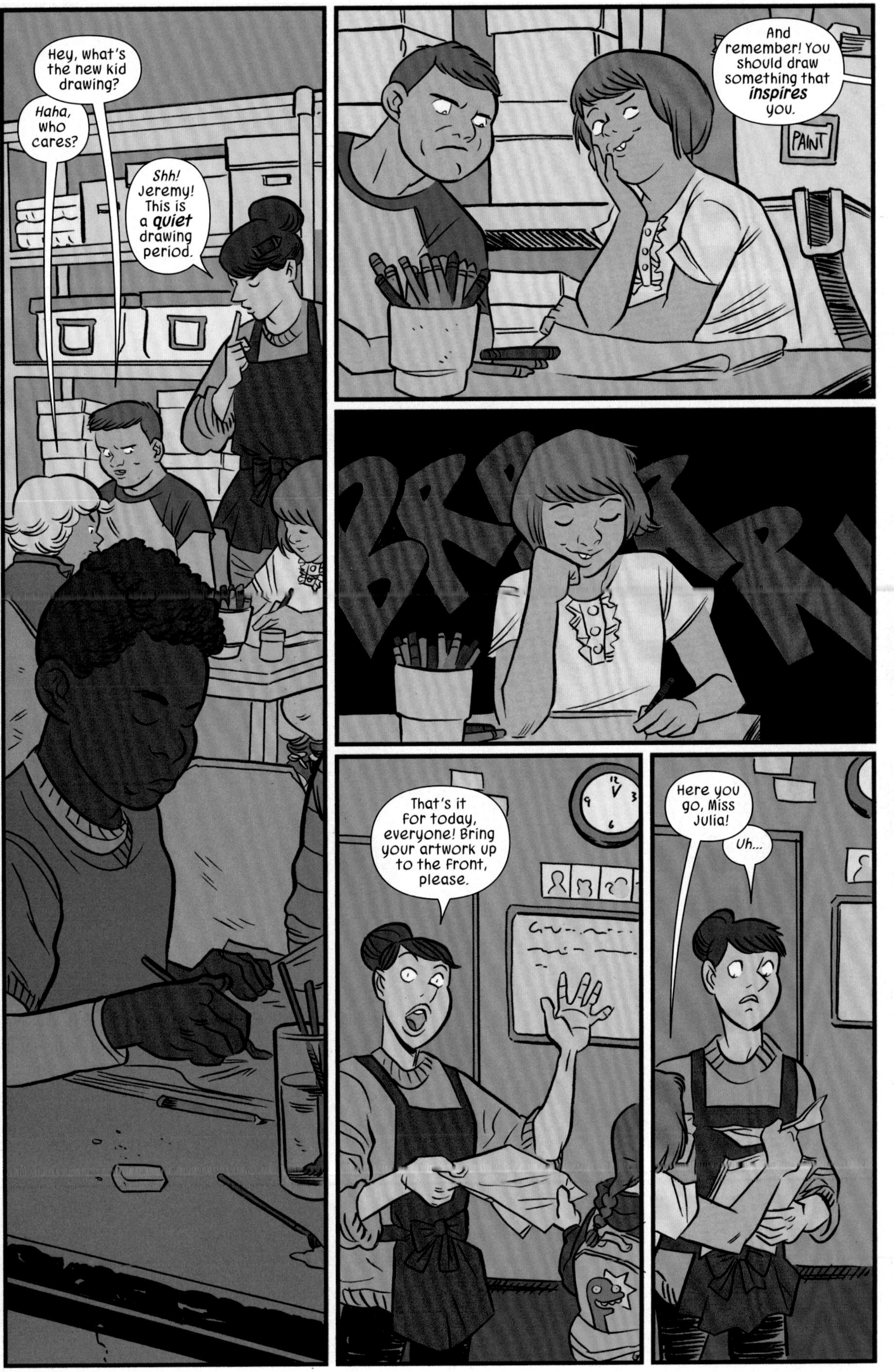
Hey, what's the new kid drawing?
Haha, who cares?
Shh! Jeremy! This is a *quiet* drawing period.
And remember! You should draw something that **inspires** you.
PAINT
That's it for today, everyone! Bring your artwork up to the front, please.
Here you go, Miss Julia!
Uh...

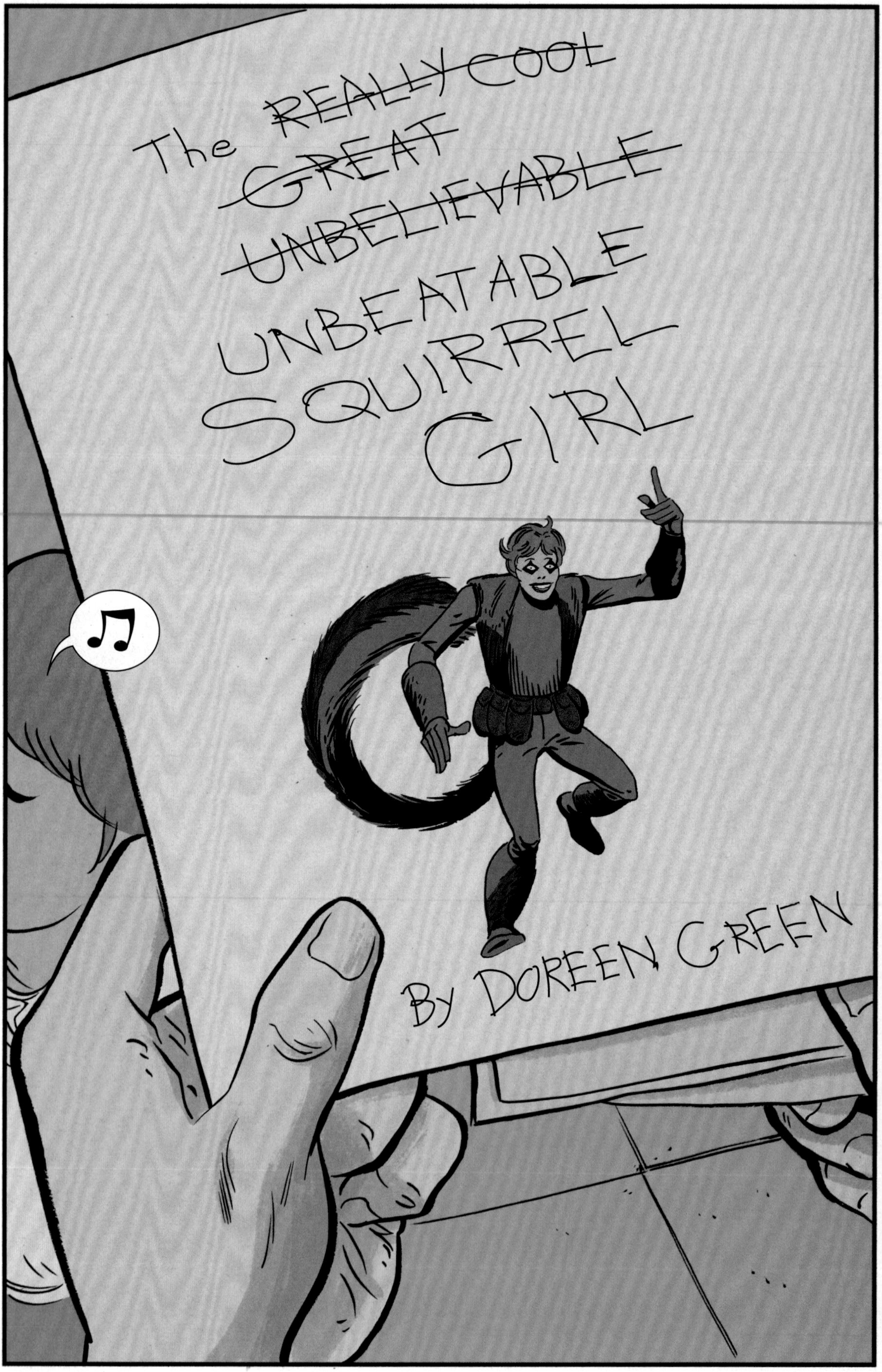

The ~~REALLY COOL~~ ~~GREAT~~ ~~UNBELIEVABLE~~ UNBEATABLE SQUIRREL GIRL
♫
By DOREEN GREEN

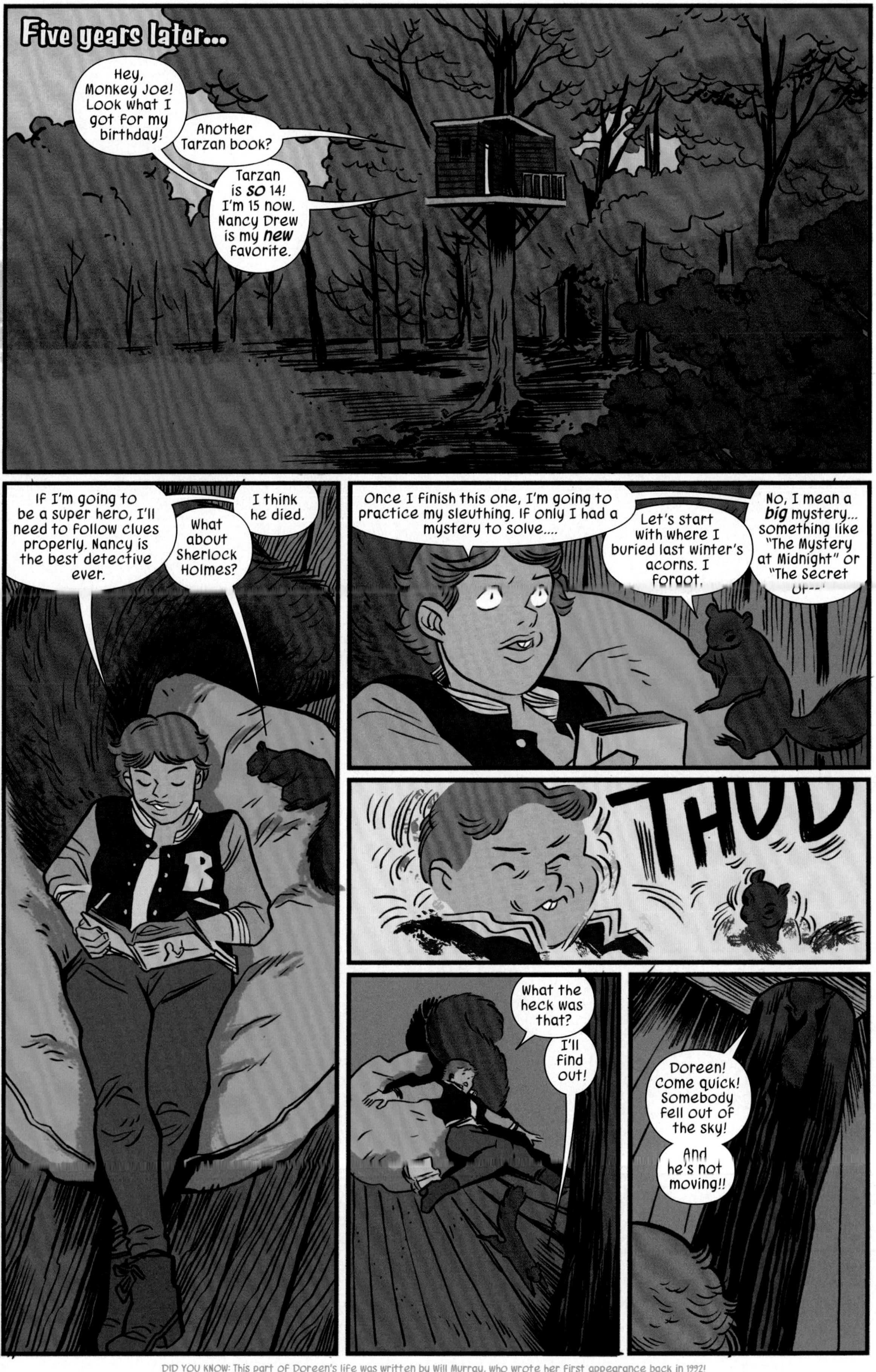
Five years later...
Hey, Monkey Joe! Look what I got for my birthday!
Another Tarzan book?
Tarzan is *SO* 14! I'm 15 now. Nancy Drew is my *new* favorite.
If I'm going to be a super hero, I'll need to follow clues properly. Nancy is the best detective ever.
What about Sherlock Holmes?
I think he died.
Once I finish this one, I'm going to practice my sleuthing. If only I had a mystery to solve....
Let's start with where I buried last winter's acorns. I forgot.
No, I mean a *big* mystery... something like "The Mystery at Midnight" or "The Secret
THUD
What the heck was that?
I'll find out!
Doreen! Come quick! Somebody fell out of the sky!
And he's not moving!!

DID YOU KNOW: This part of Doreen's life was written by Will Murray, who wrote her first appearance back in 1992! But then I added these little notes beneath his pages, because we're pals. Yes. I'm almost ***certain*** we're pals.

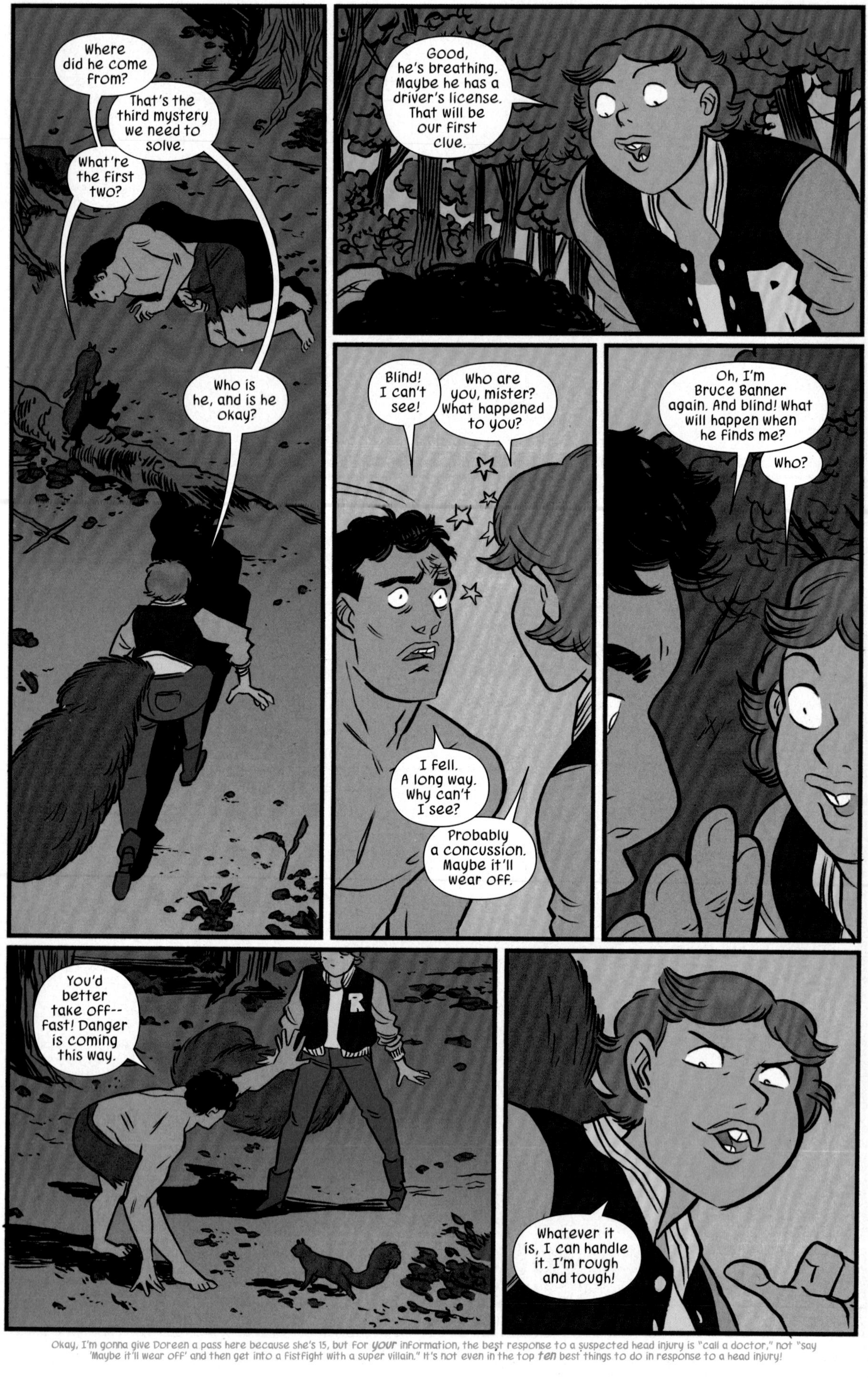
Where did he come from?
That's the third mystery we need to solve.
What're the first two?
Who is he, and is he okay?
Good, he's breathing. Maybe he has a driver's license. That will be our first clue.
Blind! I can't see!
Who are you, mister? What happened to you?
I fell. A long way. Why can't I see?
Probably a concussion. Maybe it'll wear off.
Oh, I'm Bruce Banner again. And blind! What will happen when he finds me?
Who?
You'd better take off-- fast! Danger is coming this way.
Whatever it is, I can handle it. I'm rough and tough!

Okay, I'm gonna give Doreen a pass here because she's 15, but for ***your*** information, the best response to a suspected head injury is "call a doctor," not "say 'Maybe it'll wear off' and then get into a fistfight with a super villain." It's not even in the top ***ten*** best things to do in response to a head injury!

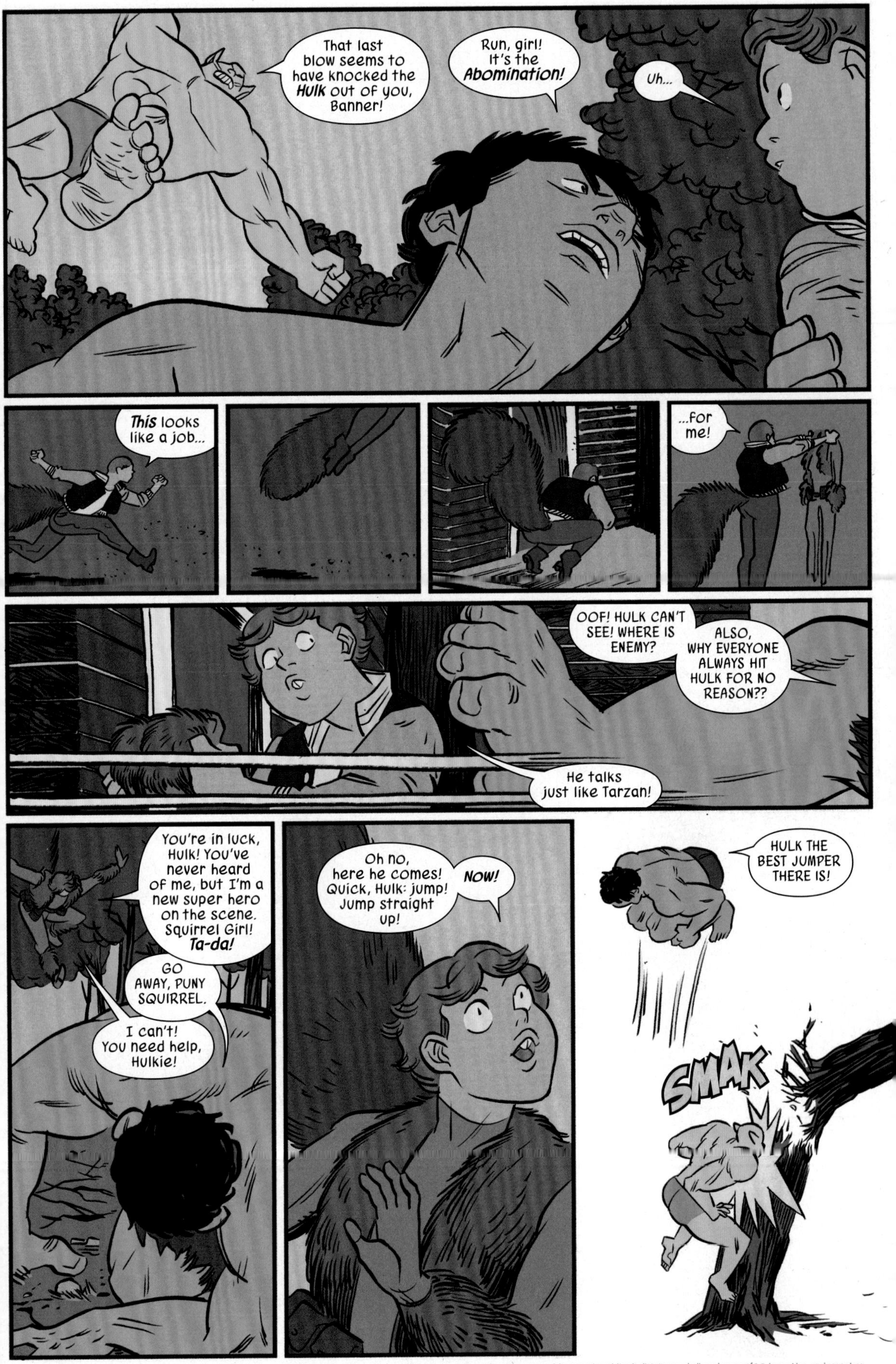
That last blow seems to have knocked the Hulk out of you, Banner!
Run, girl! It's the Abomination!
Uh...
This looks like a job...
...for me!
OOF! HULK CAN'T SEE! WHERE IS ENEMY?
ALSO, WHY EVERYONE ALWAYS HIT HULK FOR NO REASON??
He talks just like Tarzan!
You're in luck, Hulk! You've never heard of me, but I'm a new super hero on the scene. Squirrel Girl! Ta-da!
GO AWAY, PUNY SQUIRREL.
I can't! You need help, Hulkie!
Oh no, here he comes! Quick, Hulk: jump! Jump straight up!
NOW!
HULK THE BEST JUMPER THERE IS!
SMAK

That guy's Emil, and he's an enemy of the Hulk! He's got Hulk's strength and durability, but unlike him, he keeps his smarts while in "Hulk mode" and can *also* breathe underwater. Emil calls himself "The Abomination" instead of "Fishy Hulk" for reasons that I simply do not understand??

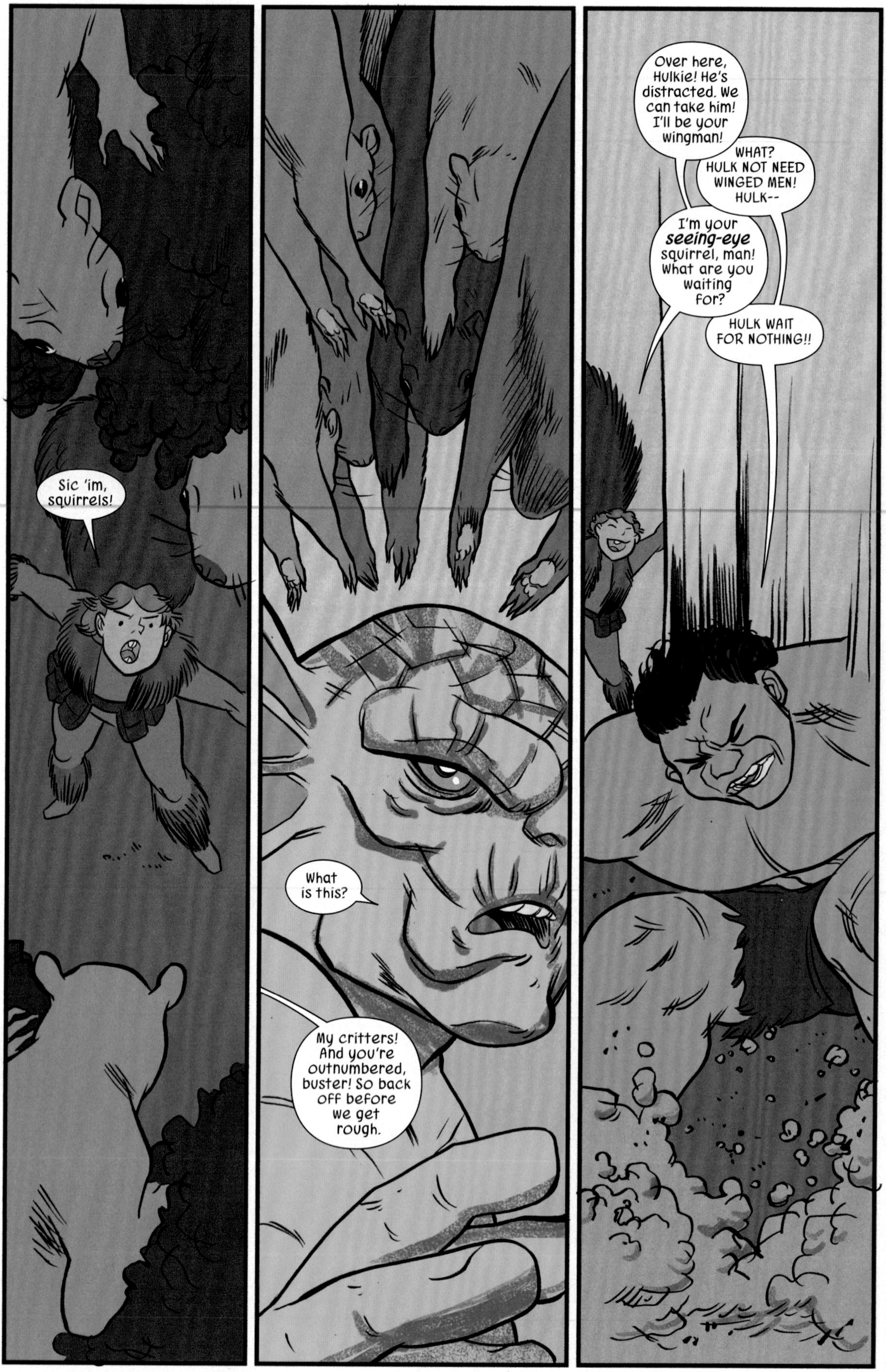
Sic 'im, squirrels!
What is this?
My critters! And you're outnumbered, buster! So back off before we get rough.
Over here, Hulkie! He's distracted. We can take him! I'll be your wingman!
WHAT? HULK NOT NEED WINGED MEN! HULK--
I'm your *seeing-eye* squirrel, man! What are you waiting for?
HULK WAIT FOR NOTHING!!

IN PARTICULAR, HULK DID NOT BECOME GIANT GREEN RAGE MONSTER SO THAT HE COULD WAIT QUIETLY IN LINE AT THE BANK, AND THAT IS ALL HULK WILL SAY ON THE MATTER!!

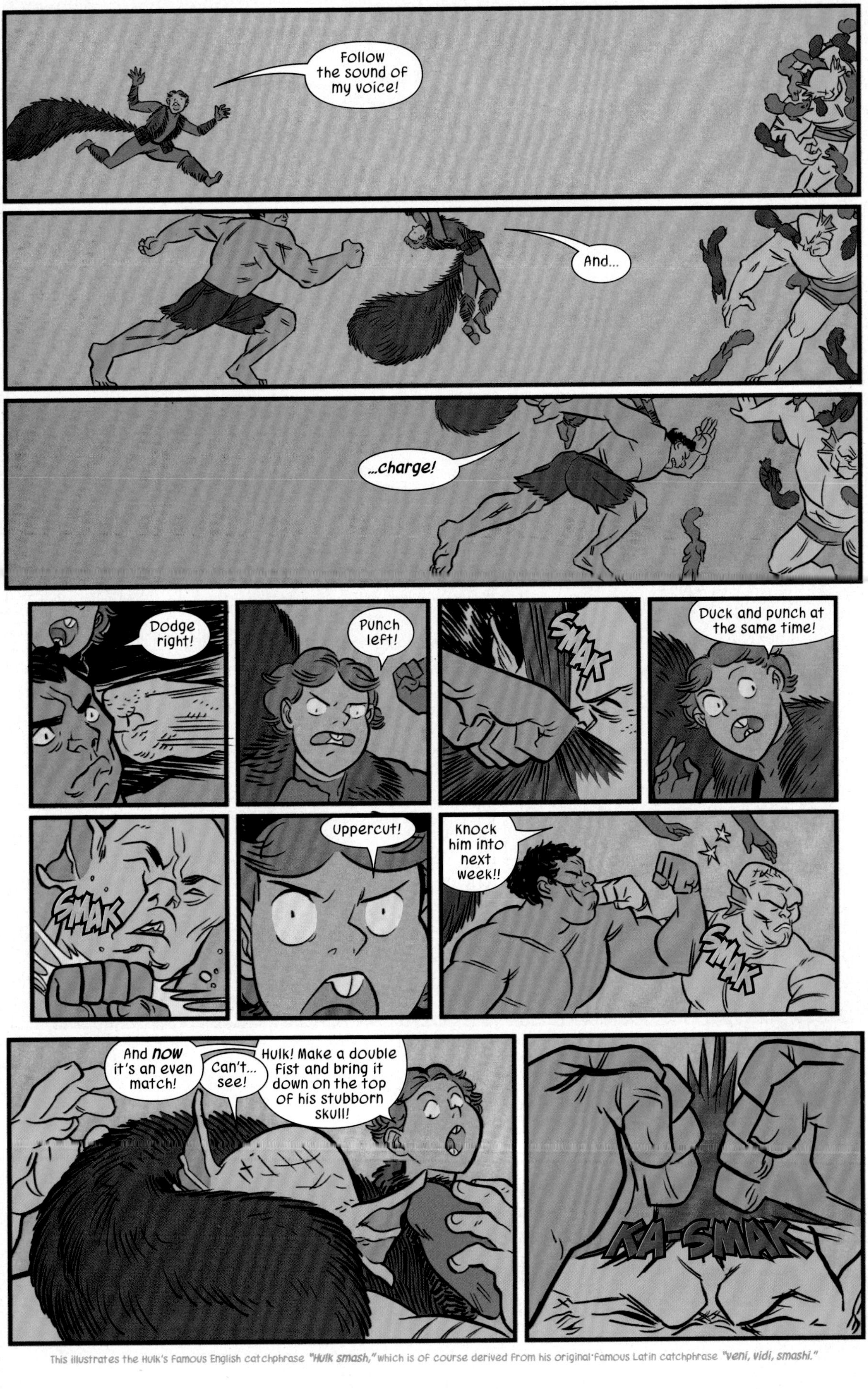
Follow the sound of my voice!
And...
...charge!
Dodge right!
Punch left!
SMAK
Duck and punch at the same time!
SMAK
Uppercut!
Knock him into next week!!
SMAK
And now it's an even match!
Can't... see!
Hulk! Make a double fist and bring it down on the top of his stubborn skull!
KA-SMAK

This illustrates the Hulk's famous English catchphrase *"Hulk smash,"* which is of course derived from his original famous Latin catchphrase *"veni, vidi, smashi."*

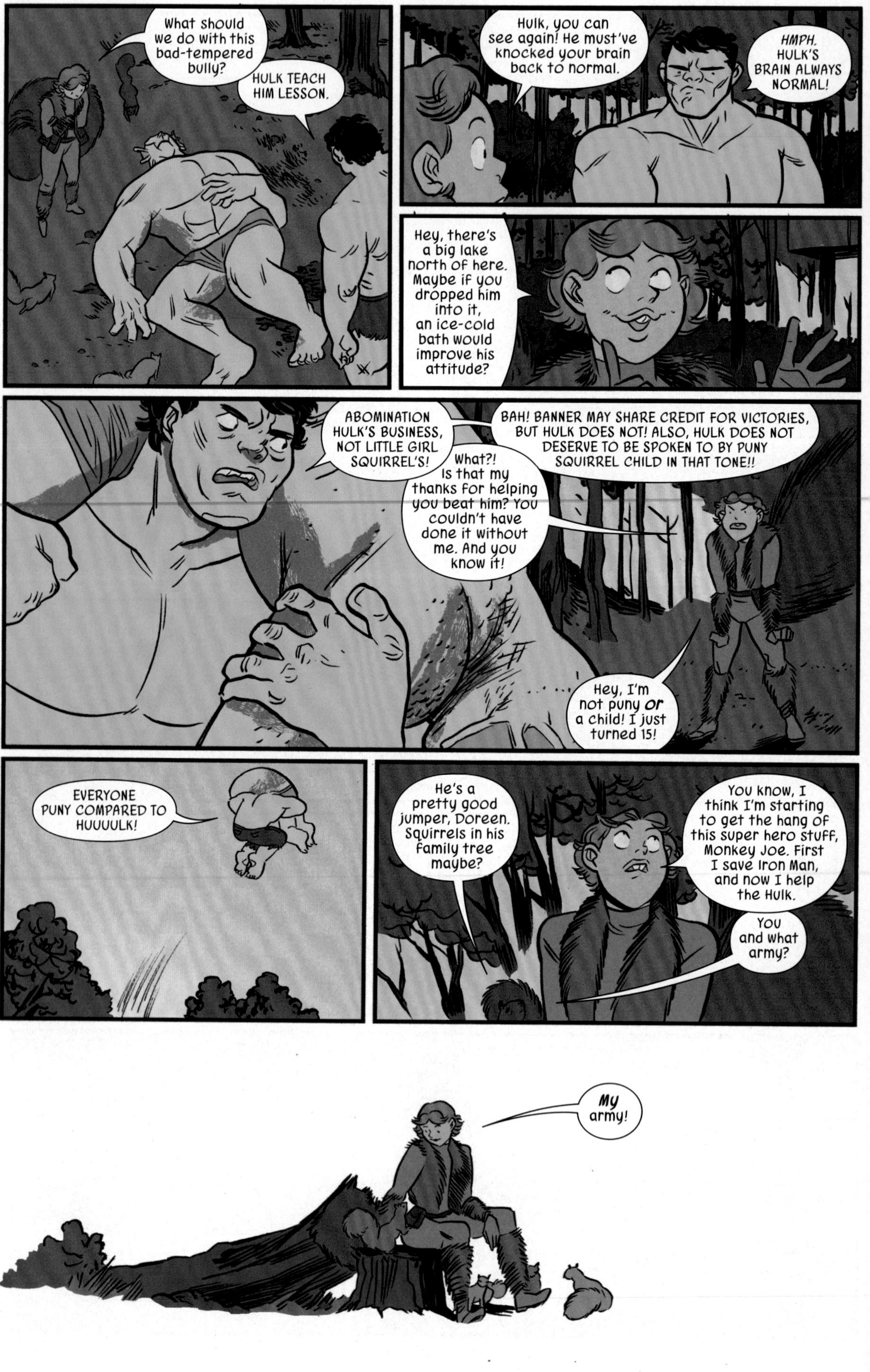
What should we do with this bad-tempered bully?
HULK TEACH HIM LESSON.
Hulk, you can see again! He must've knocked your brain back to normal.
HMPH. HULK'S BRAIN ALWAYS NORMAL!
Hey, there's a big lake north of here. Maybe if you dropped him into it, an ice-cold bath would improve his attitude?
ABOMINATION HULK'S BUSINESS, NOT LITTLE GIRL SQUIRREL'S!
What?! Is that my thanks for helping you beat him? You couldn't have done it without me. And you know it!
BAH! BANNER MAY SHARE CREDIT FOR VICTORIES, BUT HULK DOES NOT! ALSO, HULK DOES NOT DESERVE TO BE SPOKEN TO BY PUNY SQUIRREL CHILD IN THAT TONE!!
Hey, I'm not puny or a child! I just turned 15!
EVERYONE PUNY COMPARED TO HUUUULK!
He's a pretty good jumper, Doreen. Squirrels in his family tree maybe?
You know, I think I'm starting to get the hang of this super hero stuff, Monkey Joe. First I save Iron Man, and now I help the Hulk.
You and what army?
My army!

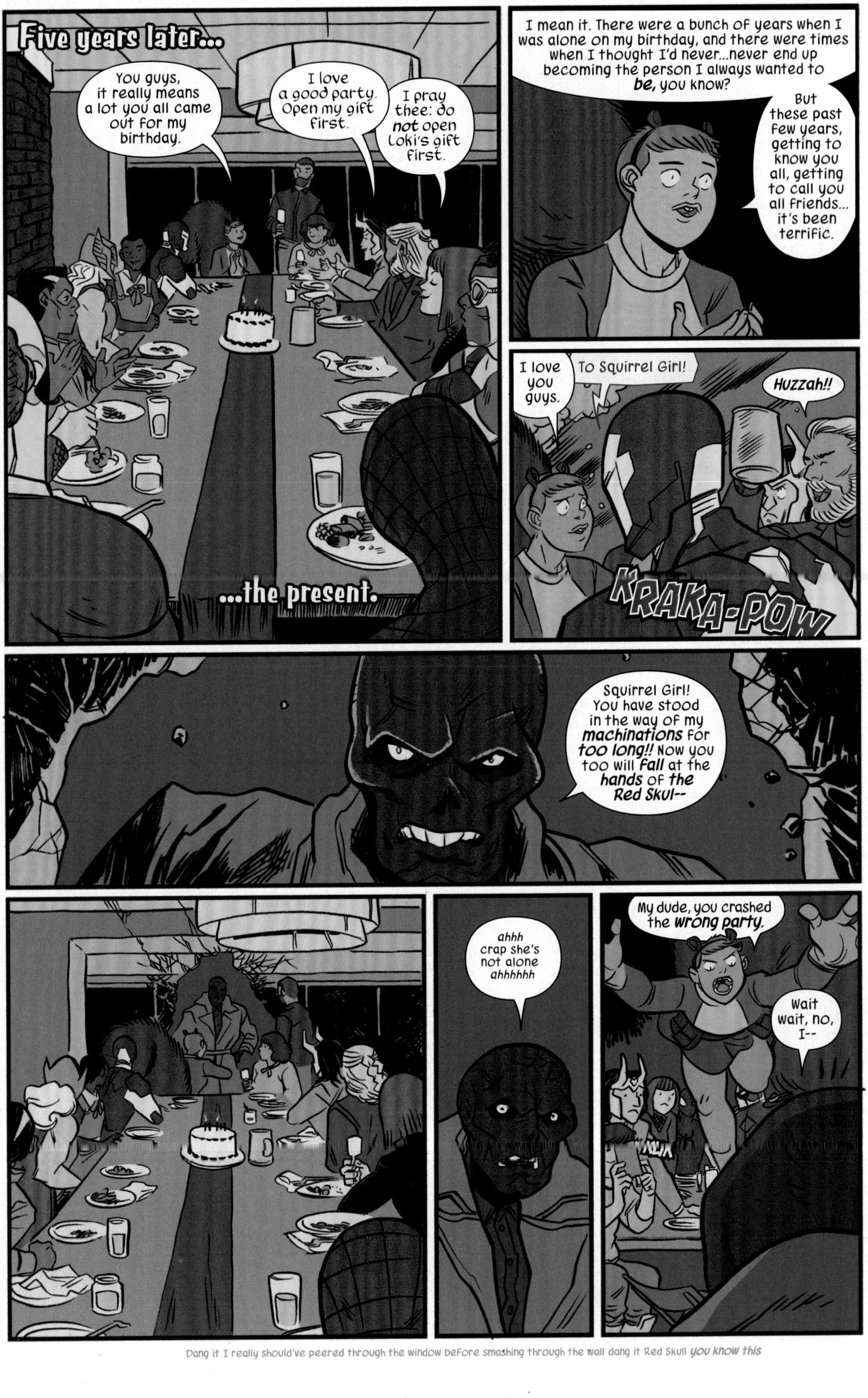
Five years later...
You guys, it really means a lot you all came out for my birthday.
I love a good party. Open my gift first.
I pray thee: do **not** open Loki's gift first.
...the present.
I mean it. There were a bunch of years when I was alone on my birthday, and there were times when I thought I'd never...never end up becoming the person I always wanted to **be,** you know?
But these past few years, getting to know you all, getting to call you all friends... it's been terrific.
I love you guys.
To Squirrel Girl!
Huzzah!!
KRAKA-POW
Squirrel Girl! You have stood in the way of my **machinations** for **too long!!** Now you too will **fall** at the **hands** of **the Red Skul--**
ahhh crap she's not alone ahhhhhh
My dude, you crashed the **wrong party.**
Wait wait, no, I--
Dang it I really should've peered through the window before smashing through the wall dang it Red Skull *you know this*

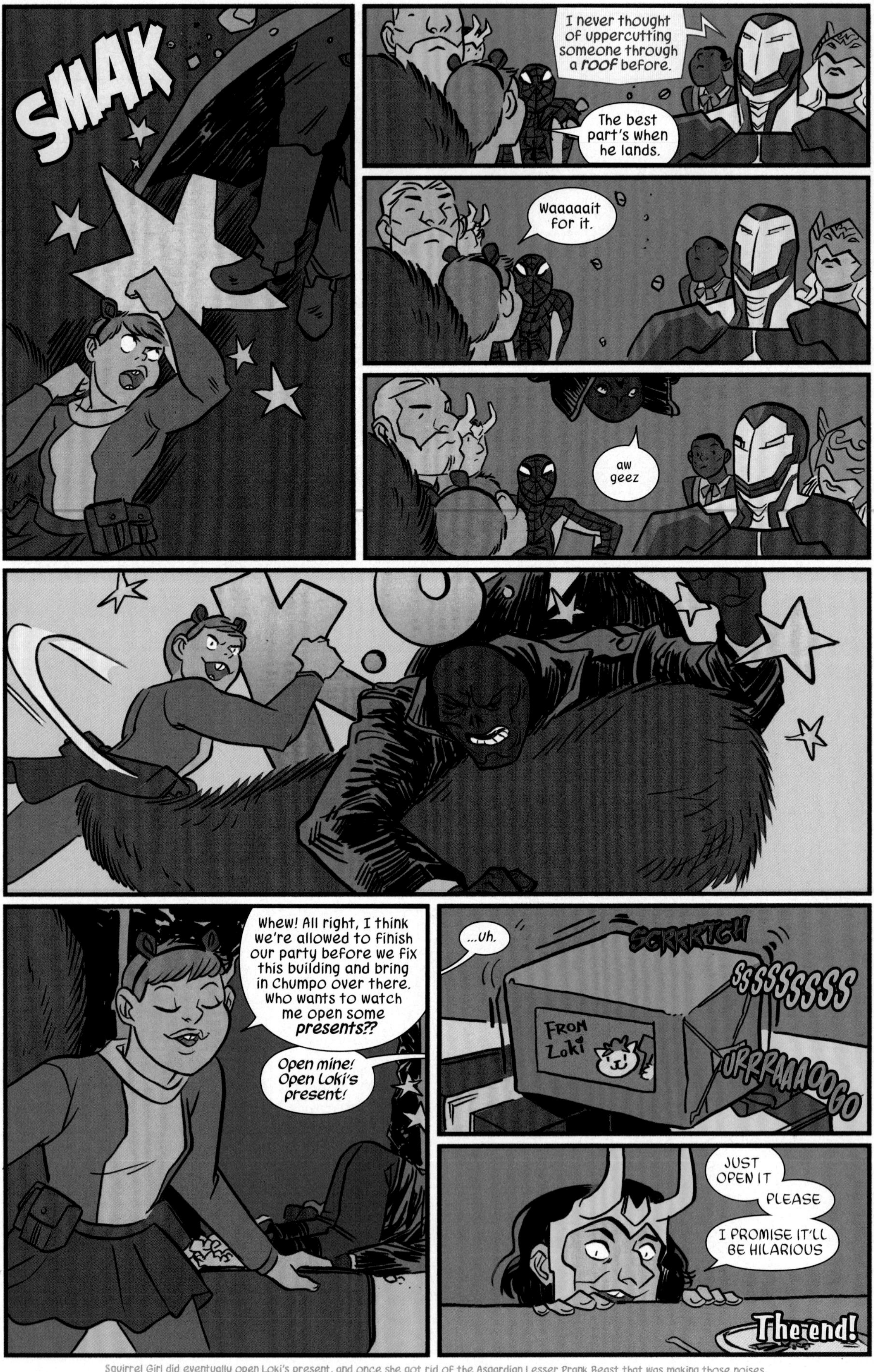
SMAK
I never thought of uppercutting someone through a *roof* before.
The best part's when he lands.
Waaaaait for it.
aw geez
Whew! All right, I think we're allowed to finish our party before we fix this building and bring in Chumpo over there. Who wants to watch me open some **presents??**
Open mine! Open Loki's present!
...uh.
SCRRRTCH
SSSSSSSSS
FROM Loki
URRRAAAOOGO
JUST OPEN IT
PLEASE
I PROMISE IT'LL BE HILARIOUS
The end!

Squirrel Girl did eventually open Loki's present, and once she got rid of the Asgardian Lesser Prank Beast that was making those noises, a lot of the stuff in there was actually really sweet. *The end.*

Ryan!

Letters From Nuts

Erica!

Send letters to mheroes@marvel.com or 135 W 50th St, 7th Floor, New York, NY 10020 (Please mark "OKAY TO PRINT")

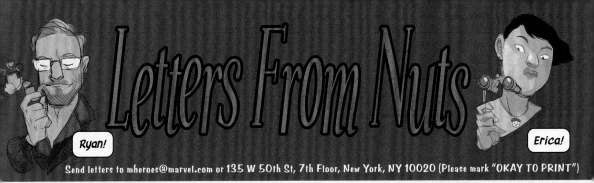

Twenty-five years ago this month, MARVEL SUPER-HEROES WINTER SPECIAL #8 hit the stands, with stories starring the X-Men, Drax, Gamora, Namor…and a brand new character named SQUIRREL GIRL!

MARVEL COMICS
80 PAGE BLOCK-BUSTER!
MARVEL SUPER-HEROES WINTER SPECIAL
X-MEN
NAMOR

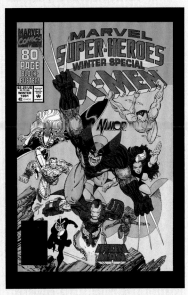

So we're all thrilled and honored to have Doreen's co-creator Will Murray contribute to this anniversary issue by writing that tale of 15-year-old Doreen and the Hulk – such a fun story, right? And we're paying tribute to SG's other co-creator, the legendary Steve Ditko, by running a panel of his art from that original story back on the page where we see Doreen's initial costume design! (So yeah, that wasn't actually Doreen's drawing – she was a talented artist for a 10-year-old, but not THAT talented!)

And TWO years ago this month, THE UNBEATABLE SQUIRREL GIRL #1 (Vol. 1) was released, so we're celebrating that milestone this issue as well! Thanks to all you readers out there for supporting this book like crazy, and for sending us your letters and your photos and your drawings – it's so great knowing these stories are connecting with you! So y'all keep that love coming, and we'll keep telling more Squirrel Girl stories! (And boy are there some exciting ones coming up…!)

Squirrel Girl team,

I couldn't believe it when I read the word "zot" in regards to sending items back in time. I am the only person I know who ever uses that word, despite its incredible usefulness. I'm guessing at least one of you played "Story Machine," that old Texas Instrument writing game with that weird purple hand monster.

Best!
Michele

RYAN: No, I've never played it! But there are few phrases more intriguing than "Texas Instrument writing game with that weird purple hand monster", so COLOR ME INTRIGUED. Since we're (tangentally) talking about calculators, let me say that I do all my calculation on an 37-year-old HP 41-CX, an RPN calculator my dad bought before I was born, and of the type that was used on Space Shuttle missions as a backup way to calculate re-entry if the main computer failed. I mostly use it to add up numbers that are too big for me to do in my head.

ERICA: I've never even owned a fancy calculator, seeing as from sixth grade on I attended arts-focused schools. My frame of reference for "Zot" is the Scott McCloud comic, which is great. There's interdimensional travel there! To a futuristic world! That's LIKE time travel, I guess. Also, according to Google, zot is god in Albanian. We learn something new every day.

Ryan and Erica,

I'd never been into reading comics before my husband put your first issue of SQUIRREL GIRL into my hands. I've been hooked from page one when she starts singing her own theme song to the tune of Spider-Man's theme! (Though, admittedly, I had to look up Spider-Man's theme online so I knew the tune because that's how out of touch I started with comics and super heroes…) Still! SQUIRREL GIRL has made me a comics convert thanks to her commitment to kicking butt but also to solving problems with smarts and friendship. She is basically a huge inspiration to anyone who ever wondered if it was possible to eat nuts AND save the world with some smart observations and a few well-placed butt-kicks!

Your delightful comic inspired my own crafts-building as well, and now I have my very own cobbled-together Squirrel Girl doll crew assembled as well as a crocheted Tippy Toe that I used to make a stop motion of the first scene of issue #v1 that drew me into this fabulous squirrelly world so quickly! I attached a few pictures of the dolls I've made (I even have Nancy in anticipation of future films, wearing a shirt that I hope Mew would approve of!) and here's the link to the short stop motion: https://youtu.be/1otZ-PJcCi8

Many thanks for all you do, can't wait for the next nutty adventure!

April Duclos
Massachusetts

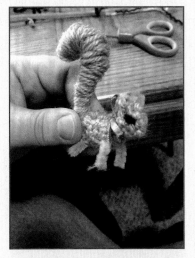

RYAN: April, I love your Tippy AND I LOVE YOUR STOP-MOTION SQUIRREL GIRL RECREATION. My friends and I made stop motion films with action figures when we were in high school, but sadly none of them were a) as good, and b) put on the Internet. However I remember one: it starred Spider-Man (um, don't sue me Marvel) and it was about 10 seconds long. Spider-Man said "Time for some heavy reading" and then tried to lift up a newspaper (giant, compared to his action-figure size), and then it collapsed on top of him and he said "Oh no, maybe a little TOO heavy!" I have no regrets.

ERICA: Ryan.

Dear Unbeatable Squirrel Warriors

I just finished 14 and must say, I am impressed with the level of thought that you put into your stories, whether using binary to count on one hand, acting like yelp for Galactus, or physics to defeat Enigmo, Doreen is truly unbeatable. It is great how Doreen and Nancy work so well together!

I have been a longtime fan of SG and am currently working on owning every single one of her appearances, so far I am ten issues away from completion! I am loving every comic you both have put out and know I will continue to enjoy Squirrel Girl's adventures forever!

Ryan, when will we learn more about Nancy? we know so little about her besides she loves Mew, Doreen, knitting, writing Cat-Thor fan fics and maybe has a tattoo?

Erica what has been your favorite panel to draw to date? Is there a character from the Marvel Universe that you would love to draw in a future issue?

P.S. I have enclosed a picture I drew of Doreen and Nancy having a bit of fun!

P.P.S. Just want to finally say that you guys are so lucky working for in my opinion for the best comic company AND the BEST character in the world! keep up the great work Ryan, Erica, Rico, and Travis, I am seriously jealous of all of you!

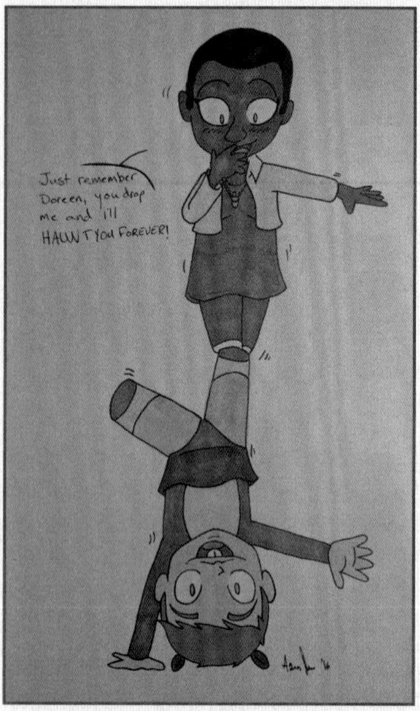
Just remember Doreen, you drop me and i'll HAUNT YOU FOREVER!

RYAN: Ah, such a cute drawing!! Besides the fun reveal of FUTURE NANCY in this issue, I also hope we'll be finding out more about Present Nancy soon. Including: NANCY'S MYSTERIOUS SECRETS??

ERICA: Hm. Last issue I got to draw Taskmaster, who I encouraged Ryan to put in a story because he is a skeleton pirate, so THAT was fun. I don't know about favorite panel, but the part that was the most surprisingly fun to draw was the multiple Squirrel Girls vs Doctor Doom fight, which I thought was just going to be terrible because it was like 20 people per panel.

Dear Squirrel Team,

I just read issue #11 (I know, I'm late, it's embarrassing) and, as a Computer Science student, I couldn't resist sending you my opinion in the form of an algorithm.

```
WHILE (reading){
    I_am_mesmerized();
    IF (Doc Ock appears){
        I_dont_realize_its_weird();
    }
}
I_love_it();
I_think_it_is_perfect();
IF (Someone wants to learn about CS){
    I_give_him_or_her_this_issue();
}ELSE{
    I_force_him_or_her_to_read_it();
```

Yours nerdly,
Roni Kaufman

P.S.: I don't know whether I'm the first one to do this. If this not the case, I apologize (another if statement?!).

RYAN: This is great, and I will gladly accept all reader letters in the form of flattering pseudocode from now on!!

ERICA: WHAT IS THIS SORCERY.

Dear Nancy, Doreen, Ryan, and Erica,

I've been a Marvel fan since I was 13 and my daughter Wanda was taught to read with Power Pack comics (POW! BAM! WHAP!). We both absolutely love THE UNBEATABLE SQUIRREL GIRL and giggle maniacally when we read the books again and again. I really like how she solves problems in new and unusual non-violent ways, yet still can appreciate a good butt-kicking occasionally. We enjoyed the Ratatosk storyline so much that we were inspired to do something special this Halloween (see attached pictures). I really hope that Squirrel Girl and Spider-Man can hang out together in the future, and Wanda wants to see more Brain Drain. Thank you so much for all your great work!

Sincerely,
Doug Smith (46) and Wanda Smith (10)

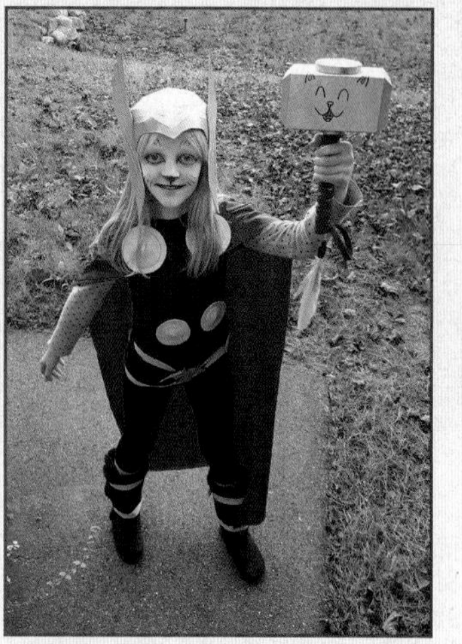

RYAN: Wanda, this part is only for you, so don't let your dad read this: that costume is amazing, there is more Brain Drain in this issue, and we can retcon that to say it was JUST FOR YOU, and thank you so much for being such a great reader! You're the first Wanda I've ever met AND THEREFORE THE BEST.

Okay Dave, this part of the answer is for you: Doreen and Spider-Man do (briefly) hang out in the SQUIRREL GIRL BEATS UP THE MARVEL UNIVERSE OGN, and it doesn't work out super well for... well, the Marvel Universe, I guess? But I'd like to see more of that too! She already seems to encounter his villains an awful lot. Also, tell Wanda her costume is awesome!

ERICA: Brain Drain is so much fun to draw. I second this. Also that is an amazing Thor outfit. I'm a proponent of capes as everyday fall wear so the choice of the word "outfit" rather than "costume" was on purpose.

Next: New Costume!

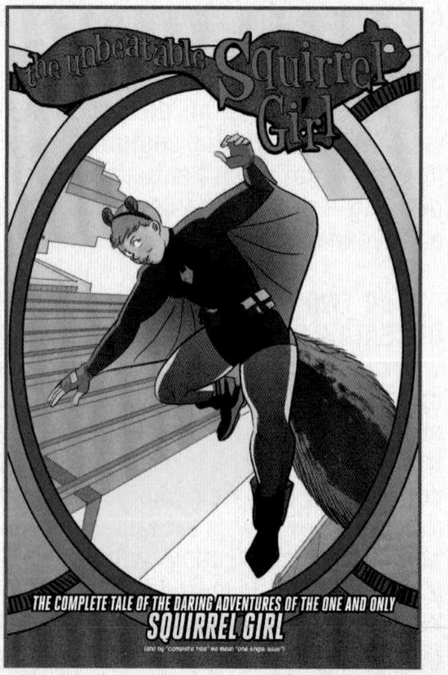
the unbeatable Squirrel Girl
THE COMPLETE TALE OF THE DARING ADVENTURES OF THE ONE AND ONLY
SQUIRREL GIRL
(and by "complete tale" we mean "one single issue")

Attention, Squirrel Scouts! Make sure to check out our production blog, **unbeatablesquirrelgirl.tumblr.com**, where we post behind-the-scenes stuff on how the book gets made, along with all sorts of cool things *you* make: fanart, cosplay, whatever!

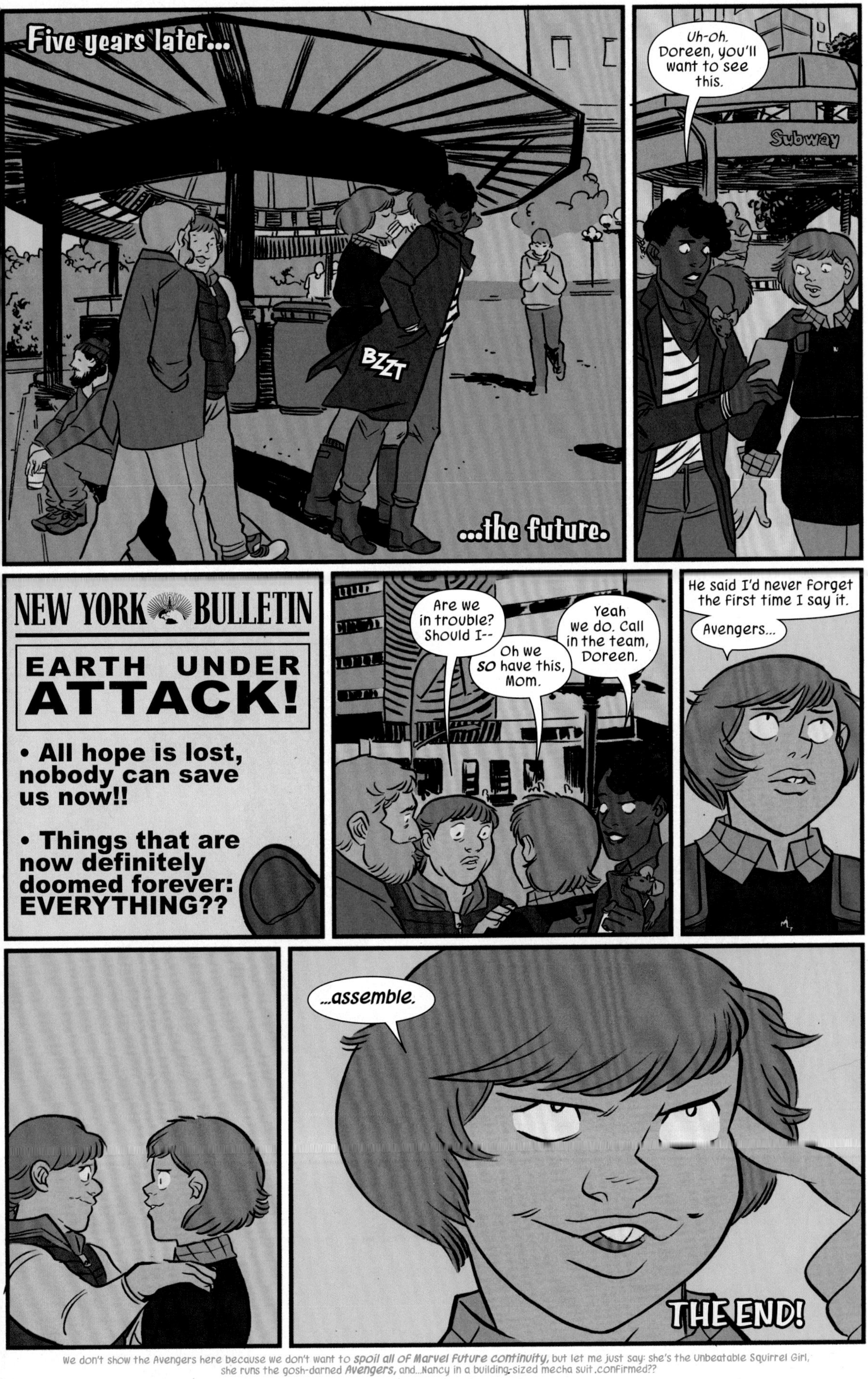
Five years later...
...the future.
BZZT
Uh-Oh. Doreen, you'll want to see this.
Subway
NEW YORK BULLETIN
EARTH UNDER ATTACK!
• All hope is lost, nobody can save us now!!
• Things that are now definitely doomed forever: EVERYTHING??
Are we in trouble? Should I--
Oh we SO have this, Mom.
Yeah we do. Call in the team, Doreen.
He said I'd never forget the first time I say it.
Avengers...
...assemble.
THE END!

We don't show the Avengers here because we don't want to *spoil all of Marvel Future continuity,* but let me just say: she's the Unbeatable Squirrel Girl, she runs the gosh-darned *Avengers,* and...Nancy in a building-sized mecha suit confirmed??

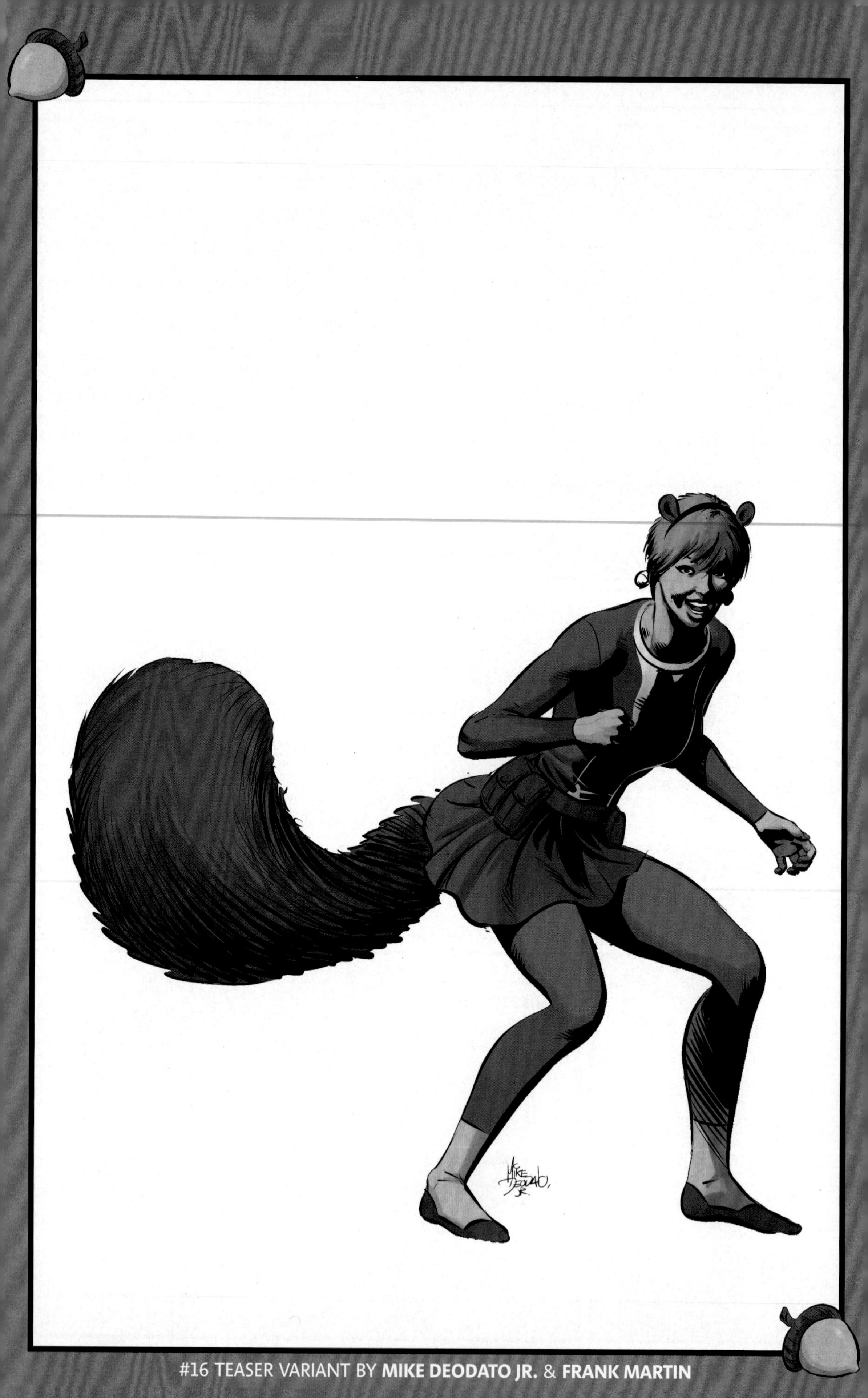
MIKE DEODATO JR.

#16 TEASER VARIANT BY **MIKE DEODATO JR.** & **FRANK MARTIN**

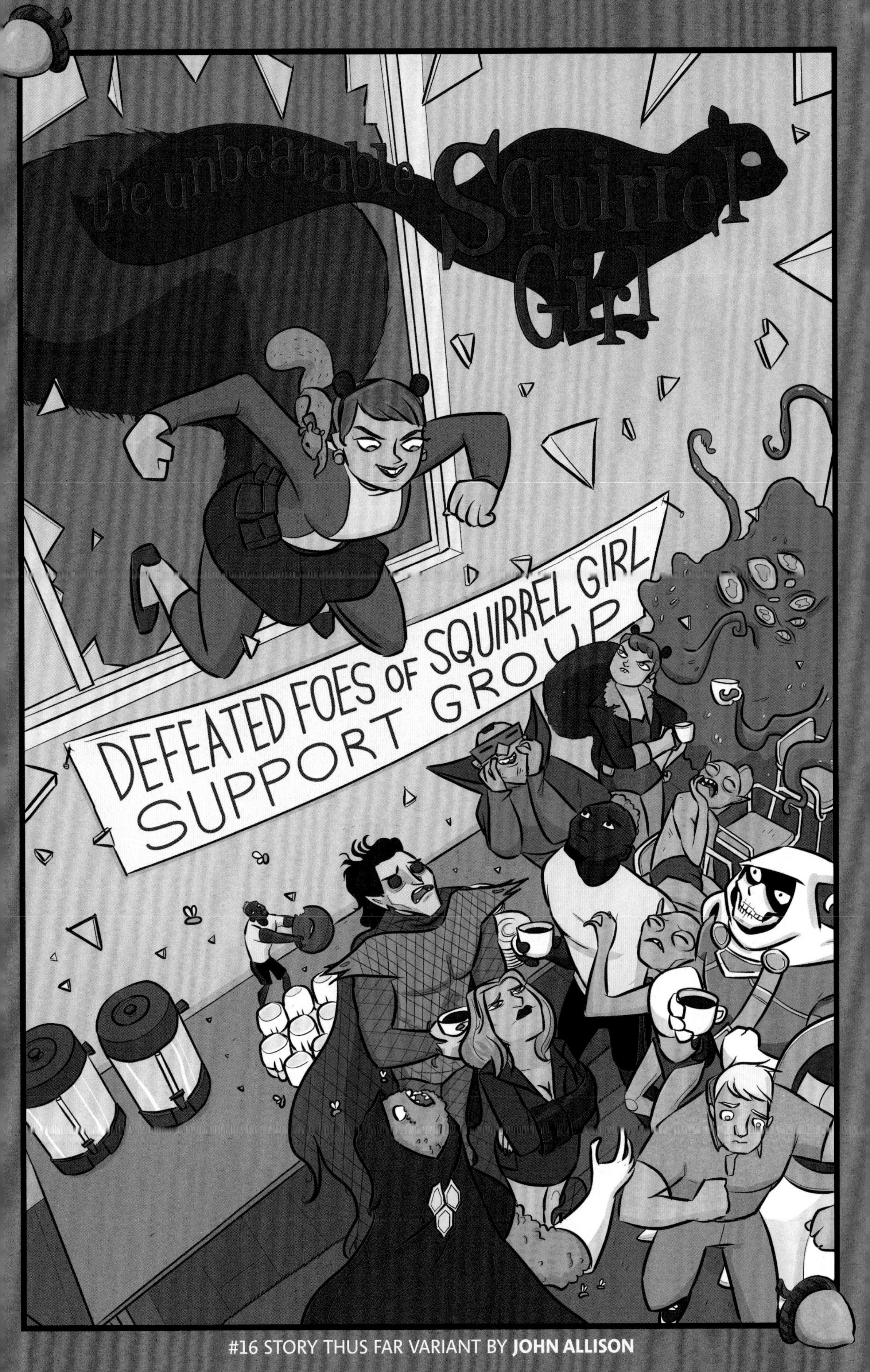
the unbeatable Squirrel Girl
DEFEATED FOES OF SQUIRREL GIRL
SUPPORT GROUP

#16 STORY THUS FAR VARIANT BY **JOHN ALLISON**

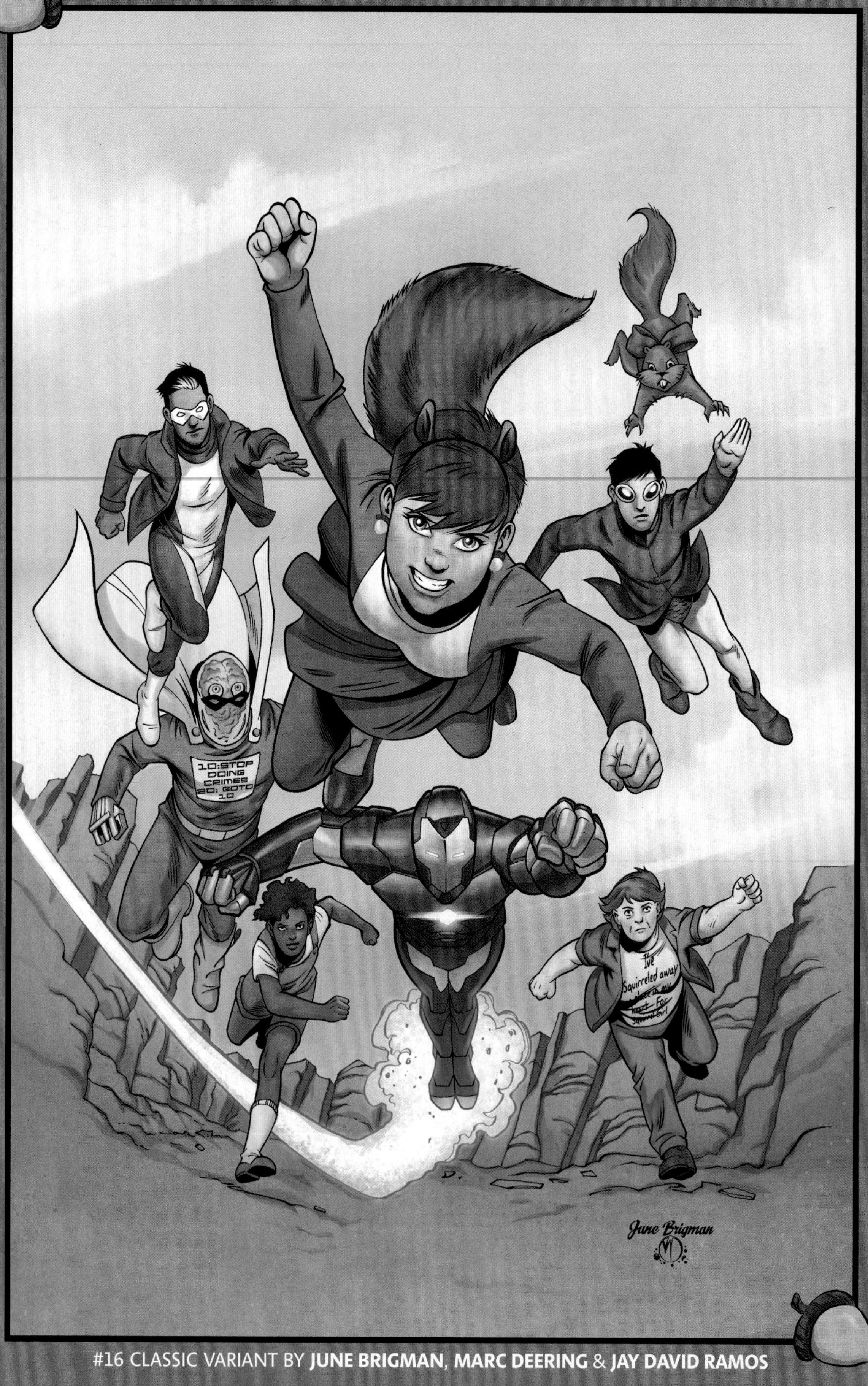
10:STOP DOING CRIMES 20: GOTO 10
Ive Squirreled away
For
June Brigman

#16 CLASSIC VARIANT BY **JUNE BRIGMAN**, **MARC DEERING** & **JAY DAVID RAMOS**

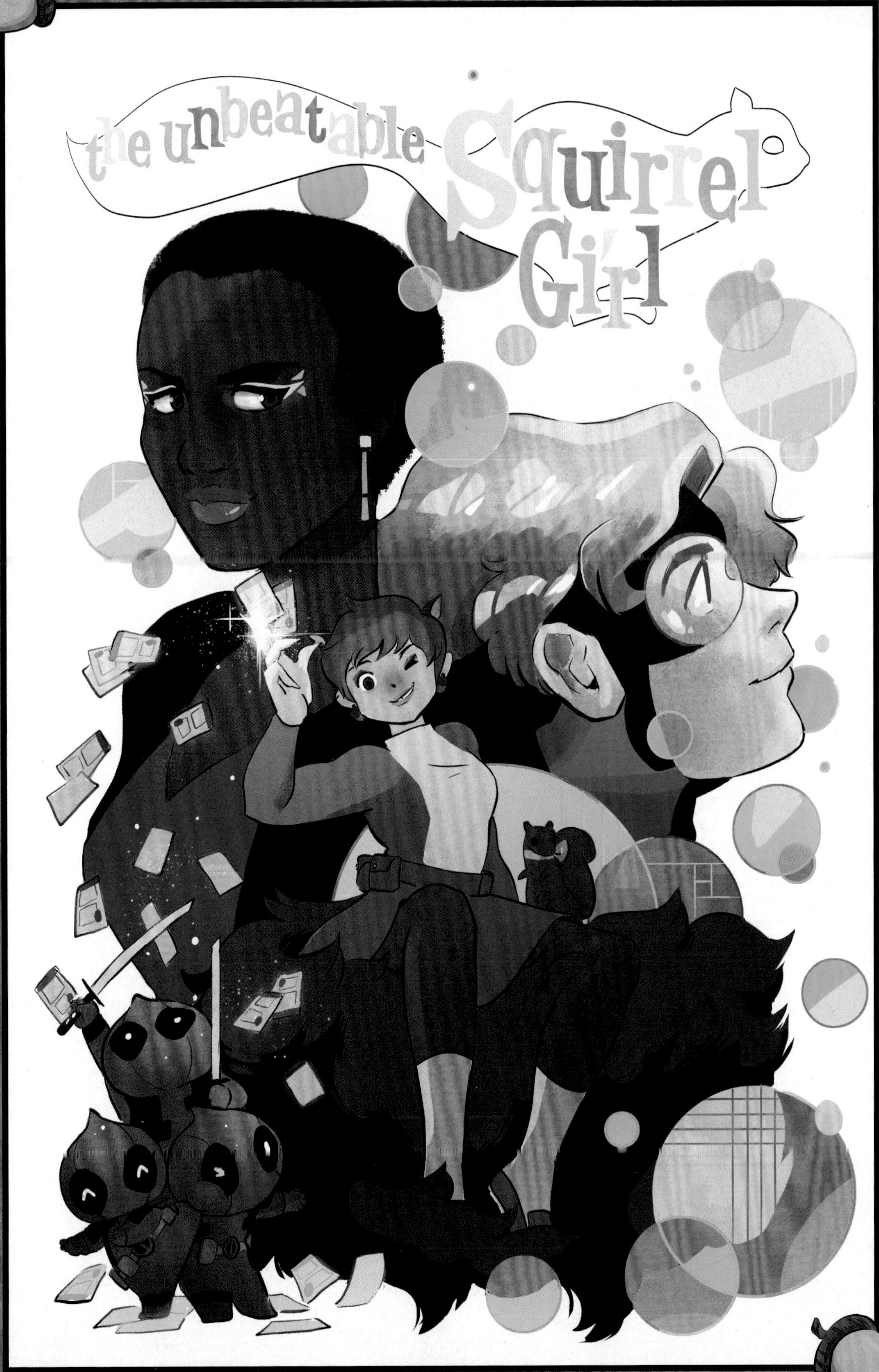
the unbeatable Squirrel Girl

#16 VARIANT BY **NATASHA ALLEGRI**

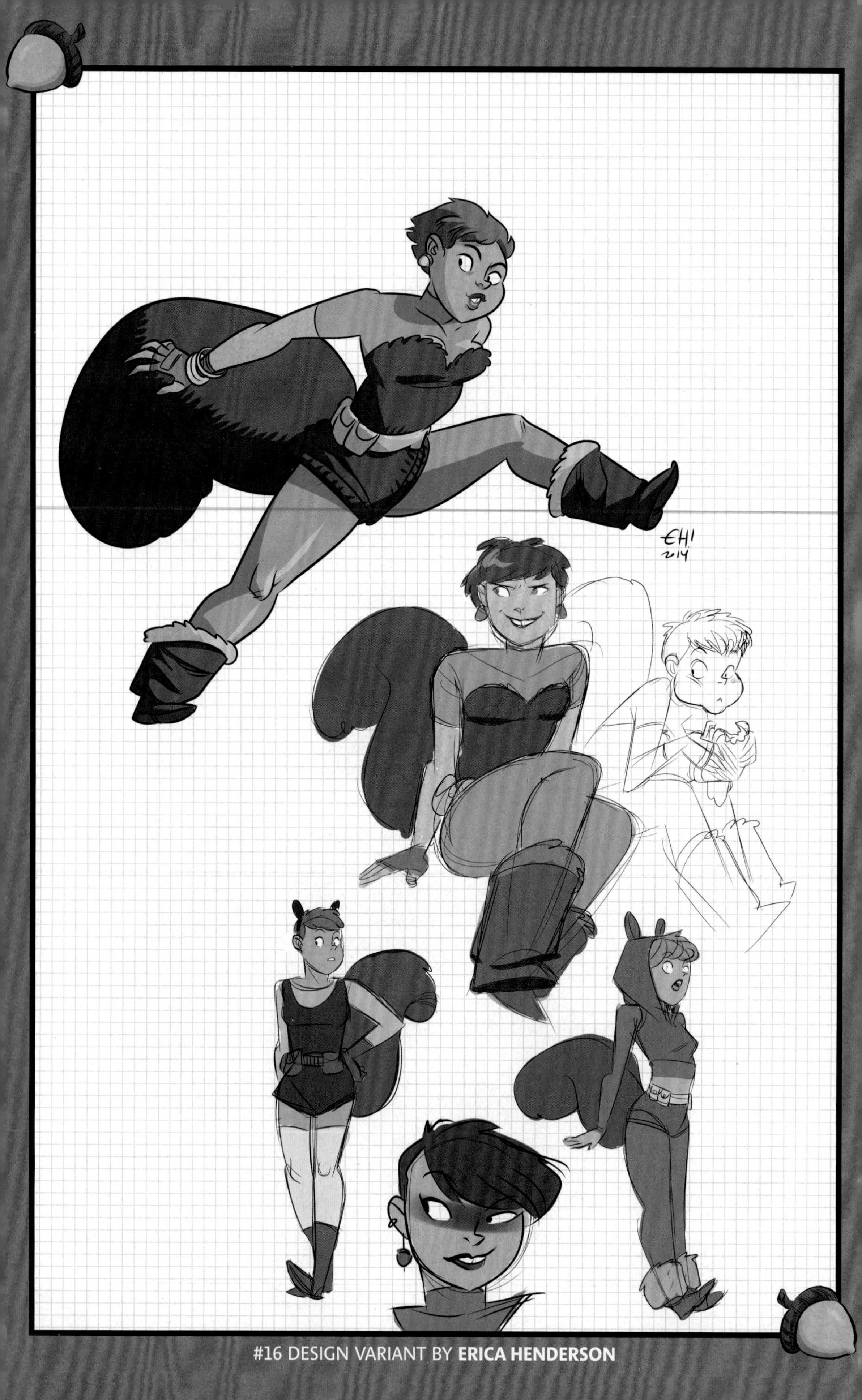
EH!
2014

#16 DESIGN VARIANT BY **ERICA HENDERSON**